THE BOOK OF LOST SOULS

INTRODUCTIONS [illegible] UND

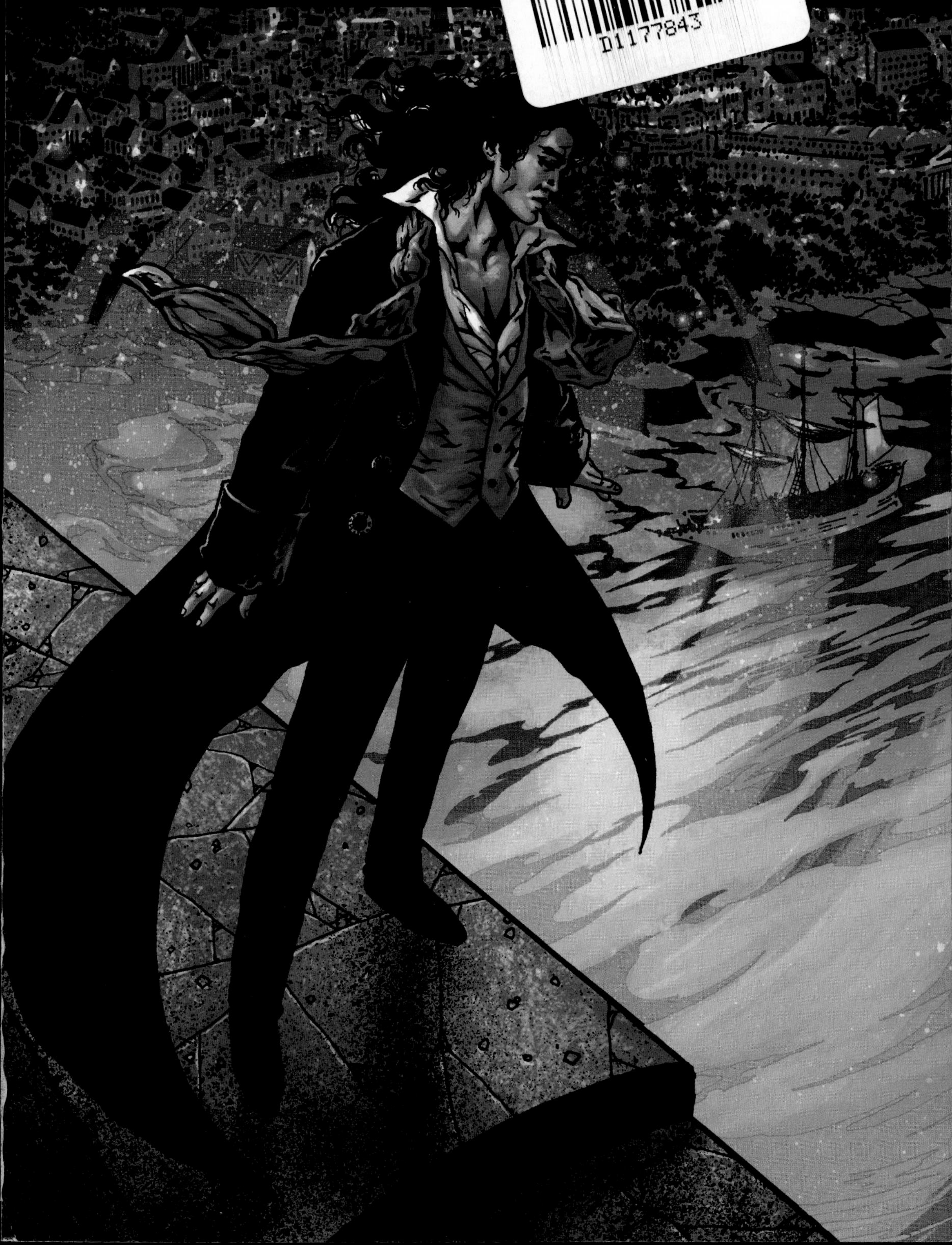

THE BOOK OF
LOST SOULS

INTRODUCTIONS ALL AROUND

WRITER:
J. Michael Straczynski

ARTIST:
Colleen Doran

COLORIST:
Dan Brown

LETTERER:
Dave Sharpe

ASSISTANT EDITORS:
Cory Sedlmeier & Michael O'Connor

EDITOR:
Axel Alonso

COLLECTION EDITOR:
Jennifer Grünwald

ASSISTANT EDITOR:
Michael Short

SENIOR EDITOR, SPECIAL PROJECTS:
Jeff Youngquist

VICE PRESIDET OF SALES:
David Gabriel

PRODUCTION:
Jerry Kalinowski

BOOK DESIGNER:
Patrick McGrath

VICE PRESIDENT OF CREATIVE:
Tom Marvelli

EDITOR IN CHIEF:
Joe Quesada

PUBLISHER:
Dan Buckley

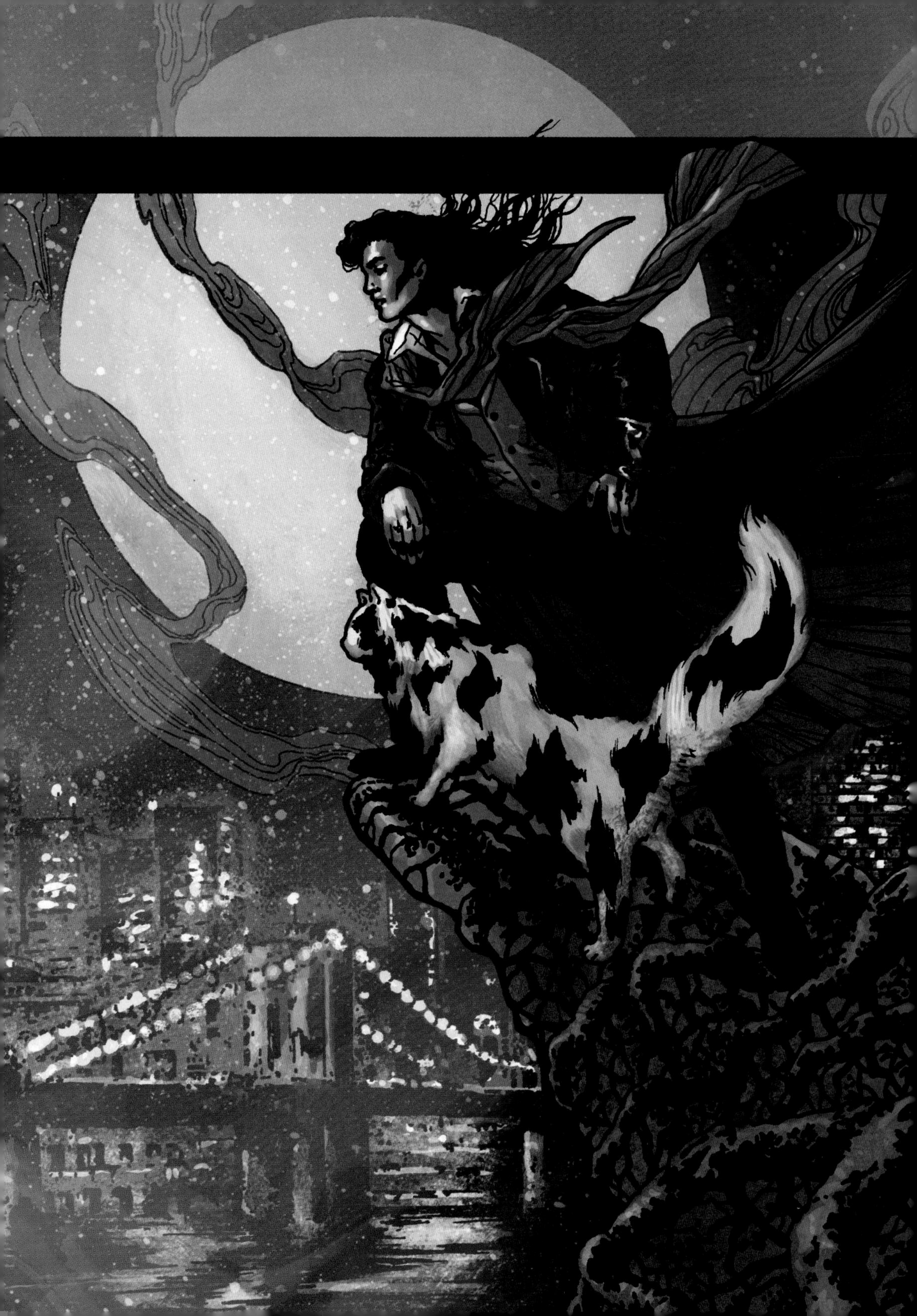

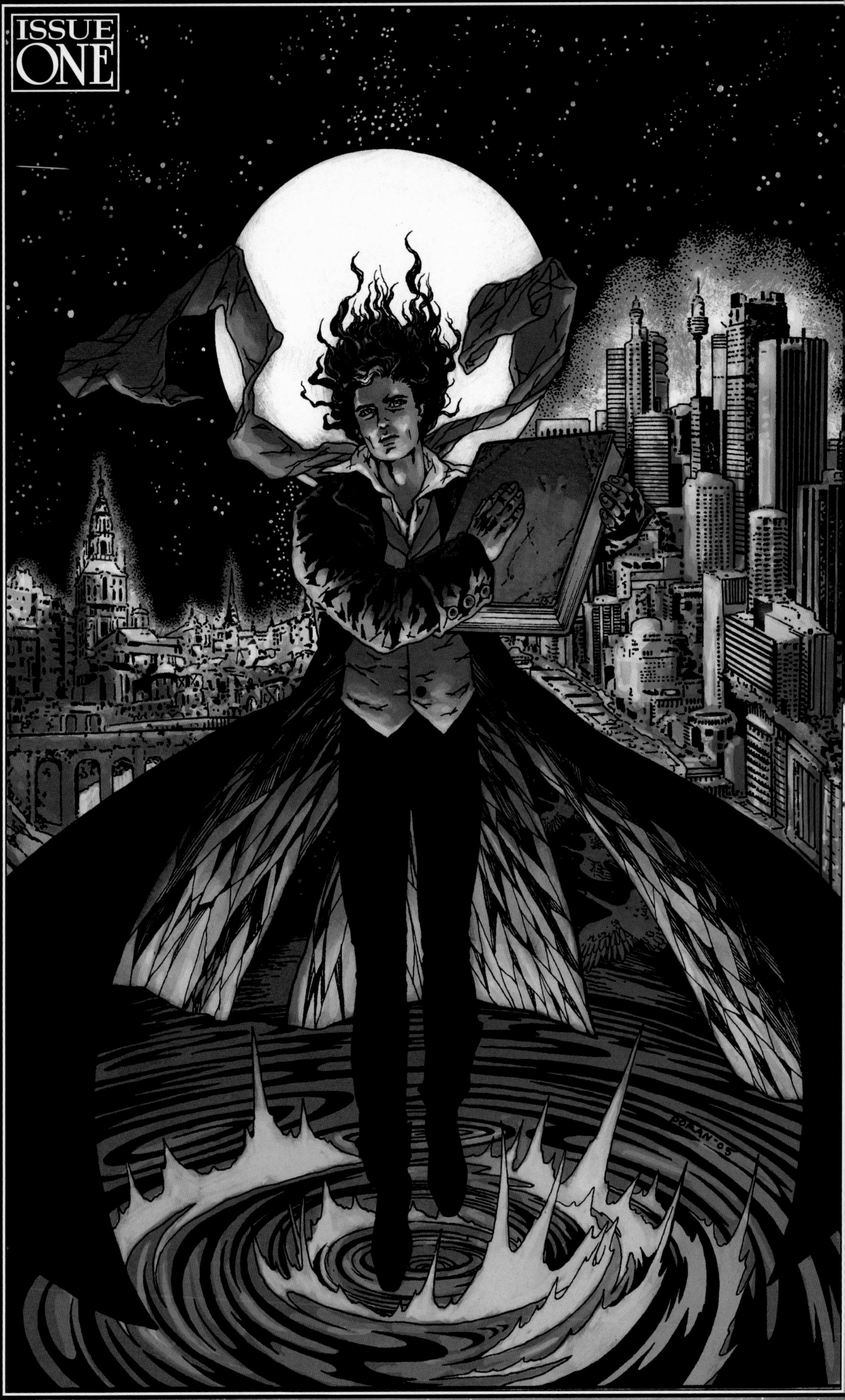
ISSUE
ONE

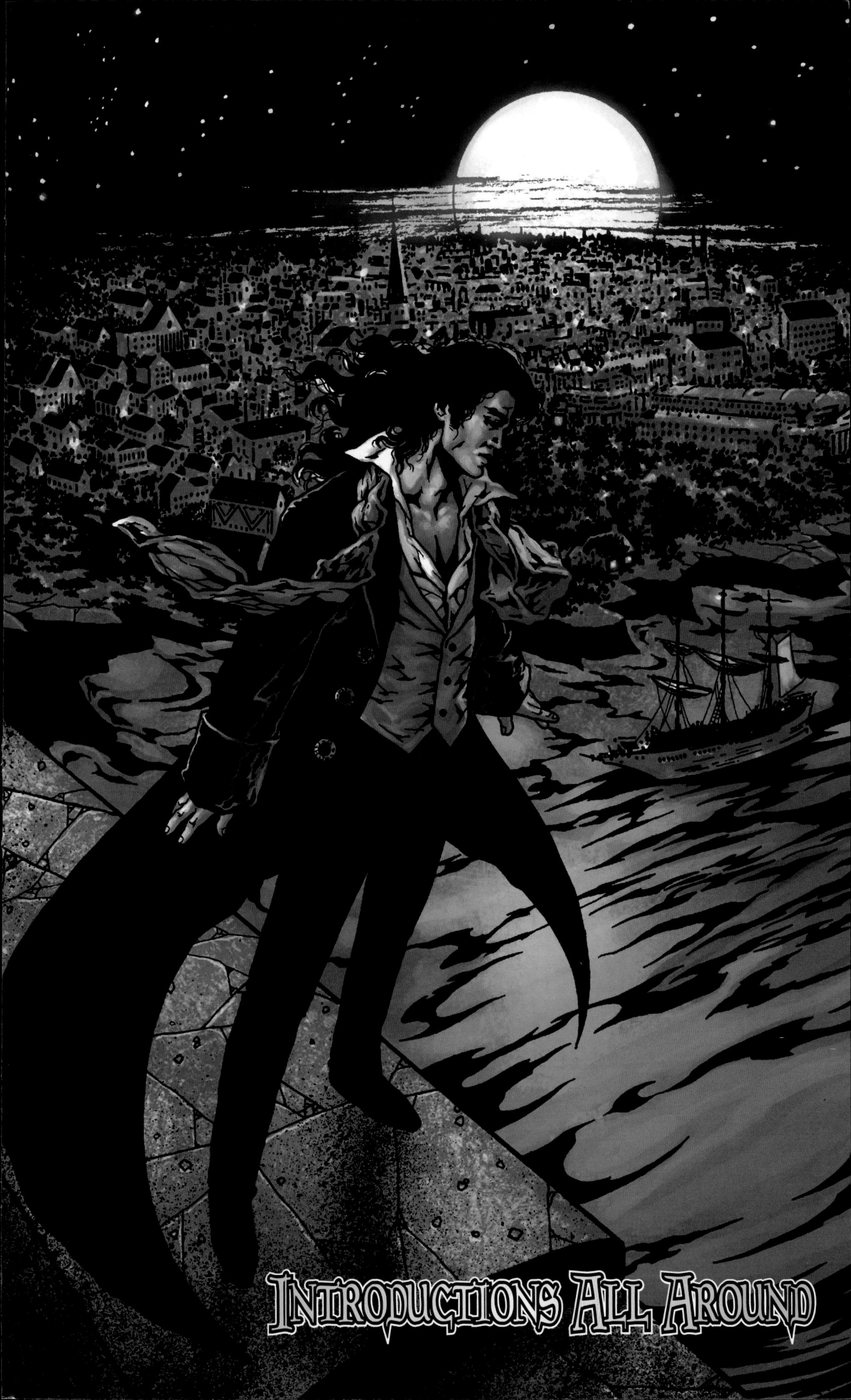
Introductions All Around

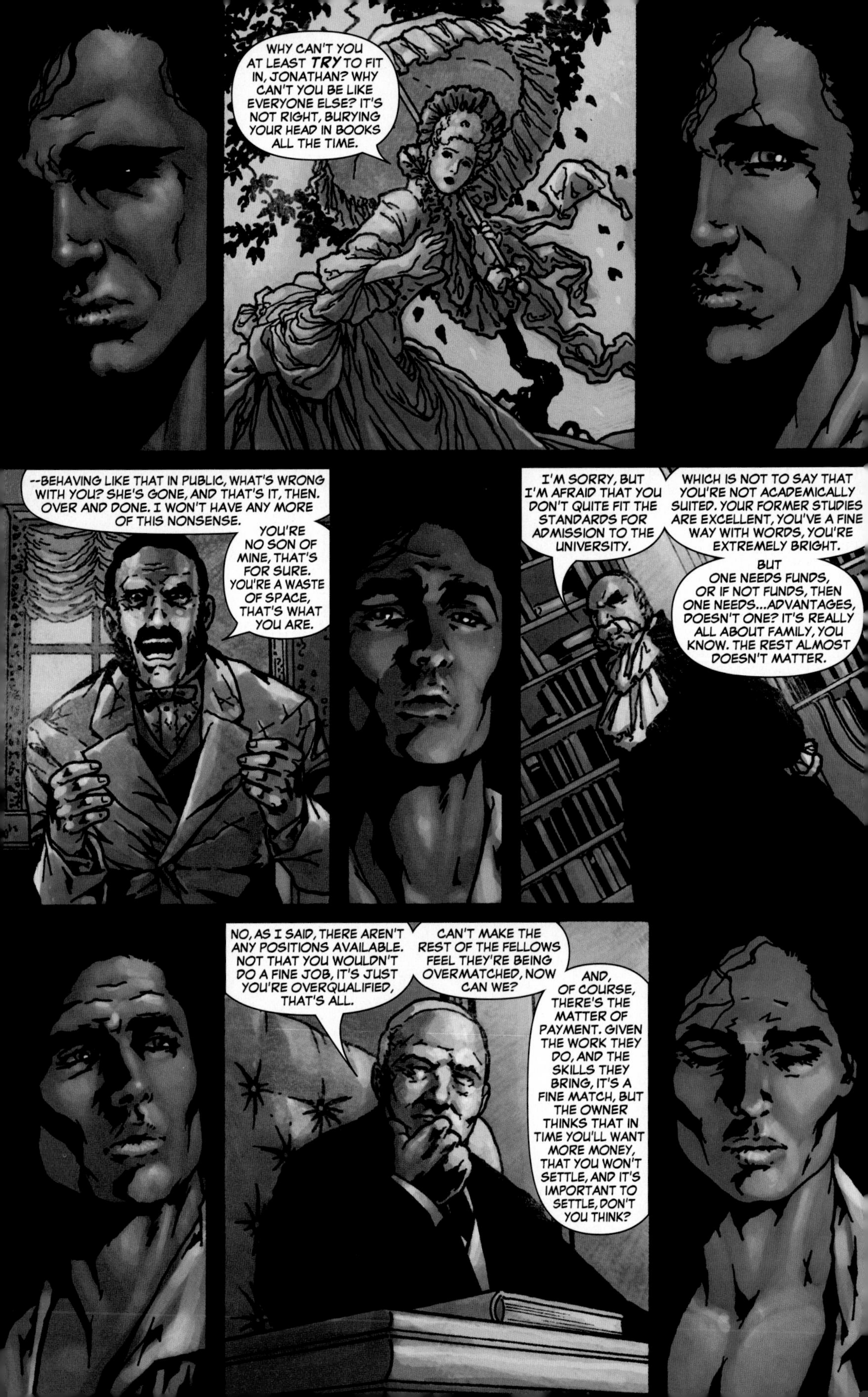
WHY CAN'T YOU AT LEAST TRY TO FIT IN, JONATHAN? WHY CAN'T YOU BE LIKE EVERYONE ELSE? IT'S NOT RIGHT, BURYING YOUR HEAD IN BOOKS ALL THE TIME.
--BEHAVING LIKE THAT IN PUBLIC, WHAT'S WRONG WITH YOU? SHE'S GONE, AND THAT'S IT, THEN. OVER AND DONE. I WON'T HAVE ANY MORE OF THIS NONSENSE.
YOU'RE NO SON OF MINE, THAT'S FOR SURE. YOU'RE A WASTE OF SPACE, THAT'S WHAT YOU ARE.
I'M SORRY, BUT I'M AFRAID THAT YOU DON'T QUITE FIT THE STANDARDS FOR ADMISSION TO THE UNIVERSITY.
WHICH IS NOT TO SAY THAT YOU'RE NOT ACADEMICALLY SUITED. YOUR FORMER STUDIES ARE EXCELLENT, YOU'VE A FINE WAY WITH WORDS, YOU'RE EXTREMELY BRIGHT.
BUT ONE NEEDS FUNDS, OR IF NOT FUNDS, THEN ONE NEEDS...ADVANTAGES, DOESN'T ONE? IT'S REALLY ALL ABOUT FAMILY, YOU KNOW. THE REST ALMOST DOESN'T MATTER.
NO, AS I SAID, THERE AREN'T ANY POSITIONS AVAILABLE. NOT THAT YOU WOULDN'T DO A FINE JOB, IT'S JUST YOU'RE OVERQUALIFIED, THAT'S ALL.
CAN'T MAKE THE REST OF THE FELLOWS FEEL THEY'RE BEING OVERMATCHED, NOW CAN WE?
AND, OF COURSE, THERE'S THE MATTER OF PAYMENT. GIVEN THE WORK THEY DO, AND THE SKILLS THEY BRING, IT'S A FINE MATCH, BUT THE OWNER THINKS THAT IN TIME YOU'LL WANT MORE MONEY, THAT YOU WON'T SETTLE, AND IT'S IMPORTANT TO SETTLE, DON'T YOU THINK?

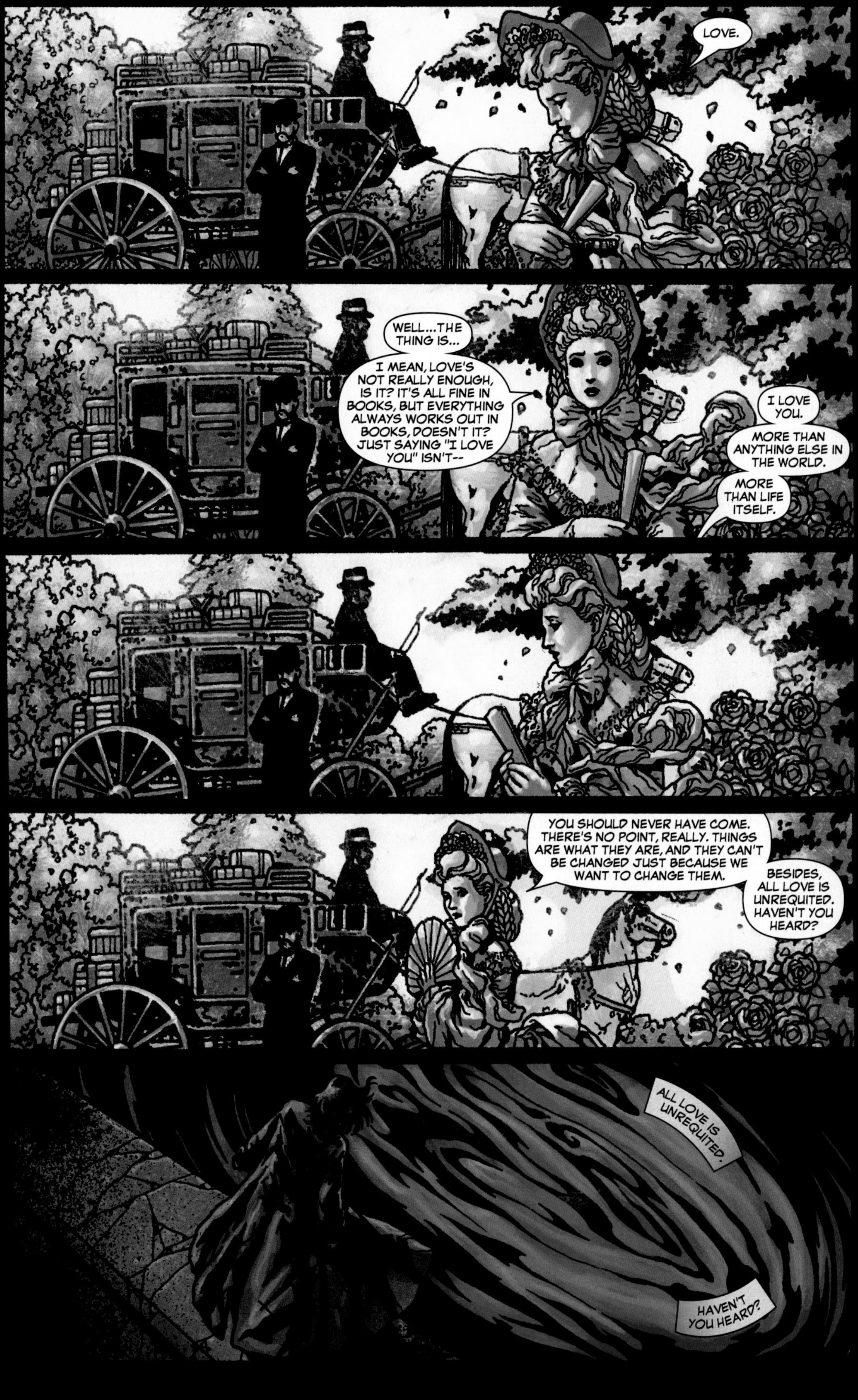
LOVE.
WELL...THE THING IS...
I MEAN, LOVE'S NOT REALLY ENOUGH, IS IT? IT'S ALL FINE IN BOOKS, BUT EVERYTHING ALWAYS WORKS OUT IN BOOKS, DOESN'T IT? JUST SAYING "I LOVE YOU" ISN'T--
I LOVE YOU.
MORE THAN ANYTHING ELSE IN THE WORLD.
MORE THAN LIFE ITSELF.
YOU SHOULD NEVER HAVE COME. THERE'S NO POINT, REALLY. THINGS ARE WHAT THEY ARE, AND THEY CAN'T BE CHANGED JUST BECAUSE WE WANT TO CHANGE THEM.
BESIDES, ALL LOVE IS UNREQUITED. HAVEN'T YOU HEARD?
ALL LOVE IS UNREQUITED.
HAVEN'T YOU HEARD?

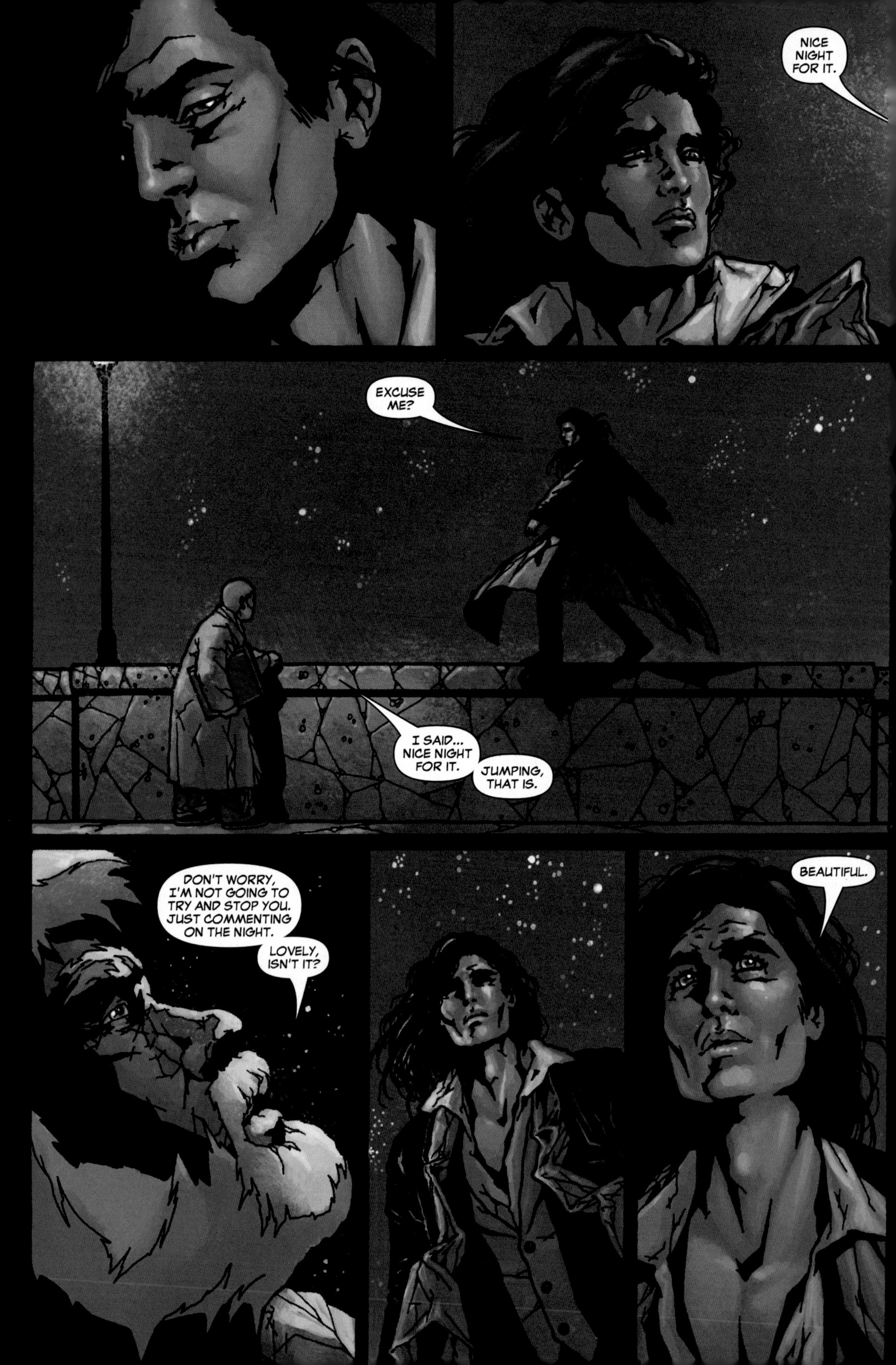
NICE NIGHT FOR IT.
EXCUSE ME?
I SAID... NICE NIGHT FOR IT.
JUMPING, THAT IS.
DON'T WORRY, I'M NOT GOING TO TRY AND STOP YOU. JUST COMMENTING ON THE NIGHT.
LOVELY, ISN'T IT?
BEAUTIFUL.

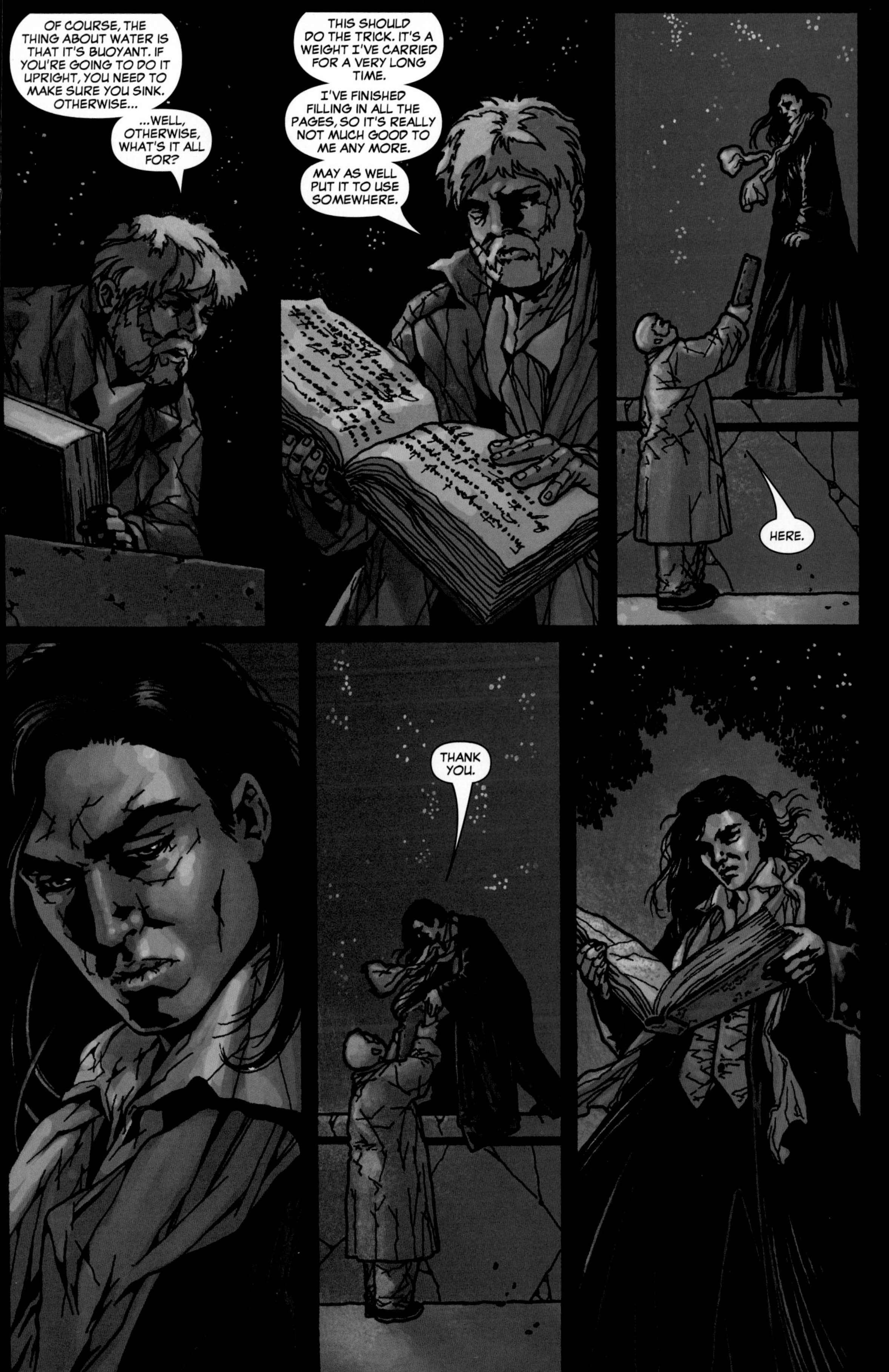
OF COURSE, THE THING ABOUT WATER IS THAT IT'S BUOYANT. IF YOU'RE GOING TO DO IT UPRIGHT, YOU NEED TO MAKE SURE YOU SINK. OTHERWISE...
...WELL, OTHERWISE, WHAT'S IT ALL FOR?
THIS SHOULD DO THE TRICK. IT'S A WEIGHT I'VE CARRIED FOR A VERY LONG TIME.
I'VE FINISHED FILLING IN ALL THE PAGES, SO IT'S REALLY NOT MUCH GOOD TO ME ANY MORE.
MAY AS WELL PUT IT TO USE SOMEWHERE.
HERE.
THANK YOU.

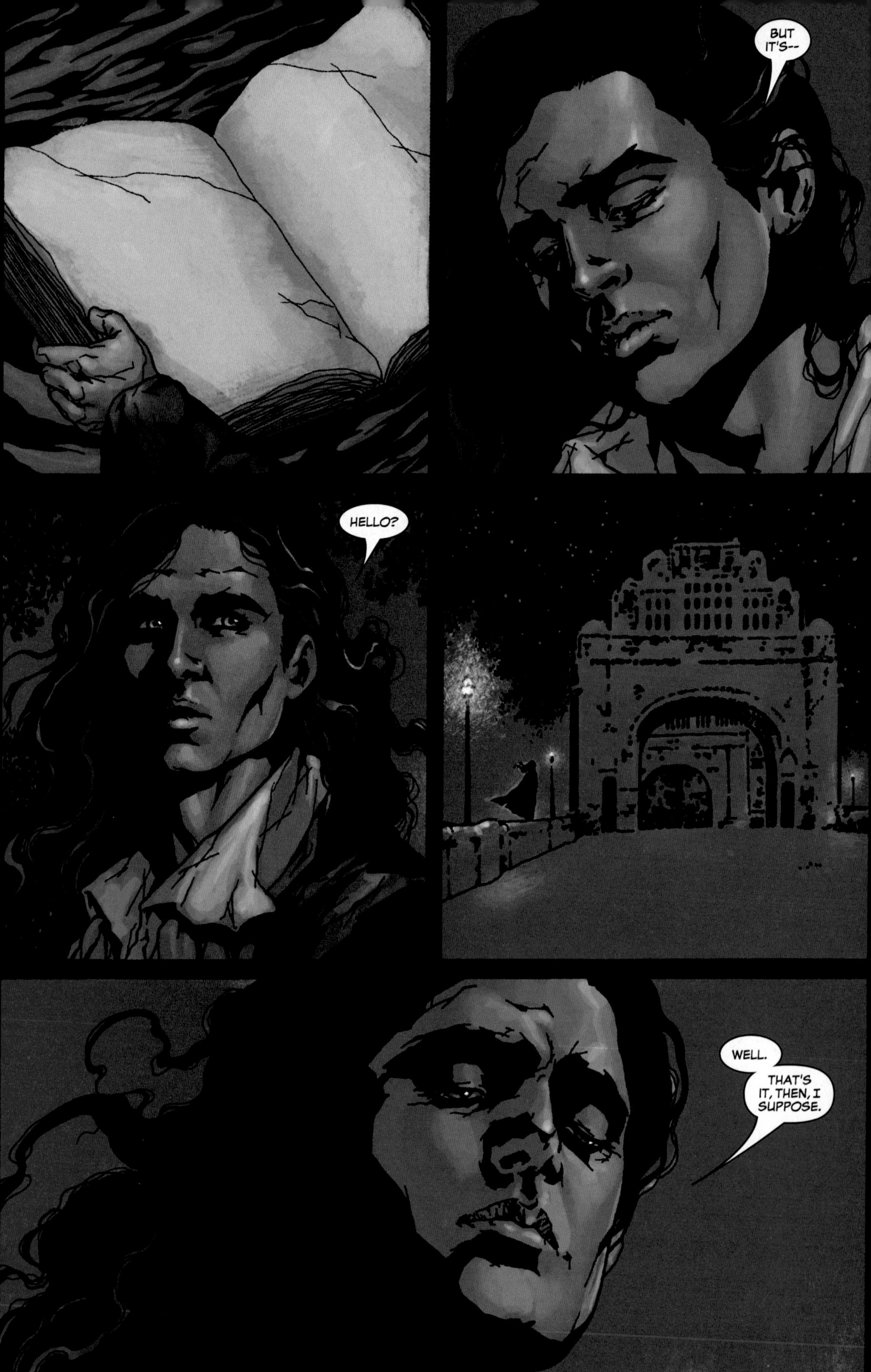
BUT IT'S--
HELLO?
WELL.
THAT'S IT, THEN, I SUPPOSE.

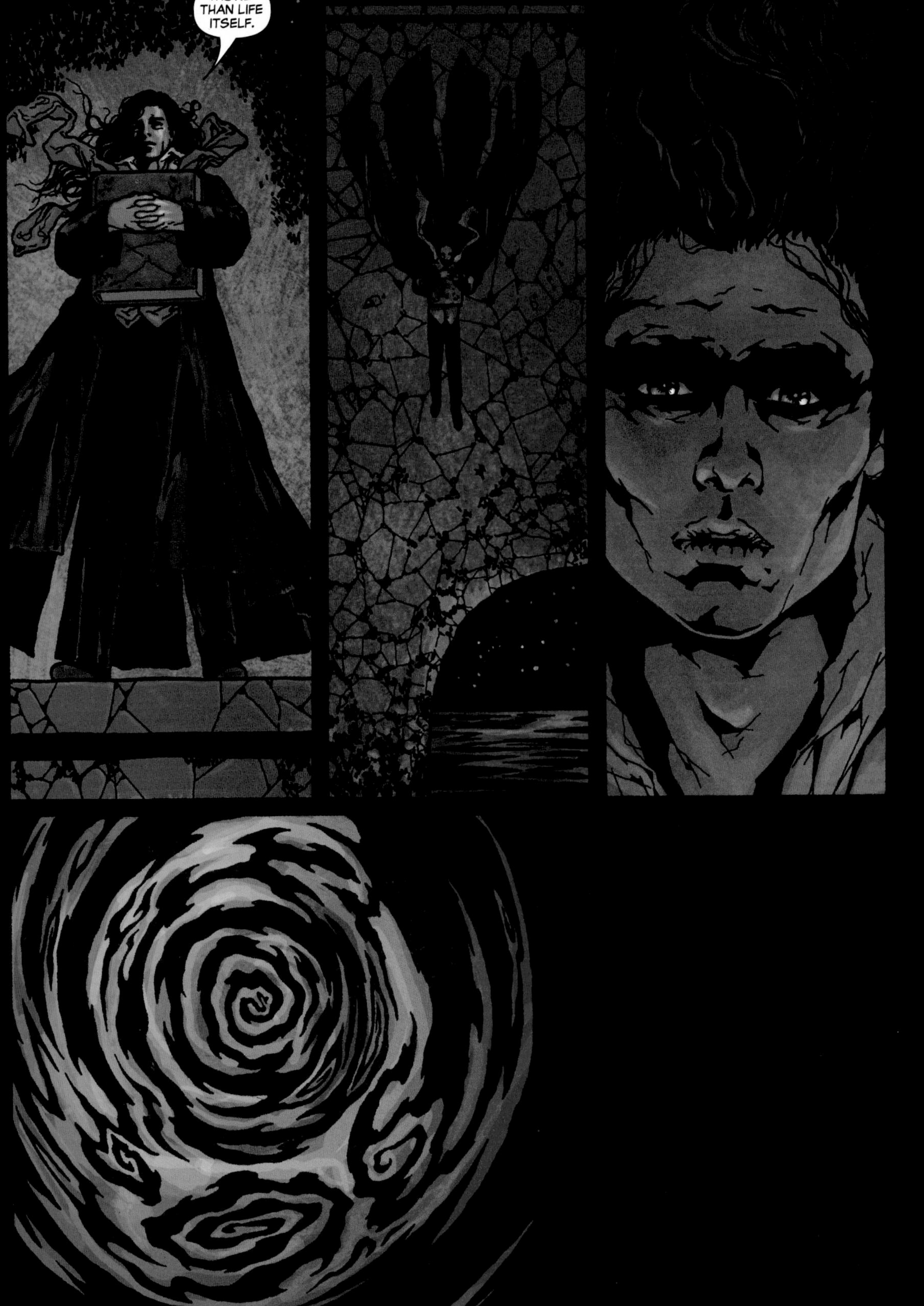
MORE THAN LIFE ITSELF.

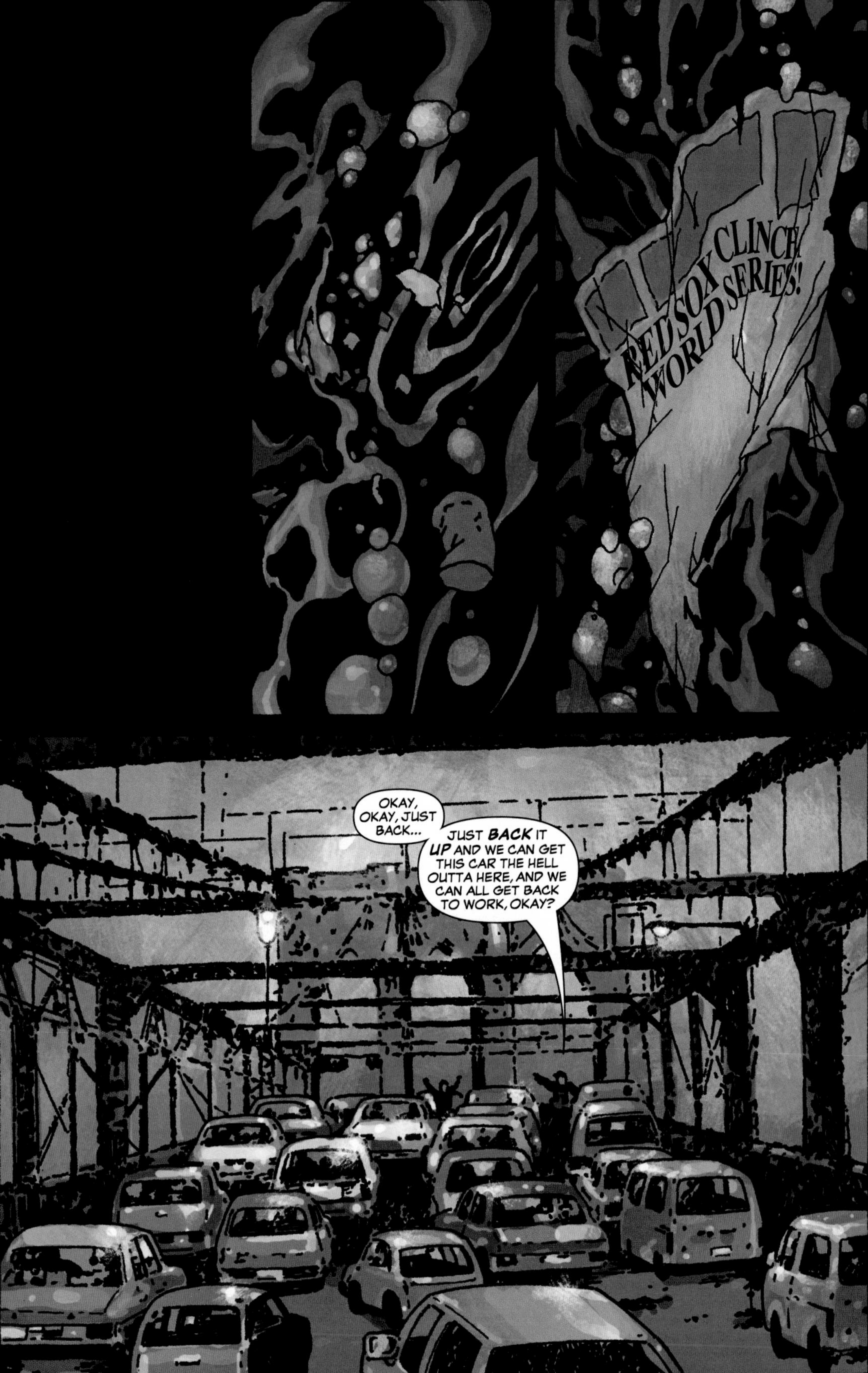
RED SOX CLINCH WORLD SERIES!
OKAY, OKAY, JUST BACK...
JUST BACK IT UP AND WE CAN GET THIS CAR THE HELL OUTTA HERE, AND WE CAN ALL GET BACK TO WORK, OKAY?

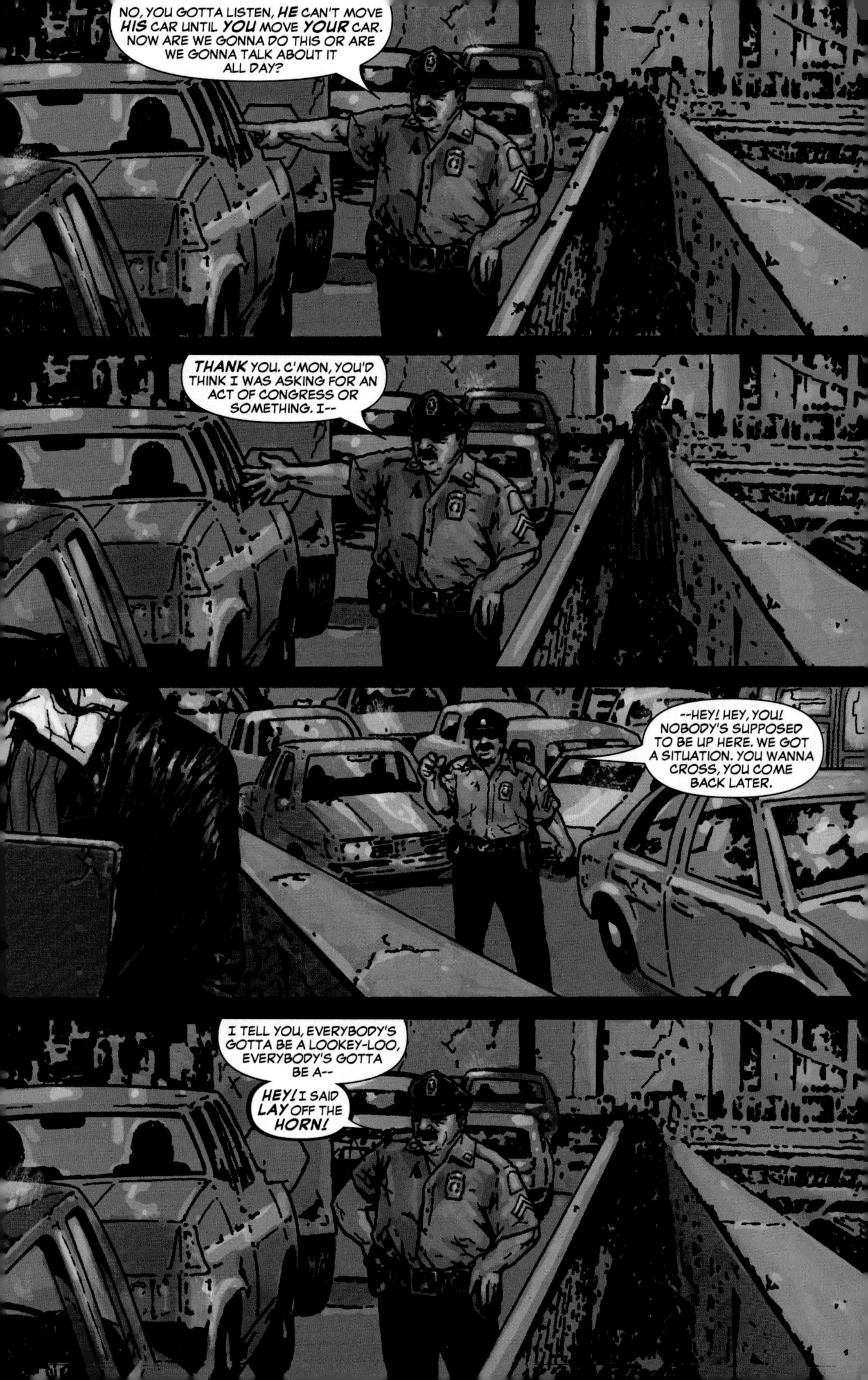
NO, YOU GOTTA LISTEN, HE CAN'T MOVE HIS CAR UNTIL YOU MOVE YOUR CAR. NOW ARE WE GONNA DO THIS OR ARE WE GONNA TALK ABOUT IT ALL DAY?
THANK YOU. C'MON, YOU'D THINK I WAS ASKING FOR AN ACT OF CONGRESS OR SOMETHING. I--
--HEY! HEY, YOU! NOBODY'S SUPPOSED TO BE UP HERE. WE GOT A SITUATION. YOU WANNA CROSS, YOU COME BACK LATER.
I TELL YOU, EVERYBODY'S GOTTA BE A LOOKEY-LOO, EVERYBODY'S GOTTA BE A--
HEY! I SAID LAY OFF THE HORN!

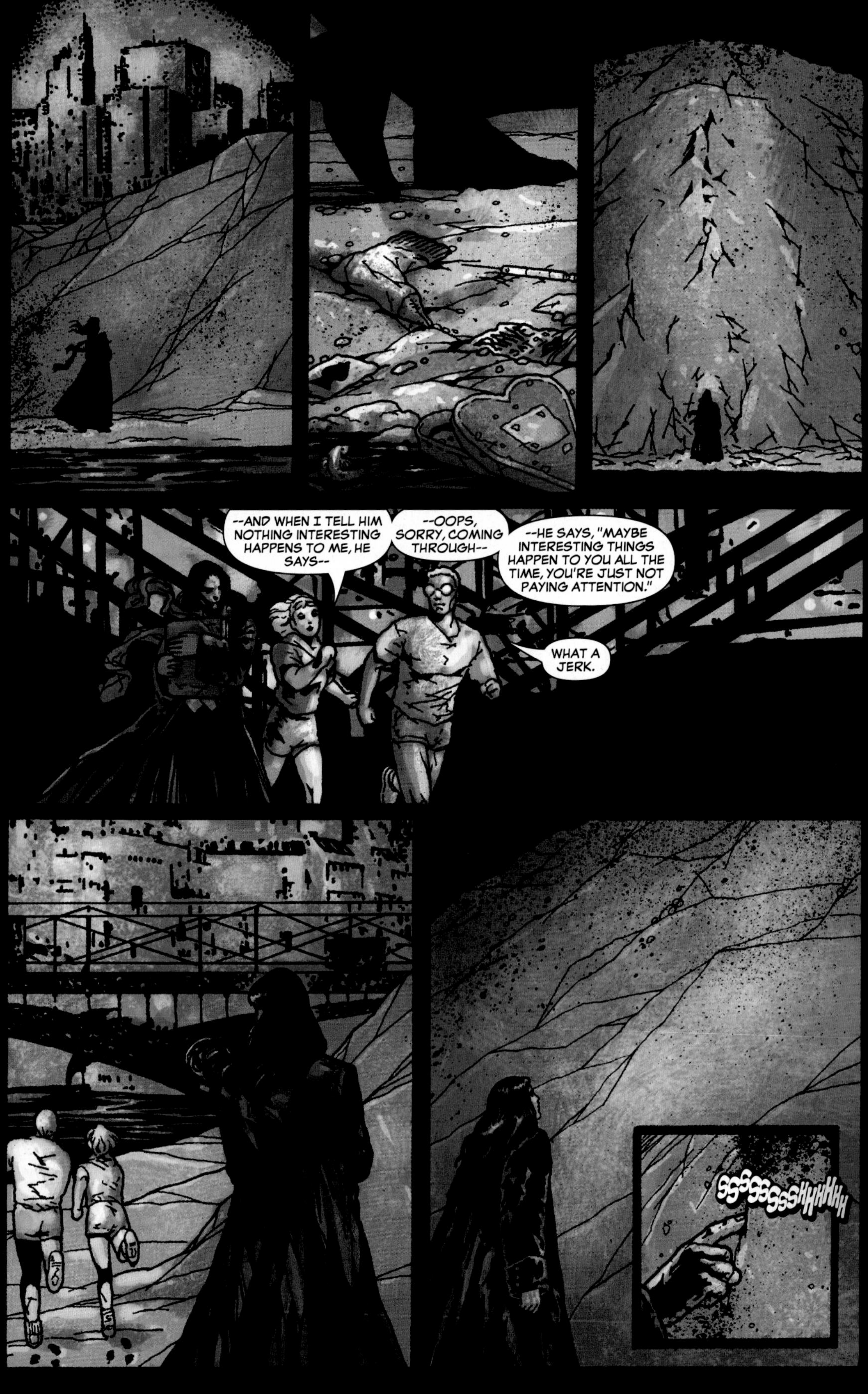
--AND WHEN I TELL HIM NOTHING INTERESTING HAPPENS TO ME, HE SAYS--
--OOPS, SORRY, COMING THROUGH--
--HE SAYS, "MAYBE INTERESTING THINGS HAPPEN TO YOU ALL THE TIME, YOU'RE JUST NOT PAYING ATTENTION."
WHAT A JERK.
SSSSSSSSHHHHHH

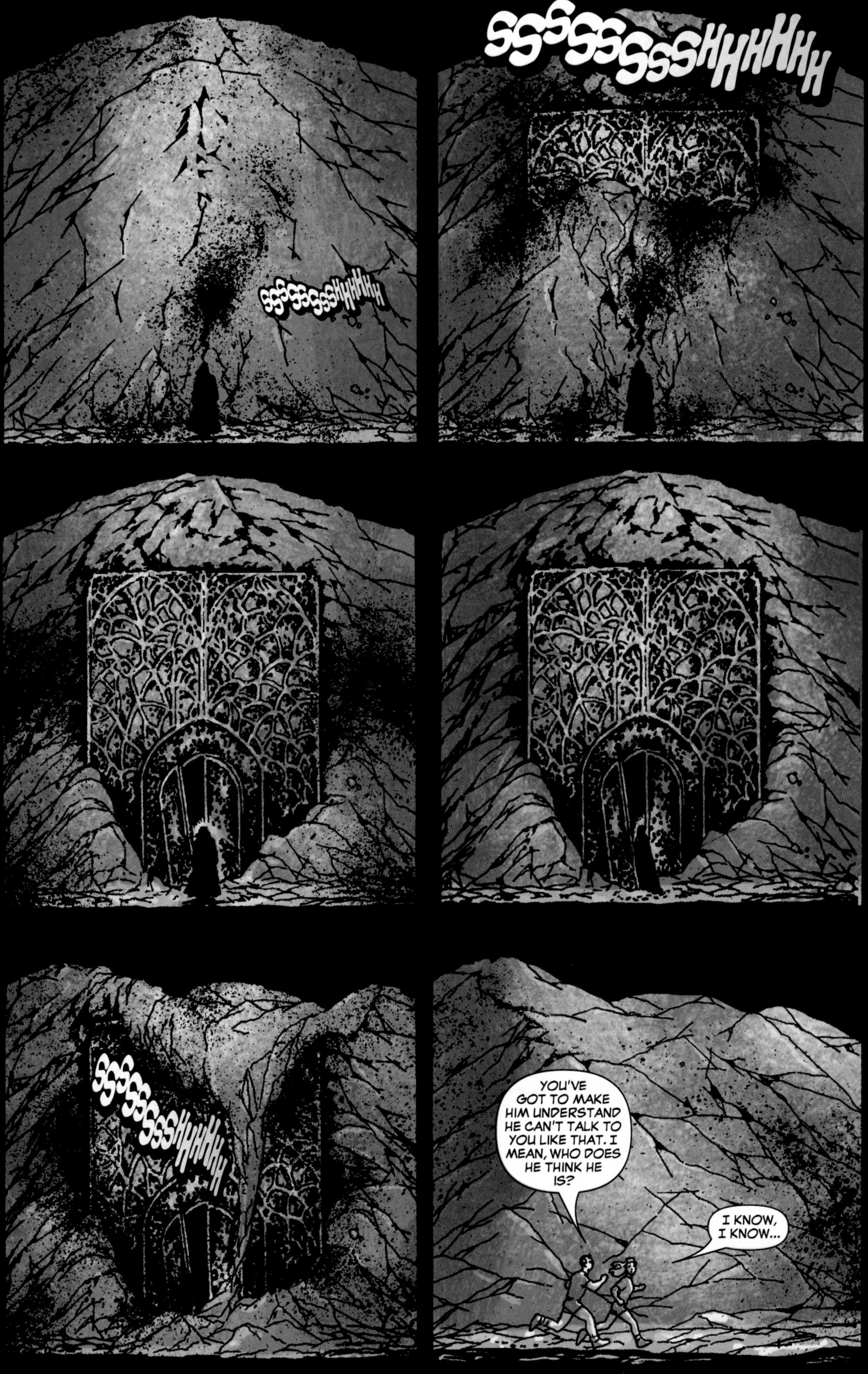
SSSSSSSSHHHHHH
SSSSSSSSSSHHHHHHH
SSSSSSSSSHHHHHH
YOU'VE GOT TO MAKE HIM UNDERSTAND HE CAN'T TALK TO YOU LIKE THAT. I MEAN, WHO DOES HE THINK HE IS?
I KNOW, I KNOW...

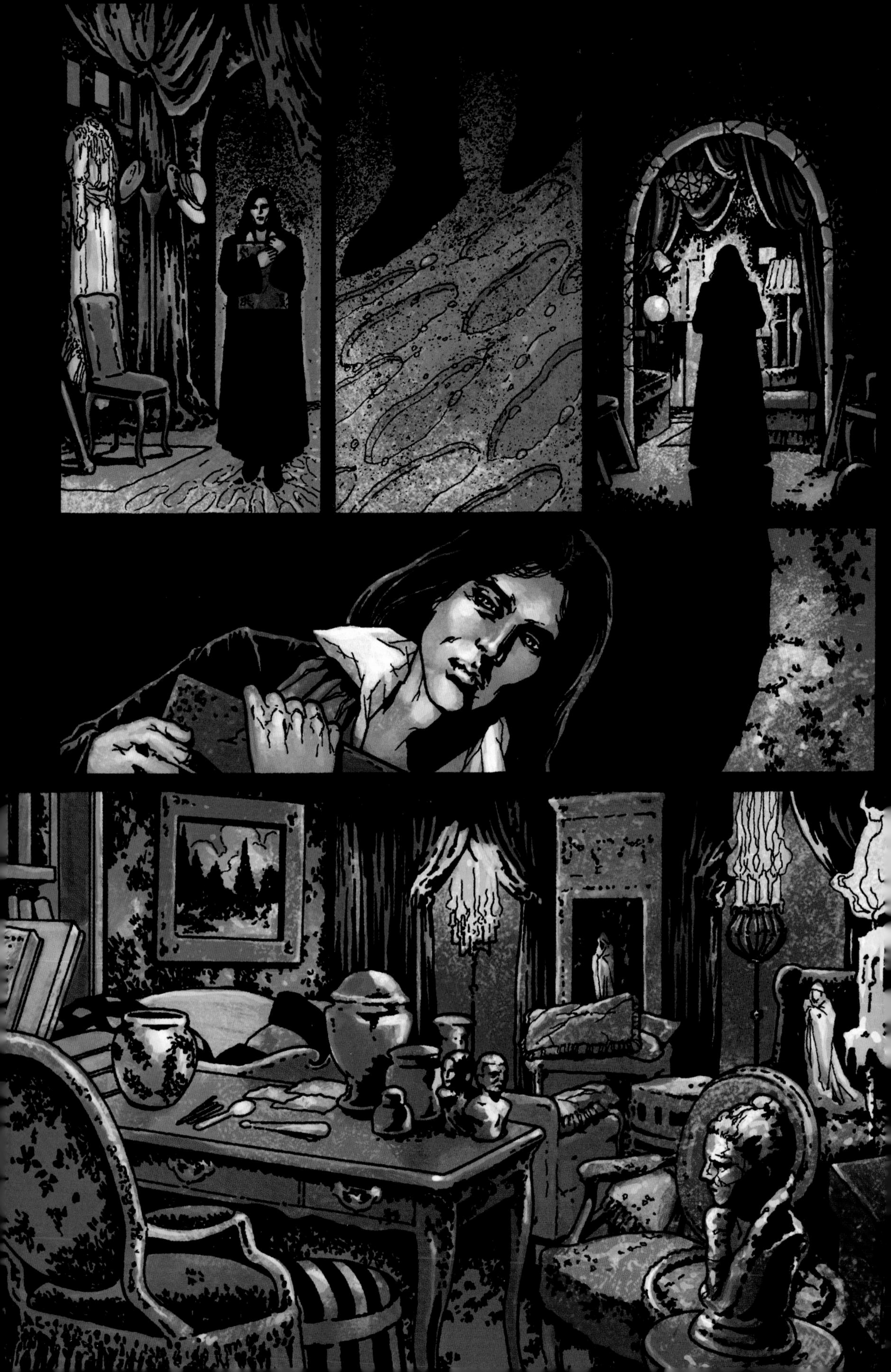

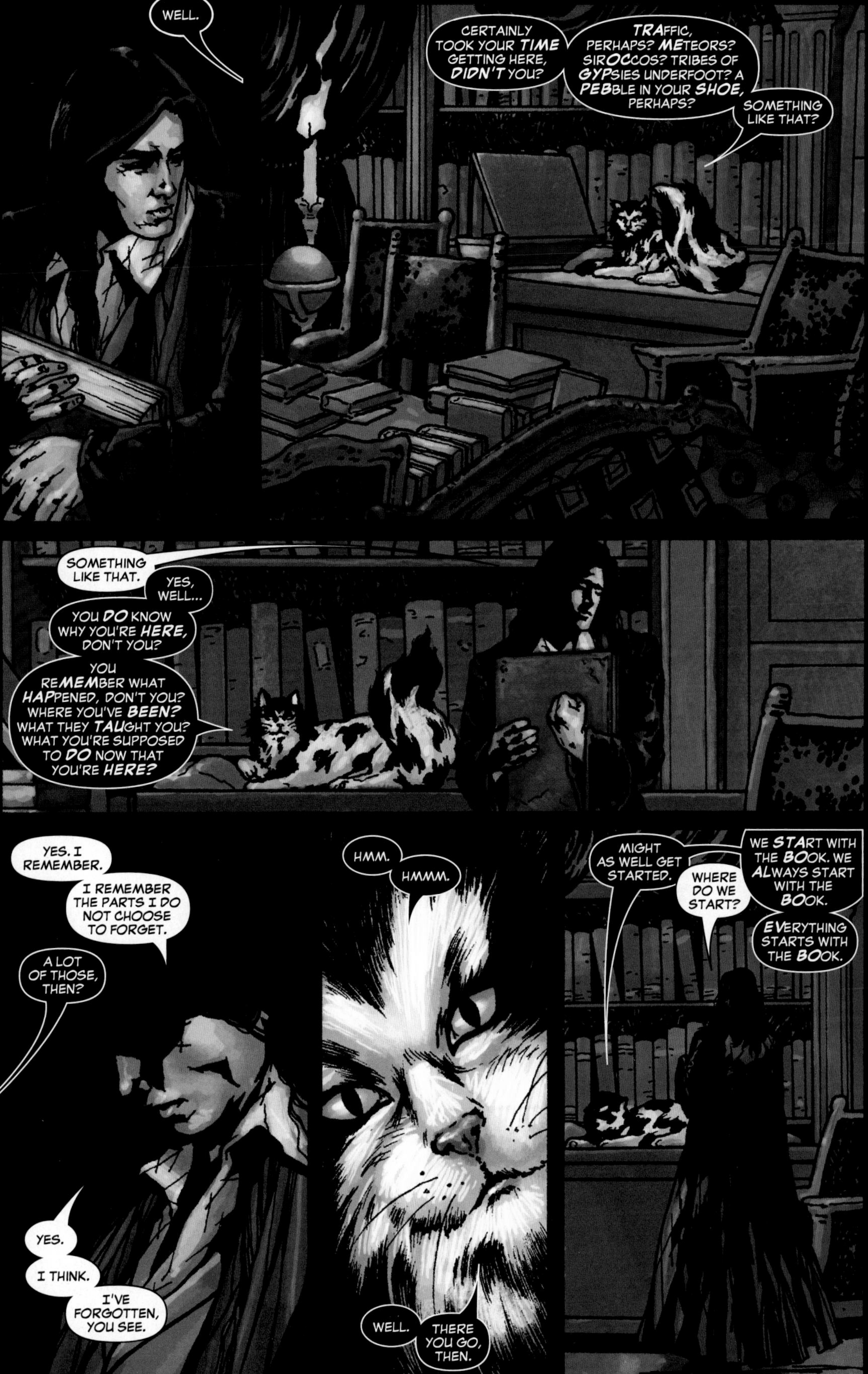

WELL.
CERTAINLY TOOK YOUR TIME GETTING HERE, DIDN'T YOU?
TRAFFIC, PERHAPS? METEORS? SIROCCOS? TRIBES OF GYPSIES UNDERFOOT? A PEBBLE IN YOUR SHOE, PERHAPS?
SOMETHING LIKE THAT?
SOMETHING LIKE THAT.
YES, WELL...
YOU DO KNOW WHY YOU'RE HERE, DON'T YOU?
YOU REMEMBER WHAT HAPPENED, DON'T YOU? WHERE YOU'VE BEEN? WHAT THEY TAUGHT YOU? WHAT YOU'RE SUPPOSED TO DO NOW THAT YOU'RE HERE?
YES. I REMEMBER.
I REMEMBER THE PARTS I DO NOT CHOOSE TO FORGET.
A LOT OF THOSE, THEN?
YES.
I THINK.
I'VE FORGOTTEN, YOU SEE.
HMM.
HMMM.
WELL.
THERE YOU GO, THEN.
MIGHT AS WELL GET STARTED.
WHERE DO WE START?
WE START WITH THE BOOK. WE ALWAYS START WITH THE BOOK.
EVERYTHING STARTS WITH THE BOOK.

WHERE DO I--

ON THE FRONT PAGE. IT STARTS WITH YOU.

IT ALWAYS STARTS WITH YOU.

Your name:

The words that brought you here:

The words that will release you:

YOU CAN LEAVE THE LAST LINE BLANK FOR NOW.

THAT ONE WILL HAVE TO COME LATER.

MUCH LATER.

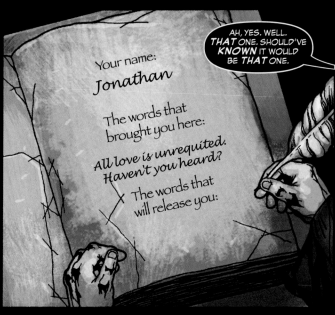

Your name:
Jonathan

The words that brought you here:

All love is unrequited. Haven't you heard?

The words that will release you:

AH, YES. WELL. THAT ONE. SHOULD'VE KNOWN IT WOULD BE THAT ONE.

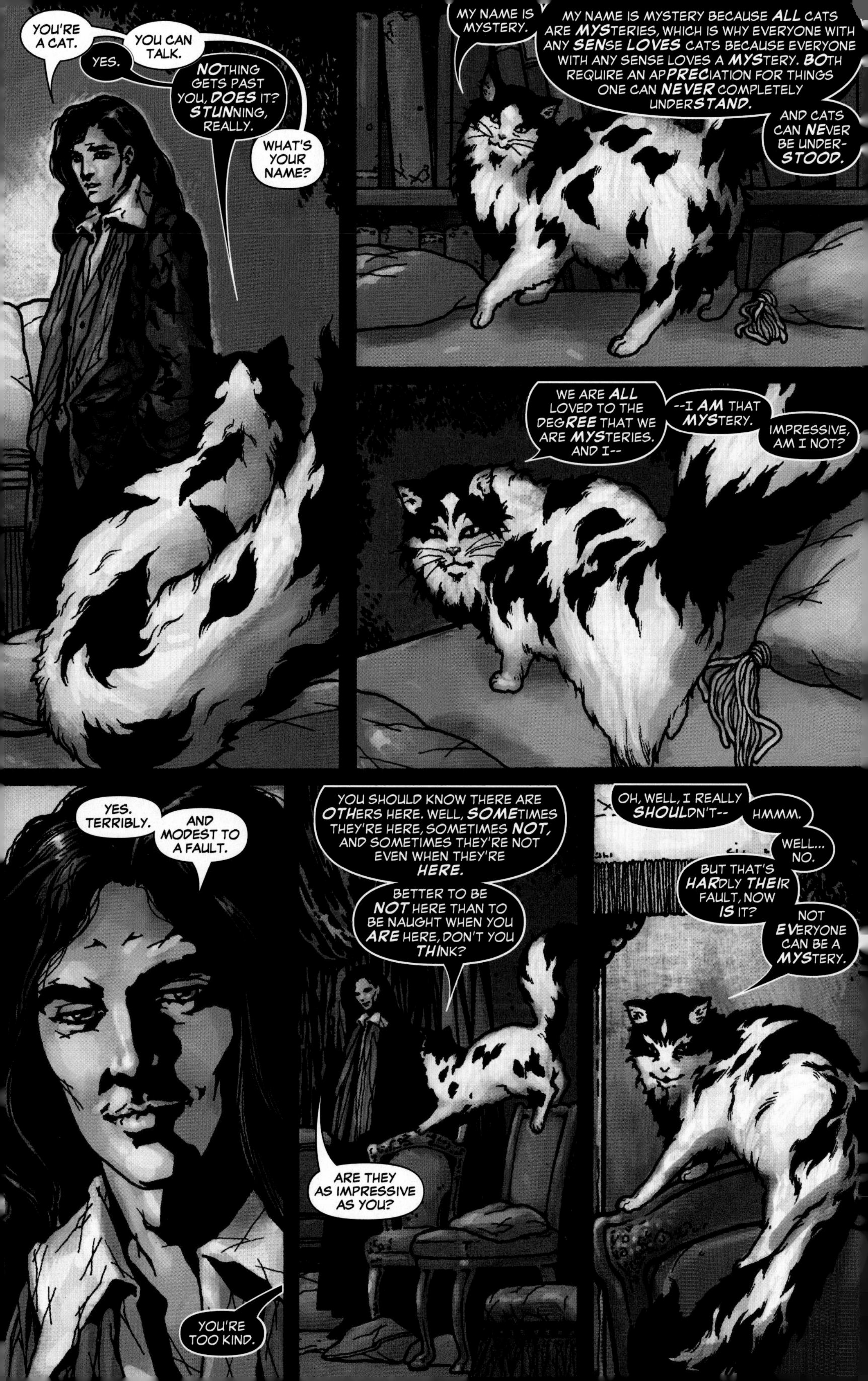
YOU'RE A CAT.
YOU CAN TALK.
YES.
NOTHING GETS PAST YOU, DOES IT? STUNNING, REALLY.
WHAT'S YOUR NAME?
MY NAME IS MYSTERY.
MY NAME IS MYSTERY BECAUSE ALL CATS ARE MYSTERIES, WHICH IS WHY EVERYONE WITH ANY SENSE LOVES CATS BECAUSE EVERYONE WITH ANY SENSE LOVES A MYSTERY. BOTH REQUIRE AN APPRECIATION FOR THINGS ONE CAN NEVER COMPLETELY UNDERSTAND.
AND CATS CAN NEVER BE UNDER-STOOD.
WE ARE ALL LOVED TO THE DEGREE THAT WE ARE MYSTERIES. AND I--
--I AM THAT MYSTERY.
IMPRESSIVE, AM I NOT?
YES. TERRIBLY.
AND MODEST TO A FAULT.
YOU'RE TOO KIND.
YOU SHOULD KNOW THERE ARE OTHERS HERE. WELL, SOMETIMES THEY'RE HERE, SOMETIMES NOT, AND SOMETIMES THEY'RE NOT EVEN WHEN THEY'RE HERE.
BETTER TO BE NOT HERE THAN TO BE NAUGHT WHEN YOU ARE HERE, DON'T YOU THINK?
ARE THEY AS IMPRESSIVE AS YOU?
OH, WELL, I REALLY SHOULDN'T--
HMMM.
WELL... NO.
BUT THAT'S HARDLY THEIR FAULT, NOW IS IT?
NOT EVERYONE CAN BE A MYSTERY.

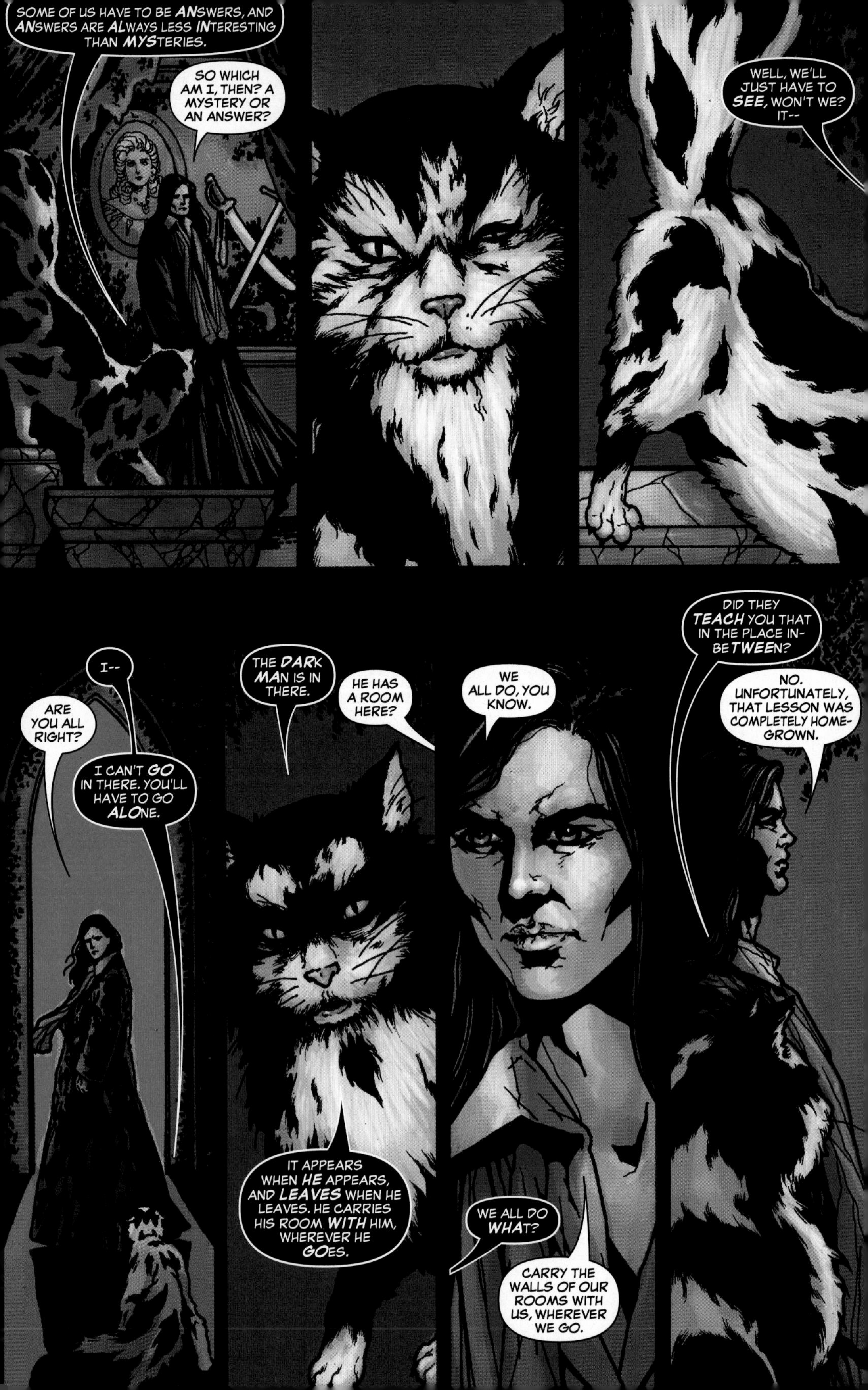
SOME OF US HAVE TO BE ANSWERS, AND ANSWERS ARE ALWAYS LESS INTERESTING THAN MYSTERIES.
SO WHICH AM I, THEN? A MYSTERY OR AN ANSWER?
WELL, WE'LL JUST HAVE TO SEE, WON'T WE? IT--
ARE YOU ALL RIGHT?
I--
I CAN'T GO IN THERE. YOU'LL HAVE TO GO ALONE.
THE DARK MAN IS IN THERE.
HE HAS A ROOM HERE?
IT APPEARS WHEN HE APPEARS, AND LEAVES WHEN HE LEAVES. HE CARRIES HIS ROOM WITH HIM, WHEREVER HE GOES.
WE ALL DO, YOU KNOW.
WE ALL DO WHAT?
CARRY THE WALLS OF OUR ROOMS WITH US, WHEREVER WE GO.
DID THEY TEACH YOU THAT IN THE PLACE IN-BETWEEN?
NO. UNFORTUNATELY, THAT LESSON WAS COMPLETELY HOME-GROWN.

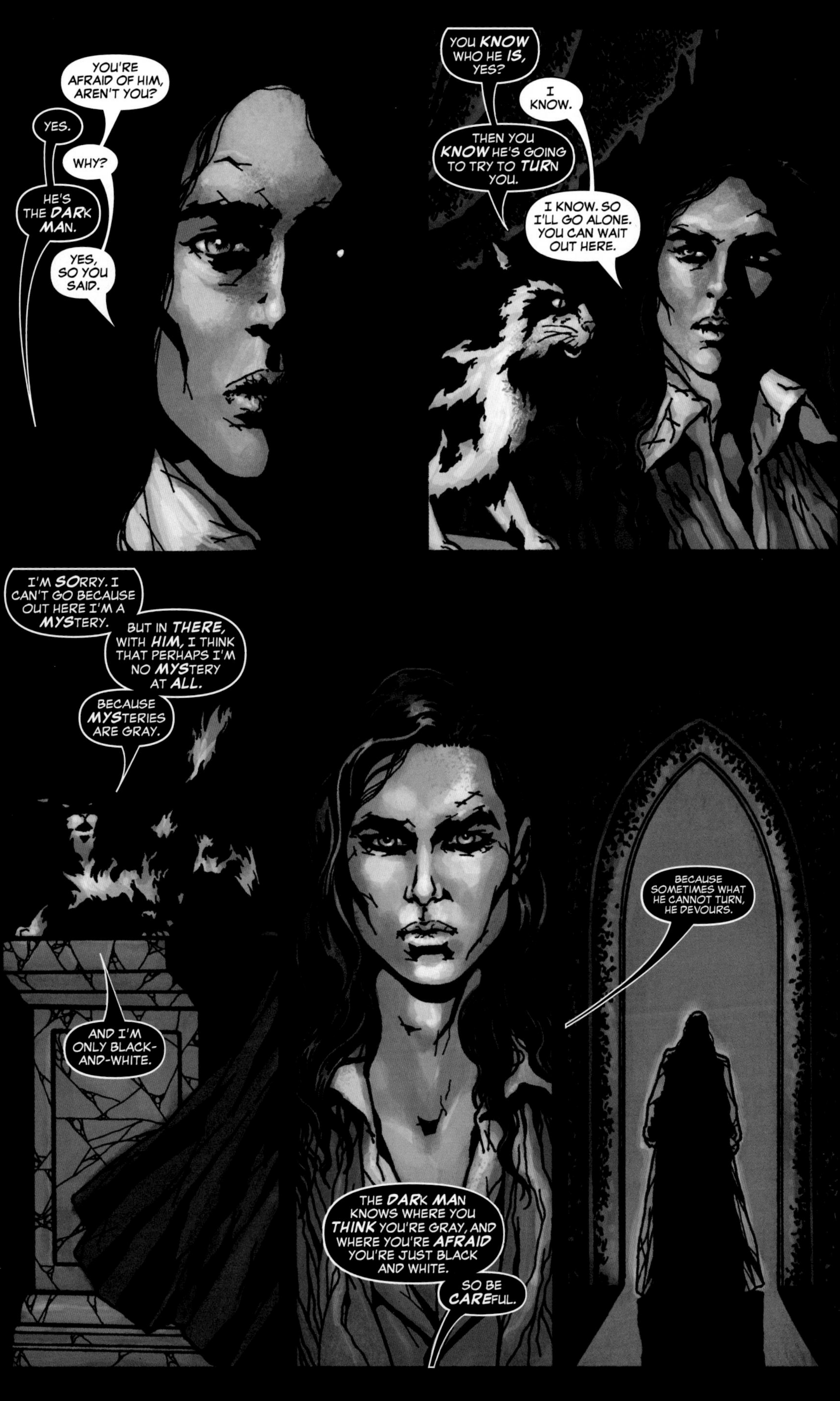
YOU'RE AFRAID OF HIM, AREN'T YOU?
YES.
WHY?
HE'S THE DARK MAN.
YES, SO YOU SAID.
YOU KNOW WHO HE IS, YES?
I KNOW.
THEN YOU KNOW HE'S GOING TO TRY TO TURN YOU.
I KNOW. SO I'LL GO ALONE. YOU CAN WAIT OUT HERE.
I'M SORRY. I CAN'T GO BECAUSE OUT HERE I'M A MYSTERY.
BUT IN THERE, WITH HIM, I THINK THAT PERHAPS I'M NO MYSTERY AT ALL.
BECAUSE MYSTERIES ARE GRAY.
AND I'M ONLY BLACK-AND-WHITE.
BECAUSE SOMETIMES WHAT HE CANNOT TURN, HE DEVOURS.
THE DARK MAN KNOWS WHERE YOU THINK YOU'RE GRAY, AND WHERE YOU'RE AFRAID YOU'RE JUST BLACK AND WHITE.
SO BE CAREFUL.

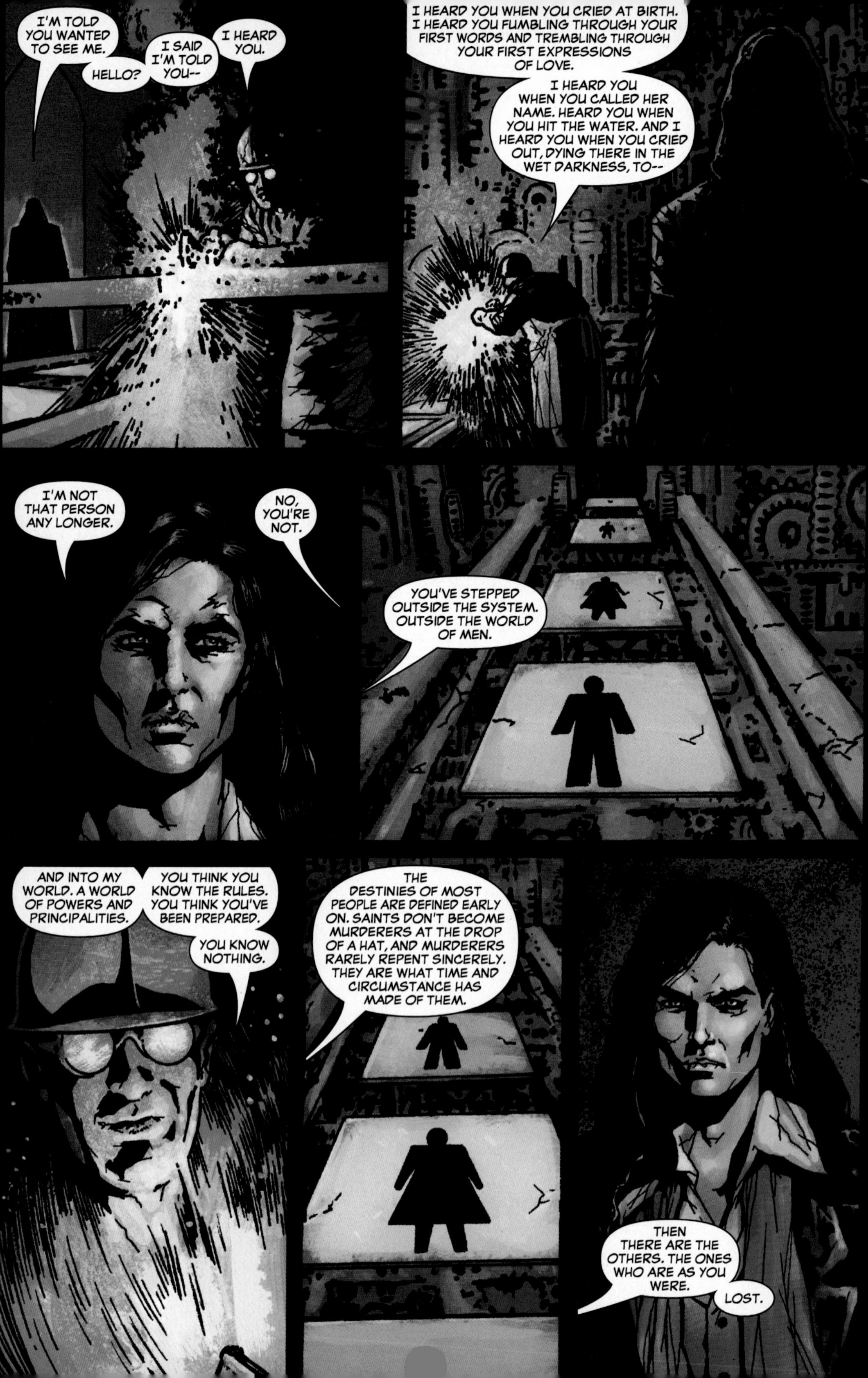
I'M TOLD YOU WANTED TO SEE ME.
HELLO?
I SAID I'M TOLD YOU--
I HEARD YOU.
I HEARD YOU WHEN YOU CRIED AT BIRTH. I HEARD YOU FUMBLING THROUGH YOUR FIRST WORDS AND TREMBLING THROUGH YOUR FIRST EXPRESSIONS OF LOVE.
I HEARD YOU WHEN YOU CALLED HER NAME. HEARD YOU WHEN YOU HIT THE WATER. AND I HEARD YOU WHEN YOU CRIED OUT, DYING THERE IN THE WET DARKNESS, TO--
I'M NOT THAT PERSON ANY LONGER.
NO, YOU'RE NOT.
YOU'VE STEPPED OUTSIDE THE SYSTEM. OUTSIDE THE WORLD OF MEN.
AND INTO MY WORLD. A WORLD OF POWERS AND PRINCIPALITIES.
YOU THINK YOU KNOW THE RULES. YOU THINK YOU'VE BEEN PREPARED.
YOU KNOW NOTHING.
THE DESTINIES OF MOST PEOPLE ARE DEFINED EARLY ON. SAINTS DON'T BECOME MURDERERS AT THE DROP OF A HAT, AND MURDERERS RARELY REPENT SINCERELY. THEY ARE WHAT TIME AND CIRCUMSTANCE HAS MADE OF THEM.
THEN THERE ARE THE OTHERS. THE ONES WHO ARE AS YOU WERE.
LOST.

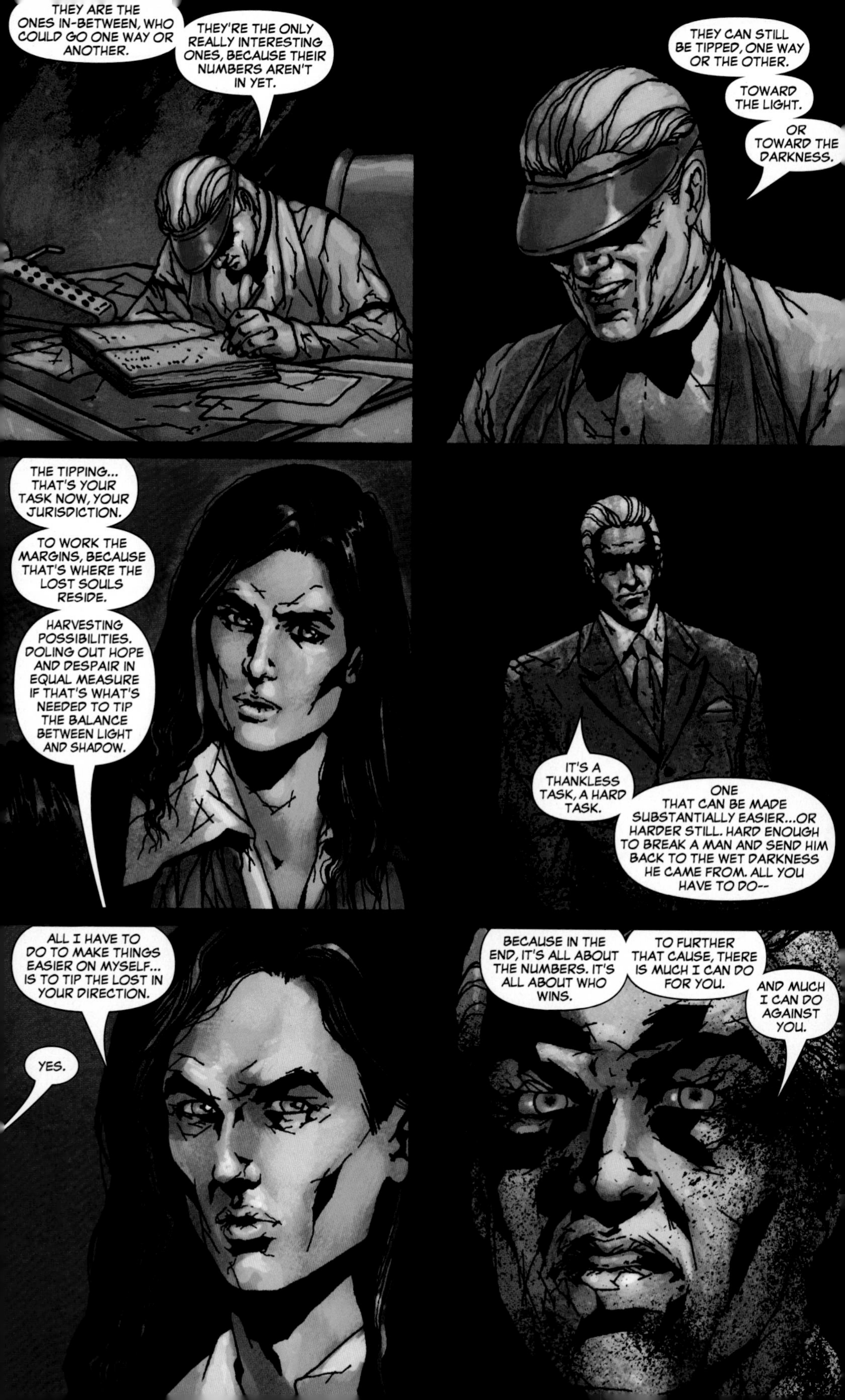
THEY ARE THE ONES IN-BETWEEN, WHO COULD GO ONE WAY OR ANOTHER.
THEY'RE THE ONLY REALLY INTERESTING ONES, BECAUSE THEIR NUMBERS AREN'T IN YET.
THEY CAN STILL BE TIPPED, ONE WAY OR THE OTHER.
TOWARD THE LIGHT.
OR TOWARD THE DARKNESS.
THE TIPPING... THAT'S YOUR TASK NOW, YOUR JURISDICTION.
TO WORK THE MARGINS, BECAUSE THAT'S WHERE THE LOST SOULS RESIDE.
HARVESTING POSSIBILITIES. DOLING OUT HOPE AND DESPAIR IN EQUAL MEASURE IF THAT'S WHAT'S NEEDED TO TIP THE BALANCE BETWEEN LIGHT AND SHADOW.
IT'S A THANKLESS TASK, A HARD TASK.
ONE THAT CAN BE MADE SUBSTANTIALLY EASIER...OR HARDER STILL. HARD ENOUGH TO BREAK A MAN AND SEND HIM BACK TO THE WET DARKNESS HE CAME FROM. ALL YOU HAVE TO DO--
ALL I HAVE TO DO TO MAKE THINGS EASIER ON MYSELF... IS TO TIP THE LOST IN YOUR DIRECTION.
YES.
BECAUSE IN THE END, IT'S ALL ABOUT THE NUMBERS. IT'S ALL ABOUT WHO WINS.
TO FURTHER THAT CAUSE, THERE IS MUCH I CAN DO FOR YOU.
AND MUCH I CAN DO AGAINST YOU.

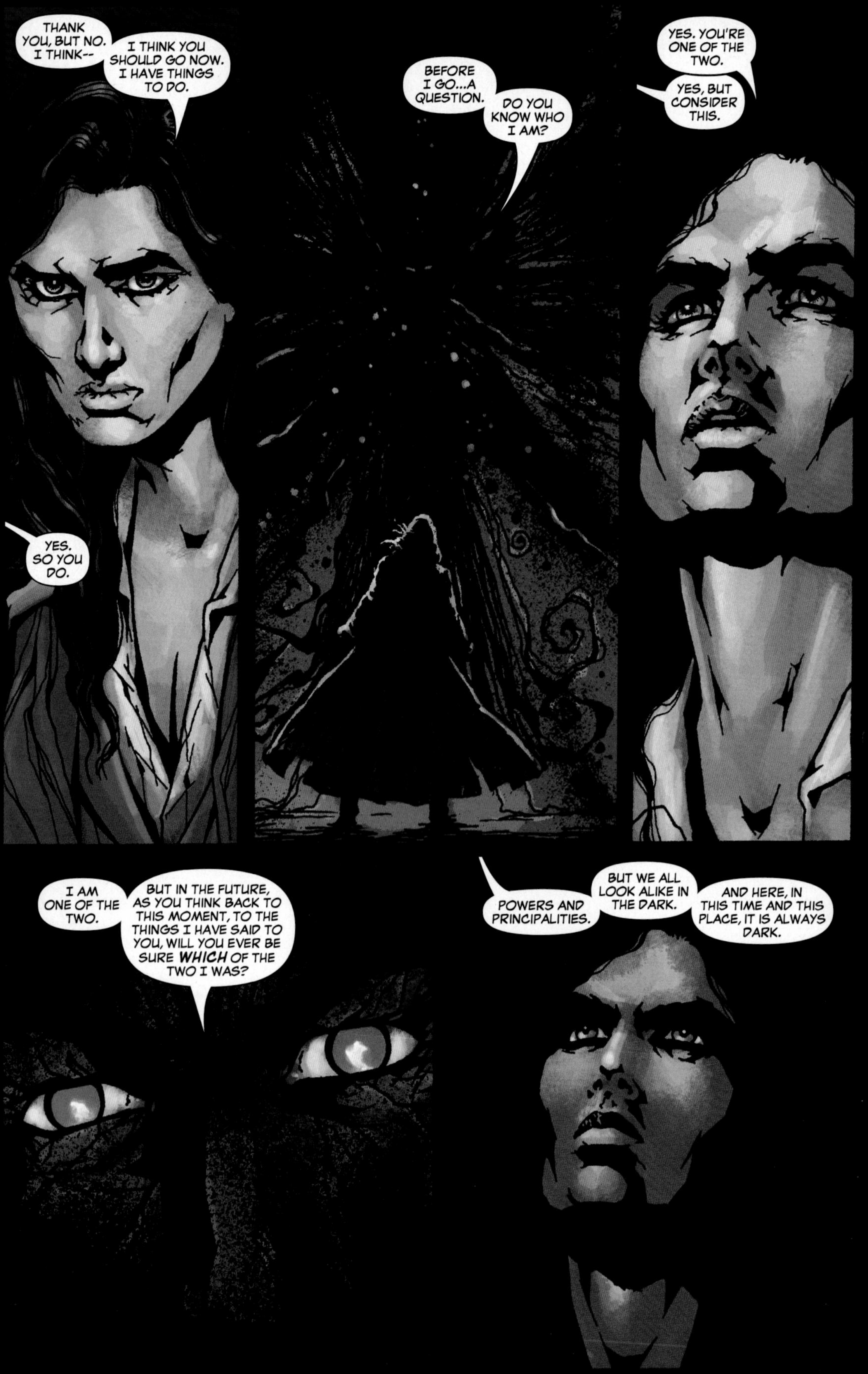
THANK YOU, BUT NO. I THINK--
I THINK YOU SHOULD GO NOW. I HAVE THINGS TO DO.
YES. SO YOU DO.
BEFORE I GO...A QUESTION.
DO YOU KNOW WHO I AM?
YES. YOU'RE ONE OF THE TWO.
YES, BUT CONSIDER THIS.
I AM ONE OF THE TWO.
BUT IN THE FUTURE, AS YOU THINK BACK TO THIS MOMENT, TO THE THINGS I HAVE SAID TO YOU, WILL YOU EVER BE SURE WHICH OF THE TWO I WAS?
POWERS AND PRINCIPALITIES.
BUT WE ALL LOOK ALIKE IN THE DARK.
AND HERE, IN THIS TIME AND THIS PLACE, IT IS ALWAYS DARK.

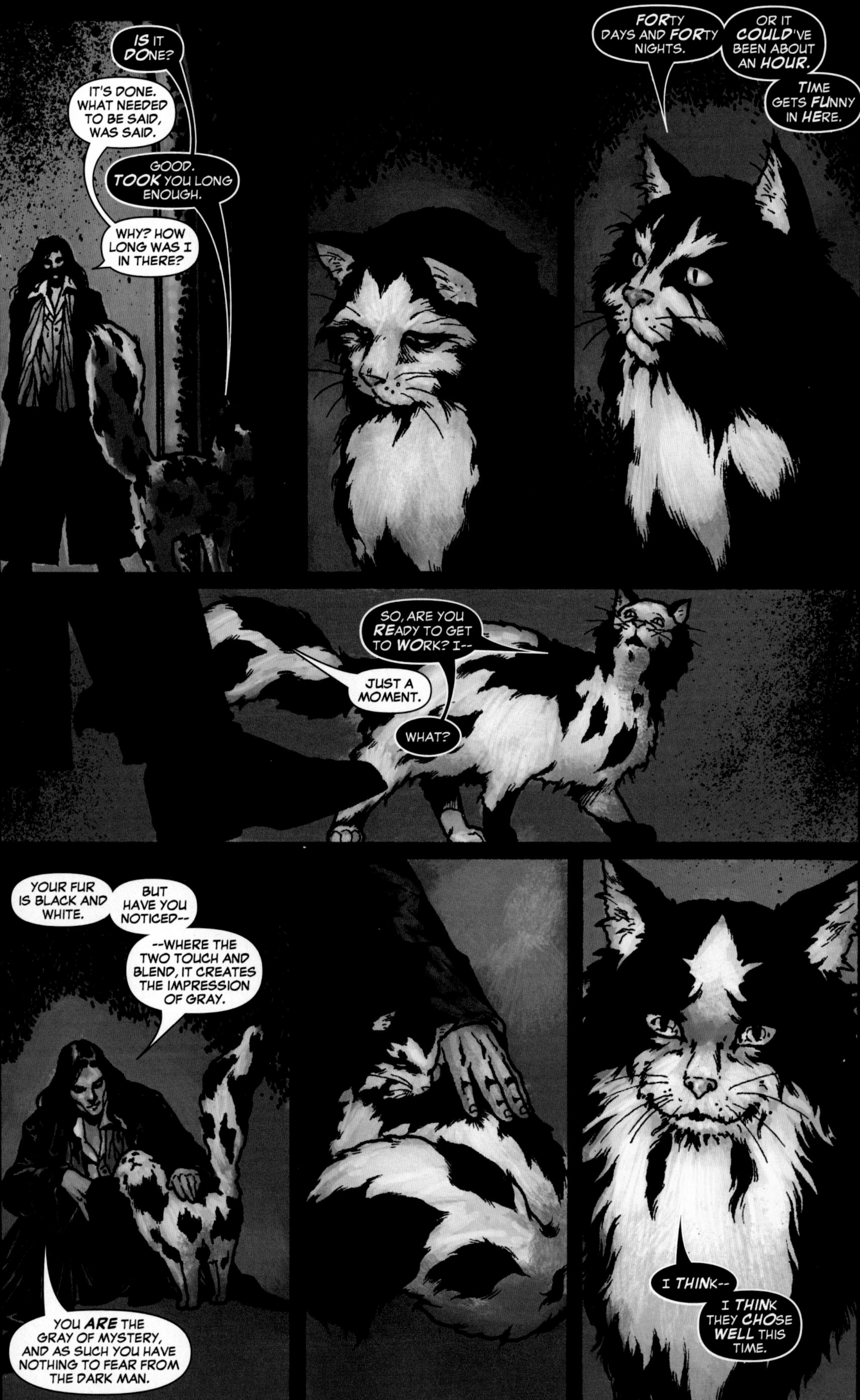
IS IT DONE?
IT'S DONE. WHAT NEEDED TO BE SAID, WAS SAID.
GOOD. TOOK YOU LONG ENOUGH.
WHY? HOW LONG WAS I IN THERE?
FORTY DAYS AND FORTY NIGHTS.
OR IT COULD'VE BEEN ABOUT AN HOUR.
TIME GETS FUNNY IN HERE.
SO, ARE YOU READY TO GET TO WORK? I--
JUST A MOMENT.
WHAT?
YOUR FUR IS BLACK AND WHITE.
BUT HAVE YOU NOTICED--
--WHERE THE TWO TOUCH AND BLEND, IT CREATES THE IMPRESSION OF GRAY.
YOU ARE THE GRAY OF MYSTERY, AND AS SUCH YOU HAVE NOTHING TO FEAR FROM THE DARK MAN.
I THINK--
I THINK THEY CHOSE WELL THIS TIME.

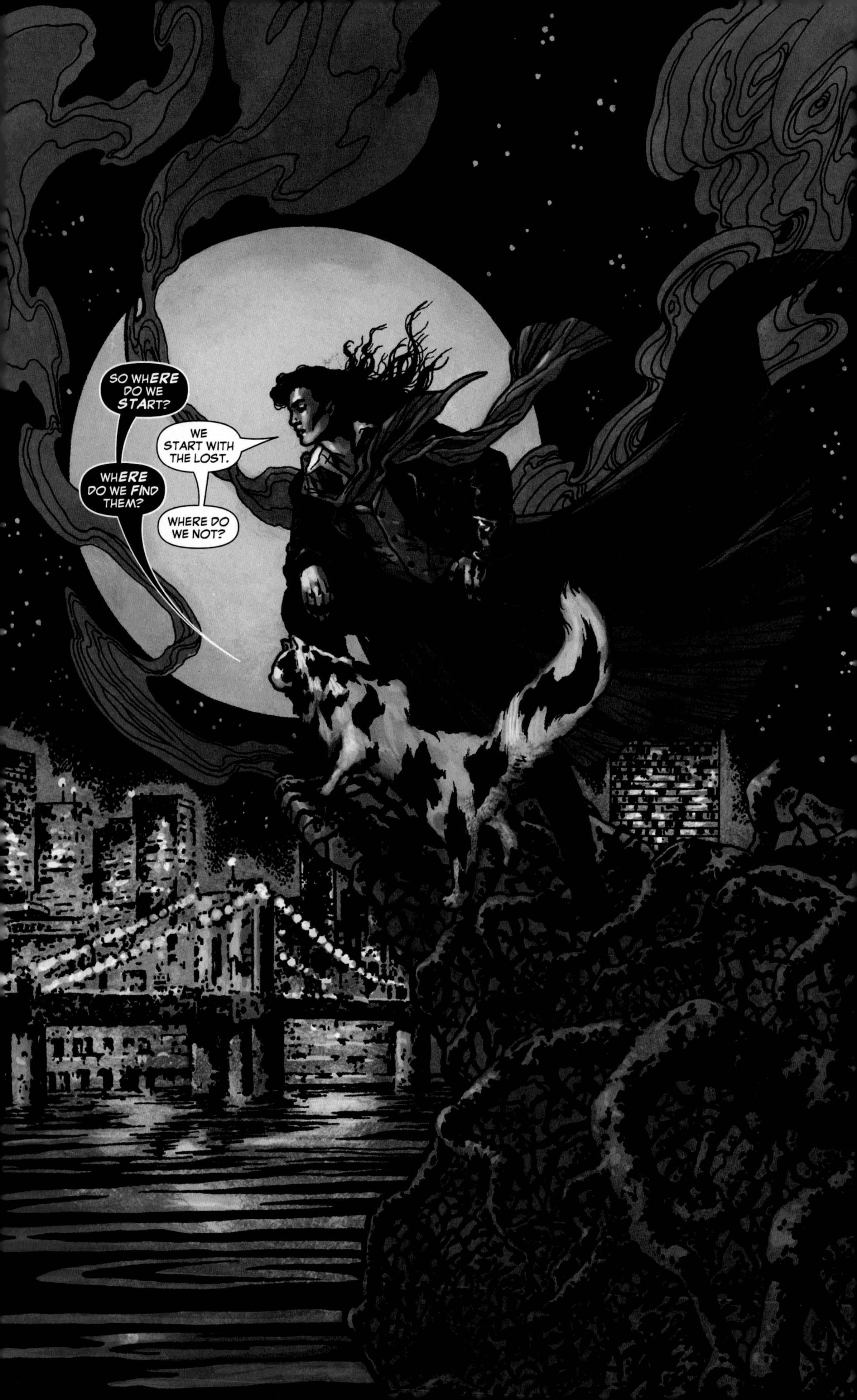

SO WHERE DO WE START?
WE START WITH THE LOST.
WHERE DO WE FIND THEM?
WHERE DO WE NOT?

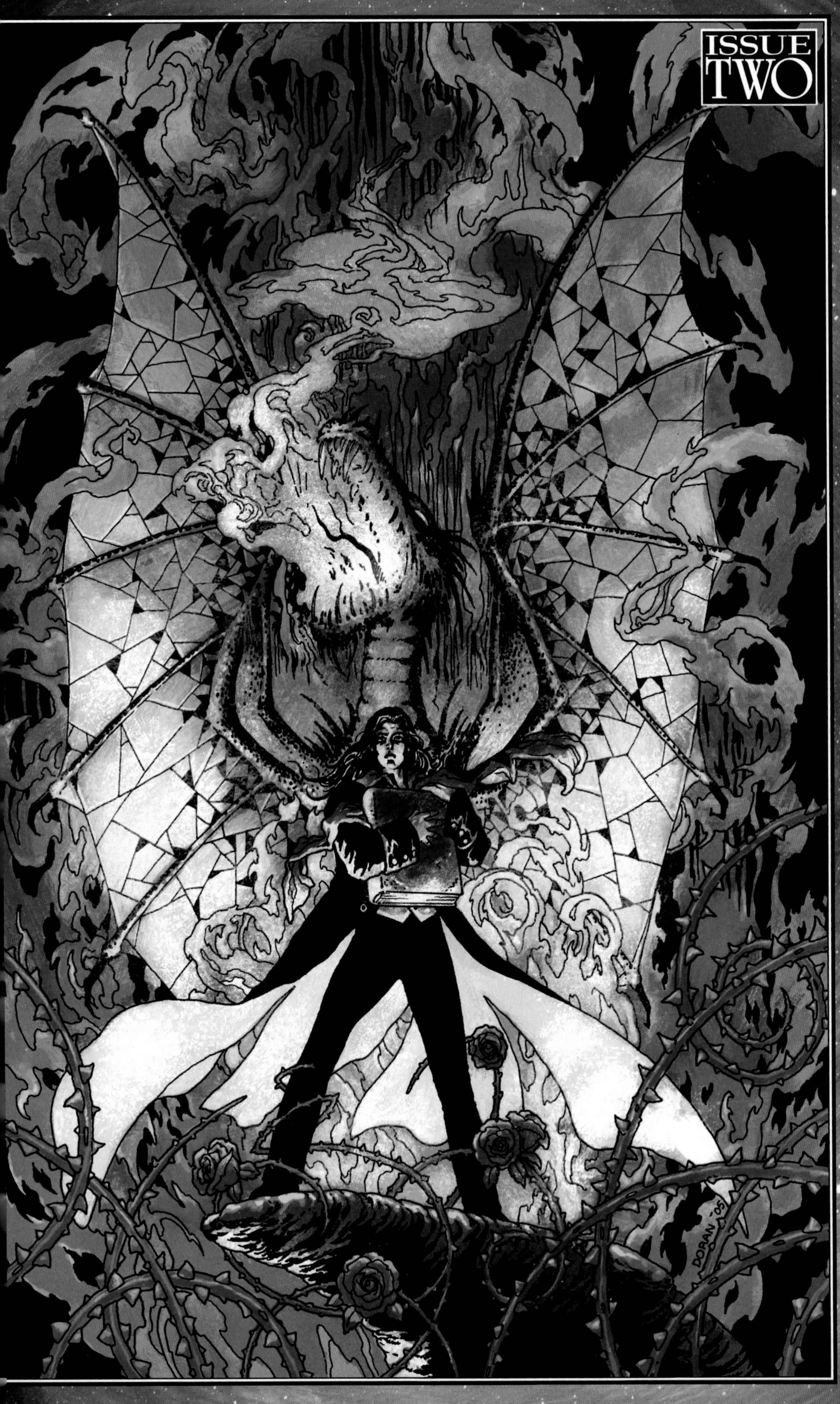
ISSUE
TWO
DORAN '05

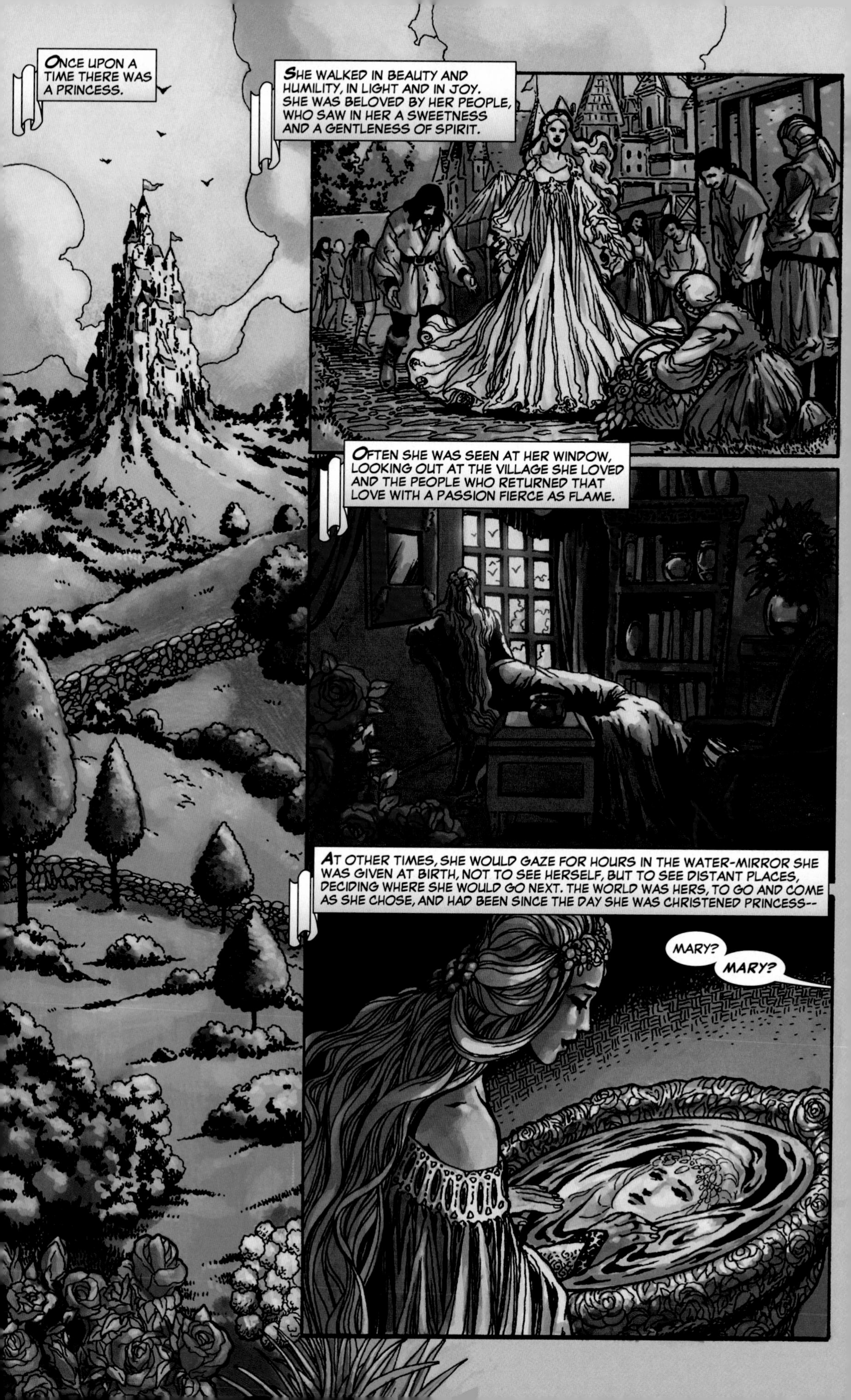
ONCE UPON A TIME THERE WAS A PRINCESS.
SHE WALKED IN BEAUTY AND HUMILITY, IN LIGHT AND IN JOY. SHE WAS BELOVED BY HER PEOPLE, WHO SAW IN HER A SWEETNESS AND A GENTLENESS OF SPIRIT.
OFTEN SHE WAS SEEN AT HER WINDOW, LOOKING OUT AT THE VILLAGE SHE LOVED AND THE PEOPLE WHO RETURNED THAT LOVE WITH A PASSION FIERCE AS FLAME.
AT OTHER TIMES, SHE WOULD GAZE FOR HOURS IN THE WATER-MIRROR SHE WAS GIVEN AT BIRTH, NOT TO SEE HERSELF, BUT TO SEE DISTANT PLACES, DECIDING WHERE SHE WOULD GO NEXT. THE WORLD WAS HERS, TO GO AND COME AS SHE CHOSE, AND HAD BEEN SINCE THE DAY SHE WAS CHRISTENED PRINCESS--
MARY?
MARY?

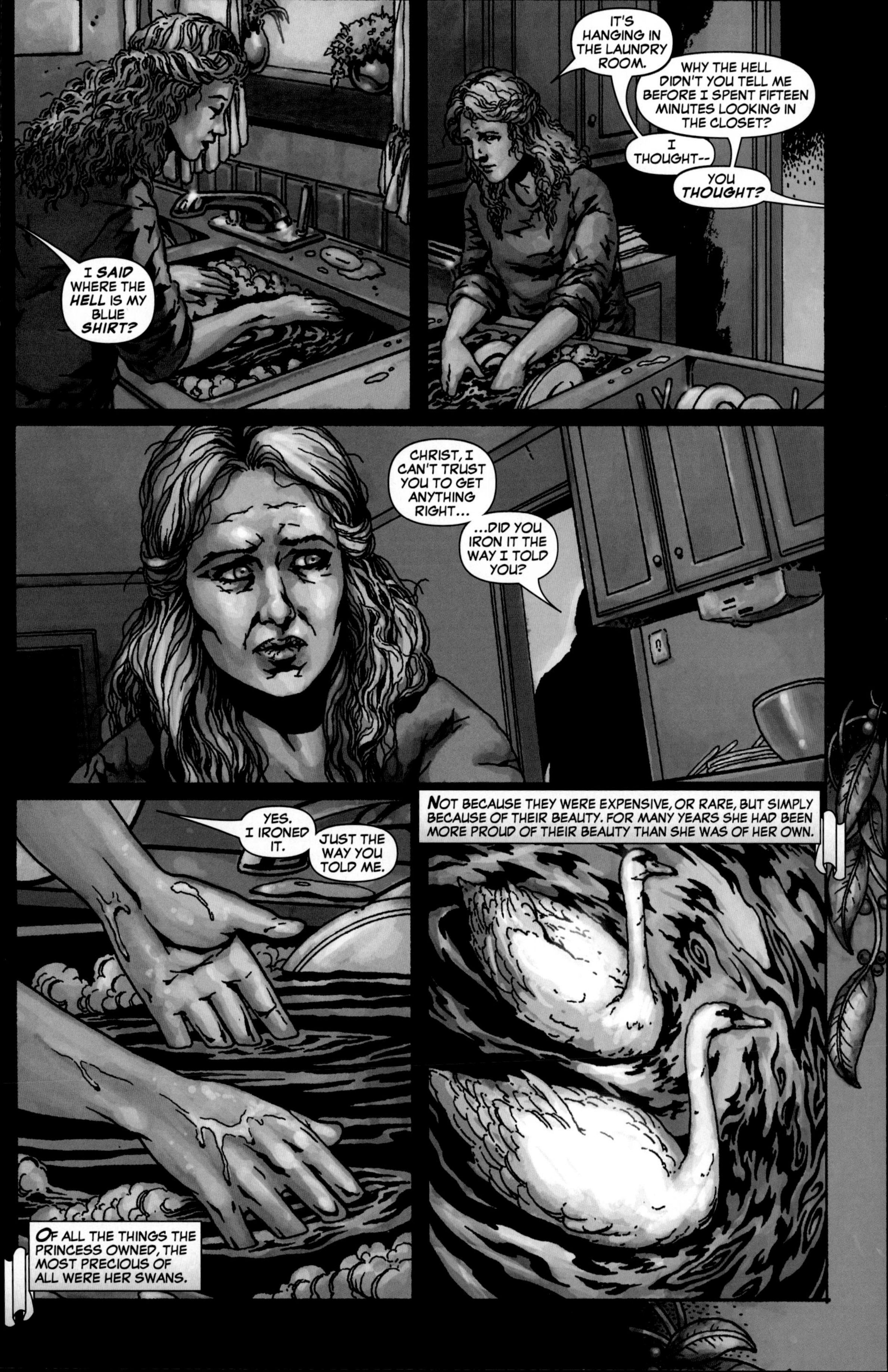
I SAID WHERE THE HELL IS MY BLUE SHIRT?
IT'S HANGING IN THE LAUNDRY ROOM.
WHY THE HELL DIDN'T YOU TELL ME BEFORE I SPENT FIFTEEN MINUTES LOOKING IN THE CLOSET?
I THOUGHT--
YOU THOUGHT?
CHRIST, I CAN'T TRUST YOU TO GET ANYTHING RIGHT...
...DID YOU IRON IT THE WAY I TOLD YOU?
YES. I IRONED IT.
JUST THE WAY YOU TOLD ME.
OF ALL THE THINGS THE PRINCESS OWNED, THE MOST PRECIOUS OF ALL WERE HER SWANS.
NOT BECAUSE THEY WERE EXPENSIVE, OR RARE, BUT SIMPLY BECAUSE OF THEIR BEAUTY. FOR MANY YEARS SHE HAD BEEN MORE PROUD OF THEIR BEAUTY THAN SHE WAS OF HER OWN.

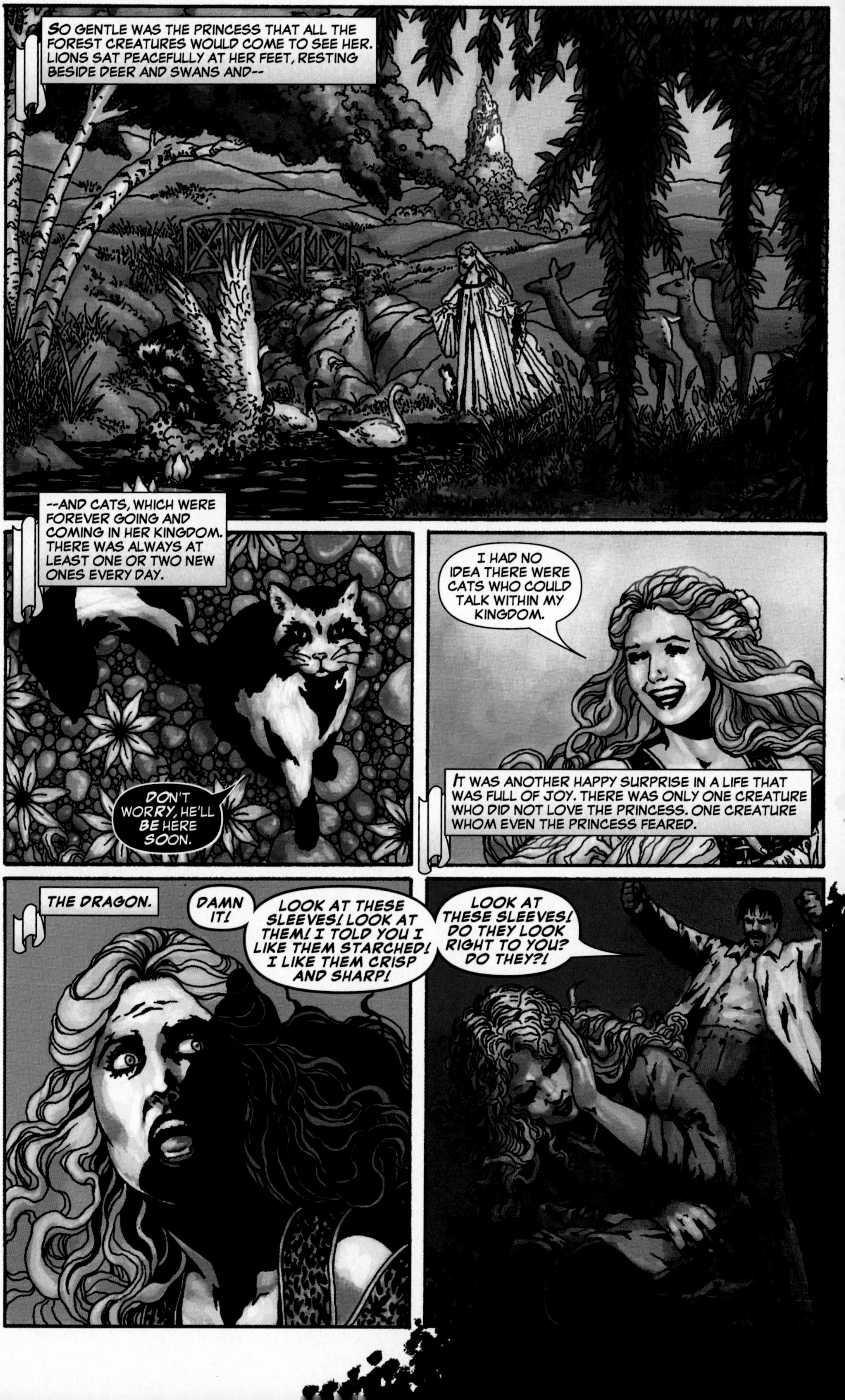
SO GENTLE WAS THE PRINCESS THAT ALL THE FOREST CREATURES WOULD COME TO SEE HER. LIONS SAT PEACEFULLY AT HER FEET, RESTING BESIDE DEER AND SWANS AND--
--AND CATS, WHICH WERE FOREVER GOING AND COMING IN HER KINGDOM. THERE WAS ALWAYS AT LEAST ONE OR TWO NEW ONES EVERY DAY.
DON'T WORRY, HE'LL BE HERE SOON.
I HAD NO IDEA THERE WERE CATS WHO COULD TALK WITHIN MY KINGDOM.
IT WAS ANOTHER HAPPY SURPRISE IN A LIFE THAT WAS FULL OF JOY. THERE WAS ONLY ONE CREATURE WHO DID NOT LOVE THE PRINCESS. ONE CREATURE WHOM EVEN THE PRINCESS FEARED.
THE DRAGON.
DAMN IT!
LOOK AT THESE SLEEVES! LOOK AT THEM! I TOLD YOU I LIKE THEM STARCHED! I LIKE THEM CRISP AND SHARP!
LOOK AT THESE SLEEVES! DO THEY LOOK RIGHT TO YOU? DO THEY?!

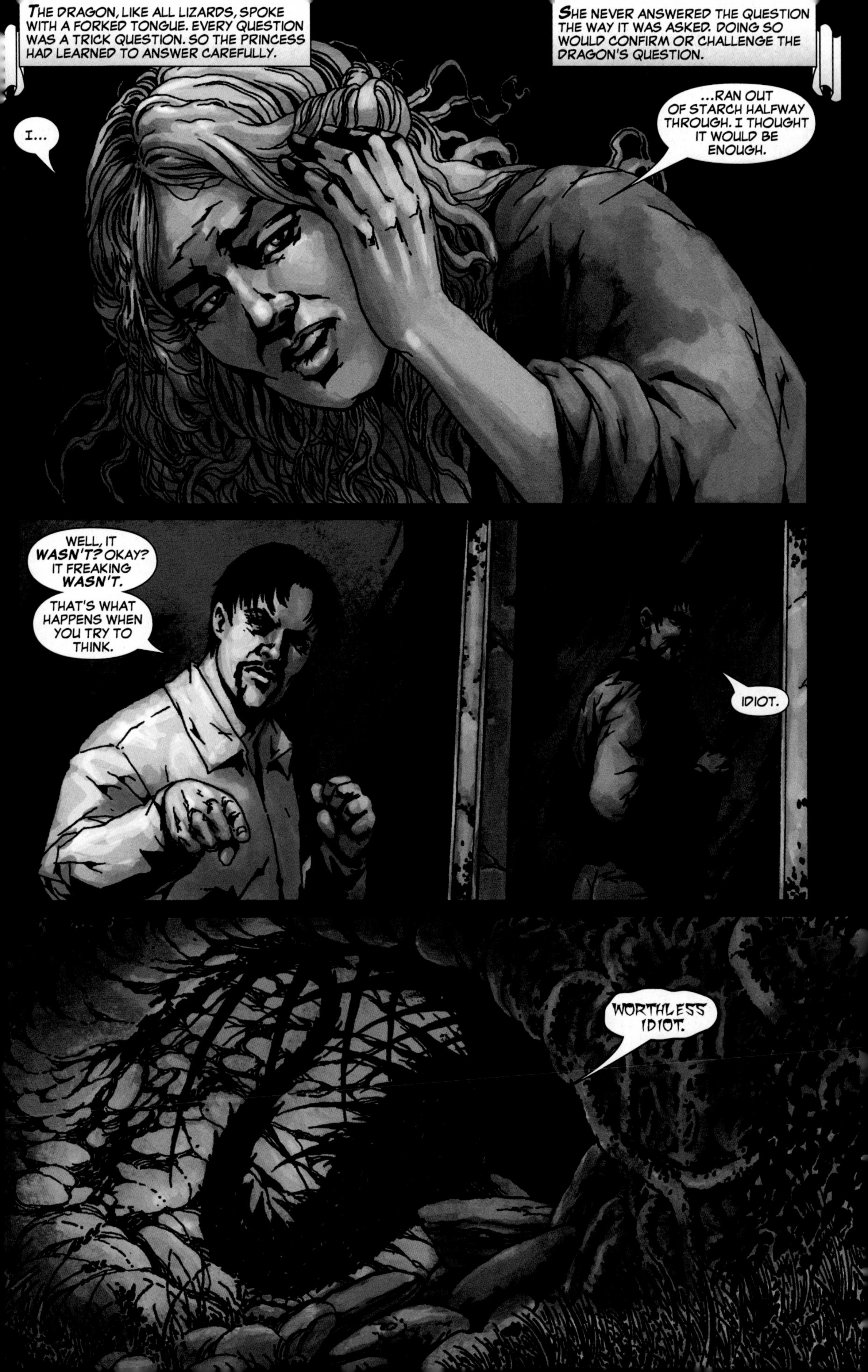
THE DRAGON, LIKE ALL LIZARDS, SPOKE WITH A FORKED TONGUE. EVERY QUESTION WAS A TRICK QUESTION. SO THE PRINCESS HAD LEARNED TO ANSWER CAREFULLY.
SHE NEVER ANSWERED THE QUESTION THE WAY IT WAS ASKED. DOING SO WOULD CONFIRM OR CHALLENGE THE DRAGON'S QUESTION.
I...
...RAN OUT OF STARCH HALFWAY THROUGH. I THOUGHT IT WOULD BE ENOUGH.
WELL, IT WASN'T? OKAY? IT FREAKING WASN'T.
THAT'S WHAT HAPPENS WHEN YOU TRY TO THINK.
IDIOT.
WORTHLESS IDIOT.

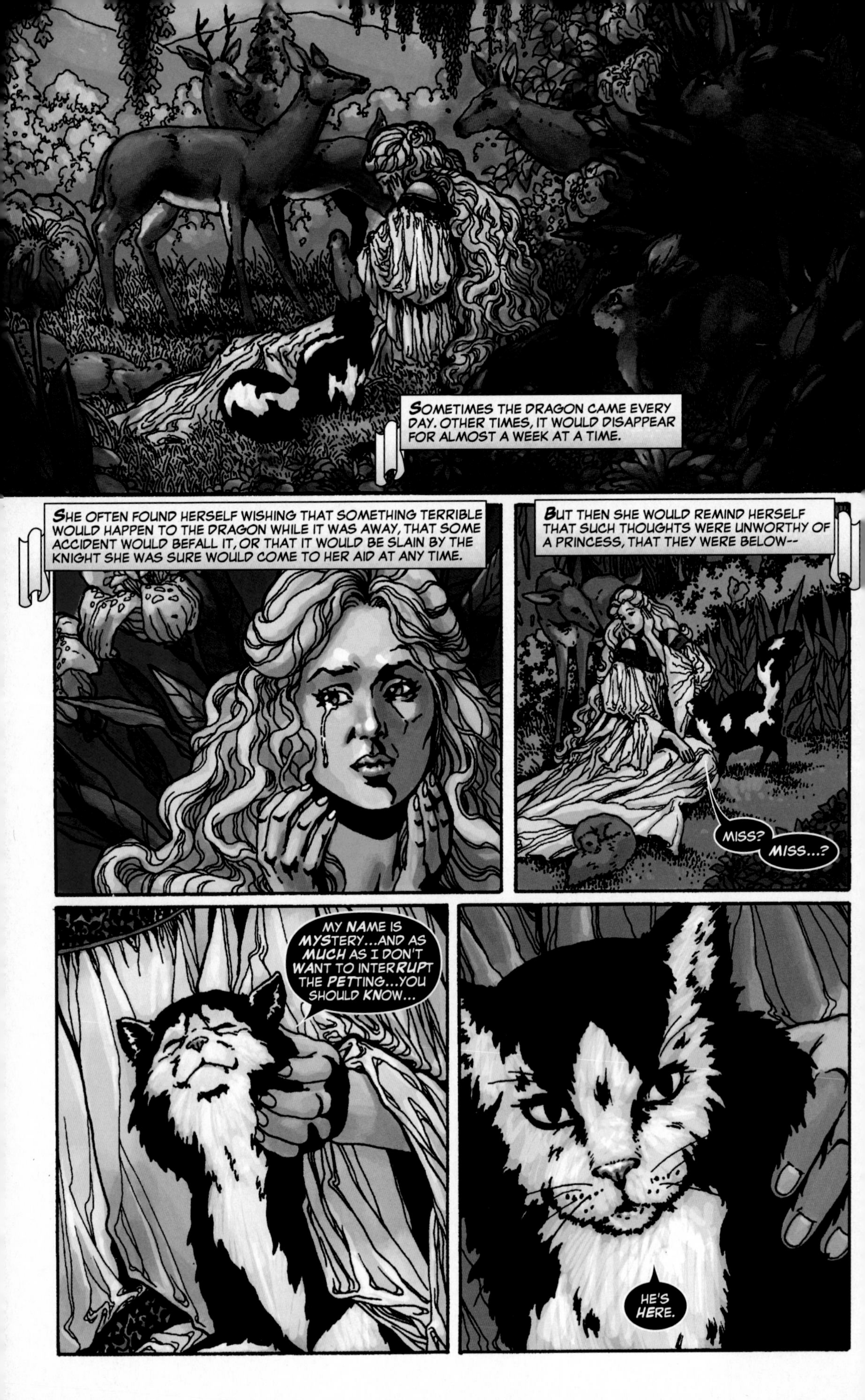
SOMETIMES THE DRAGON CAME EVERY DAY. OTHER TIMES, IT WOULD DISAPPEAR FOR ALMOST A WEEK AT A TIME.
SHE OFTEN FOUND HERSELF WISHING THAT SOMETHING TERRIBLE WOULD HAPPEN TO THE DRAGON WHILE IT WAS AWAY, THAT SOME ACCIDENT WOULD BEFALL IT, OR THAT IT WOULD BE SLAIN BY THE KNIGHT SHE WAS SURE WOULD COME TO HER AID AT ANY TIME.
BUT THEN SHE WOULD REMIND HERSELF THAT SUCH THOUGHTS WERE UNWORTHY OF A PRINCESS, THAT THEY WERE BELOW--
MISS?
MISS...?
MY NAME IS MYSTERY...AND AS MUCH AS I DON'T WANT TO INTERRUPT THE PETTING...YOU SHOULD KNOW...
HE'S HERE.

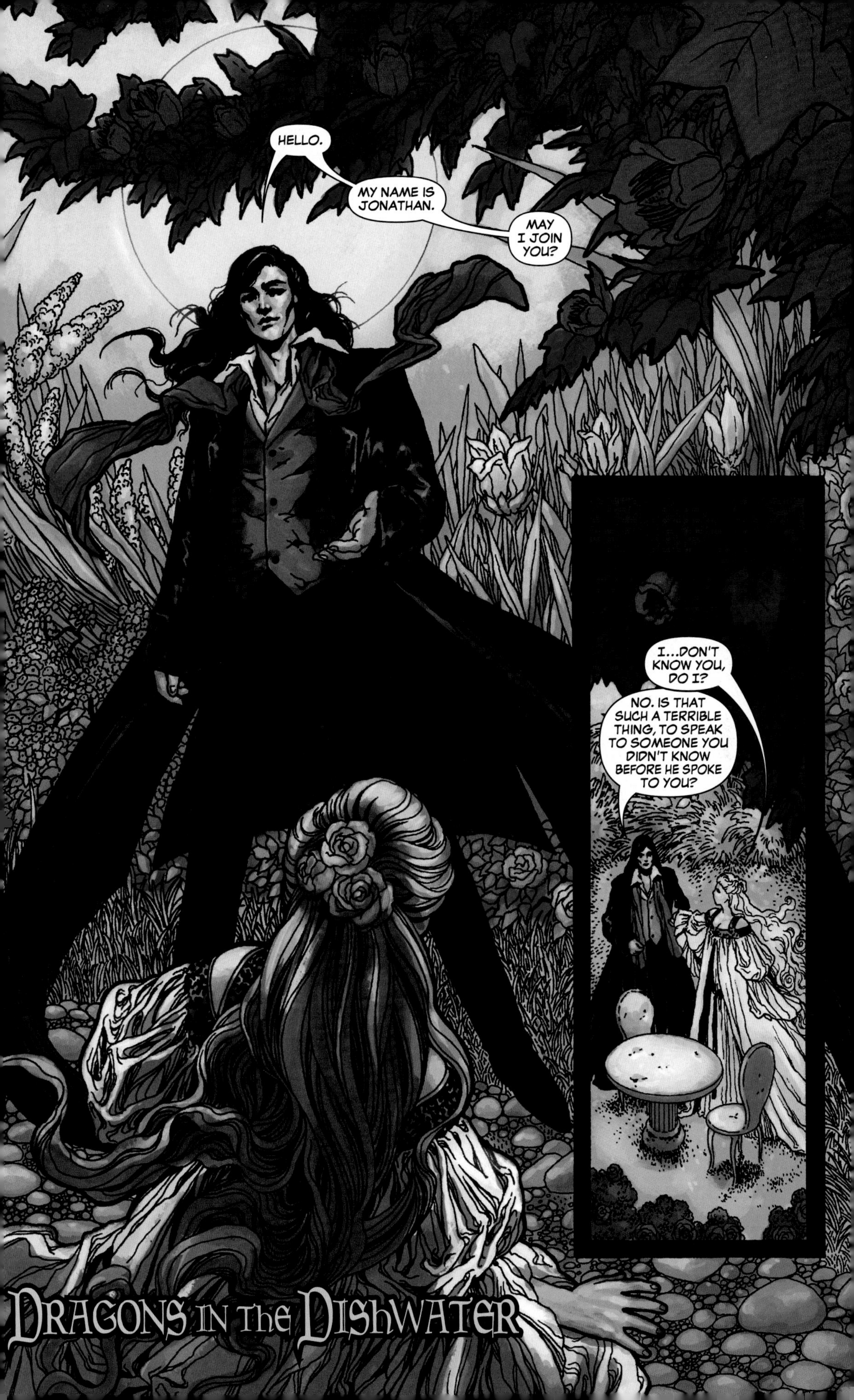
HELLO.
MY NAME IS JONATHAN.
MAY I JOIN YOU?
I...DON'T KNOW YOU, DO I?
NO. IS THAT SUCH A TERRIBLE THING, TO SPEAK TO SOMEONE YOU DIDN'T KNOW BEFORE HE SPOKE TO YOU?
DRAGONS IN THE DISHWATER

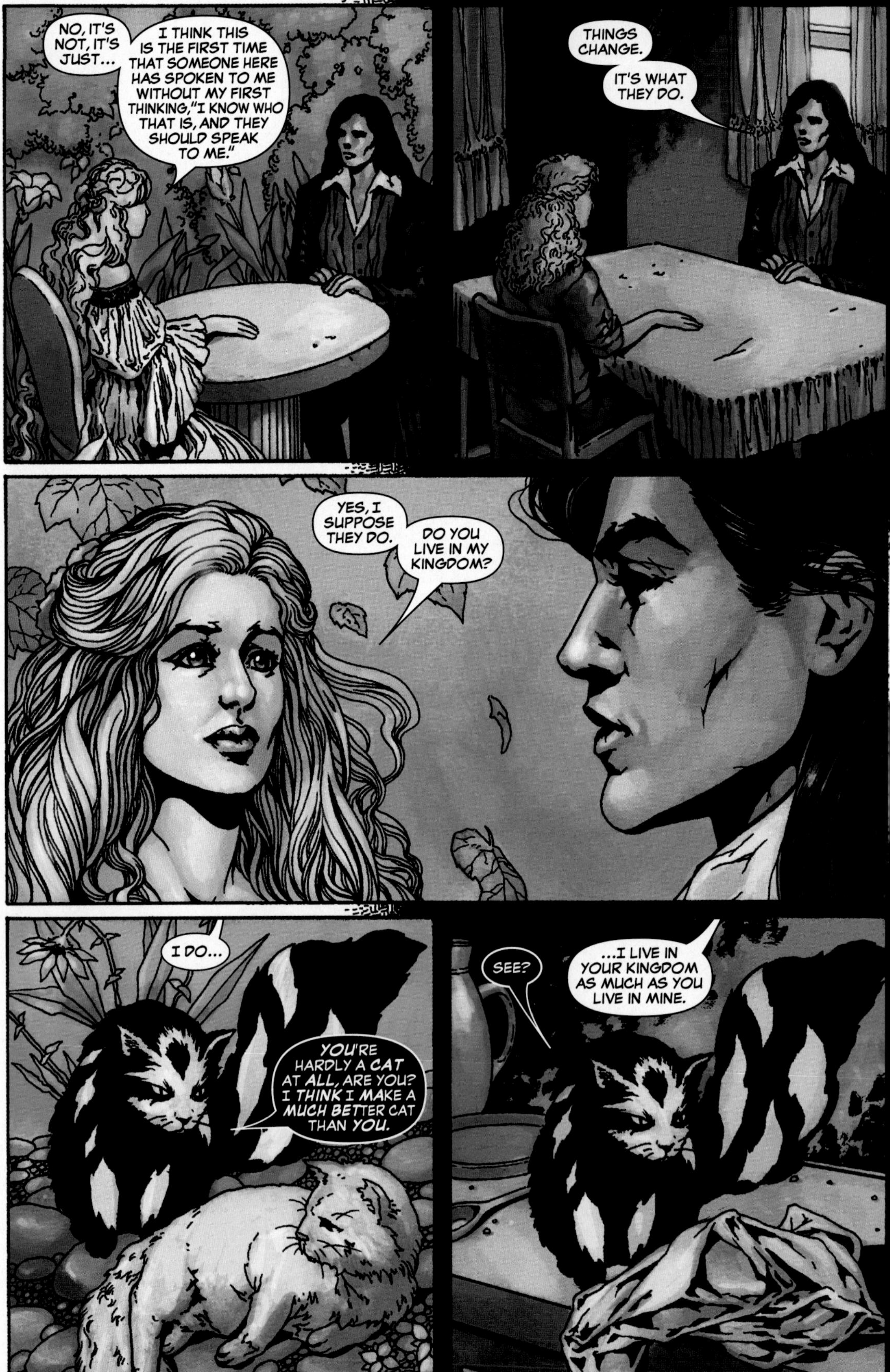
NO, IT'S NOT, IT'S JUST...
I THINK THIS IS THE FIRST TIME THAT SOMEONE HERE HAS SPOKEN TO ME WITHOUT MY FIRST THINKING, "I KNOW WHO THAT IS, AND THEY SHOULD SPEAK TO ME."
THINGS CHANGE.
IT'S WHAT THEY DO.
YES, I SUPPOSE THEY DO.
DO YOU LIVE IN MY KINGDOM?
I DO...
YOU'RE HARDLY A CAT AT ALL, ARE YOU? I THINK I MAKE A MUCH BETTER CAT THAN YOU.
SEE?
...I LIVE IN YOUR KINGDOM AS MUCH AS YOU LIVE IN MINE.

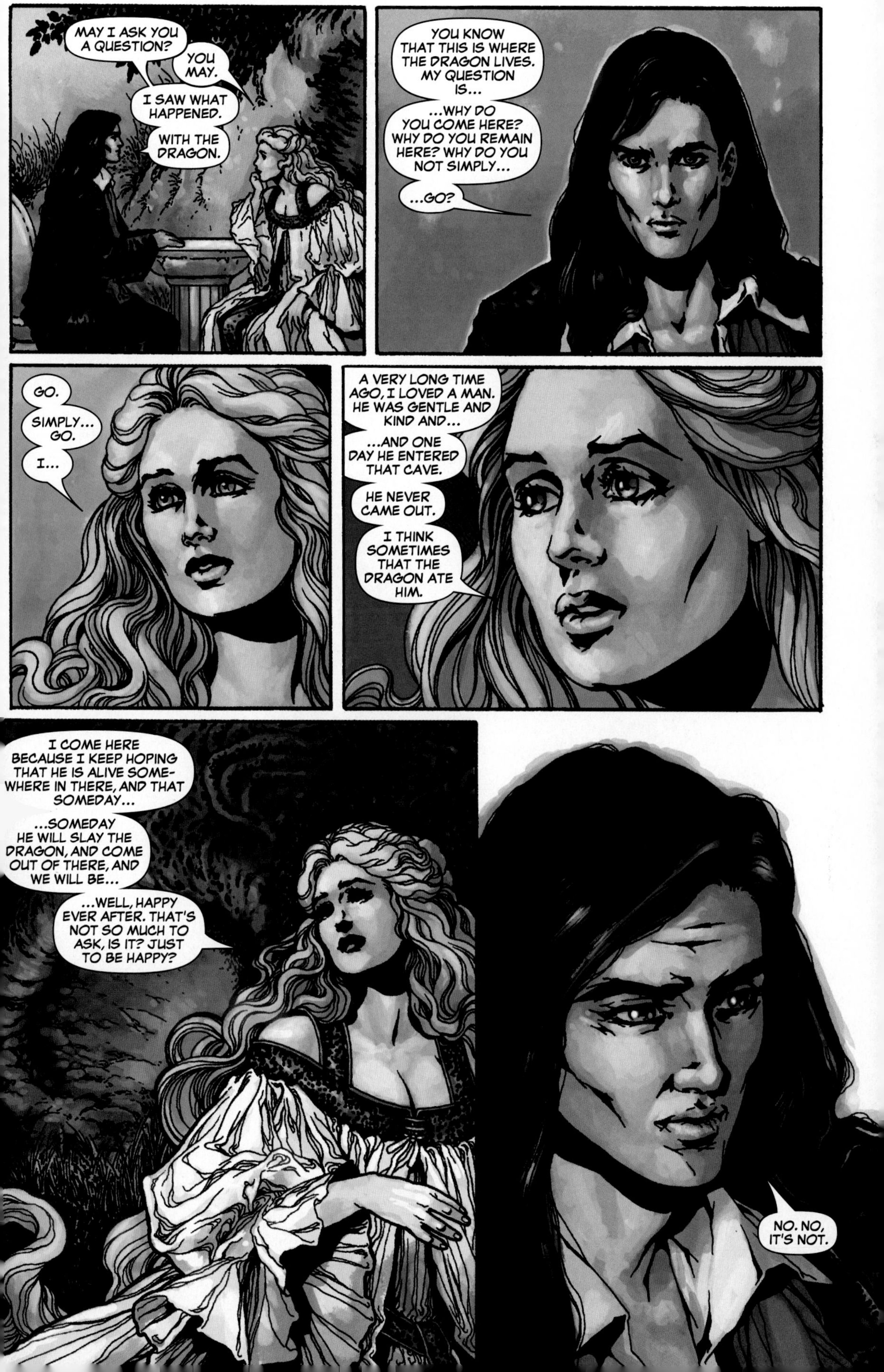
MAY I ASK YOU A QUESTION?
YOU MAY.
I SAW WHAT HAPPENED.
WITH THE DRAGON.
YOU KNOW THAT THIS IS WHERE THE DRAGON LIVES. MY QUESTION IS...
...WHY DO YOU COME HERE? WHY DO YOU REMAIN HERE? WHY DO YOU NOT SIMPLY...
...GO?
GO.
SIMPLY... GO.
I...
A VERY LONG TIME AGO, I LOVED A MAN. HE WAS GENTLE AND KIND AND...
...AND ONE DAY HE ENTERED THAT CAVE.
HE NEVER CAME OUT.
I THINK SOMETIMES THAT THE DRAGON ATE HIM.
I COME HERE BECAUSE I KEEP HOPING THAT HE IS ALIVE SOME-WHERE IN THERE, AND THAT SOMEDAY...
...SOMEDAY HE WILL SLAY THE DRAGON, AND COME OUT OF THERE, AND WE WILL BE...
...WELL, HAPPY EVER AFTER. THAT'S NOT SO MUCH TO ASK, IS IT? JUST TO BE HAPPY?
NO. NO, IT'S NOT.

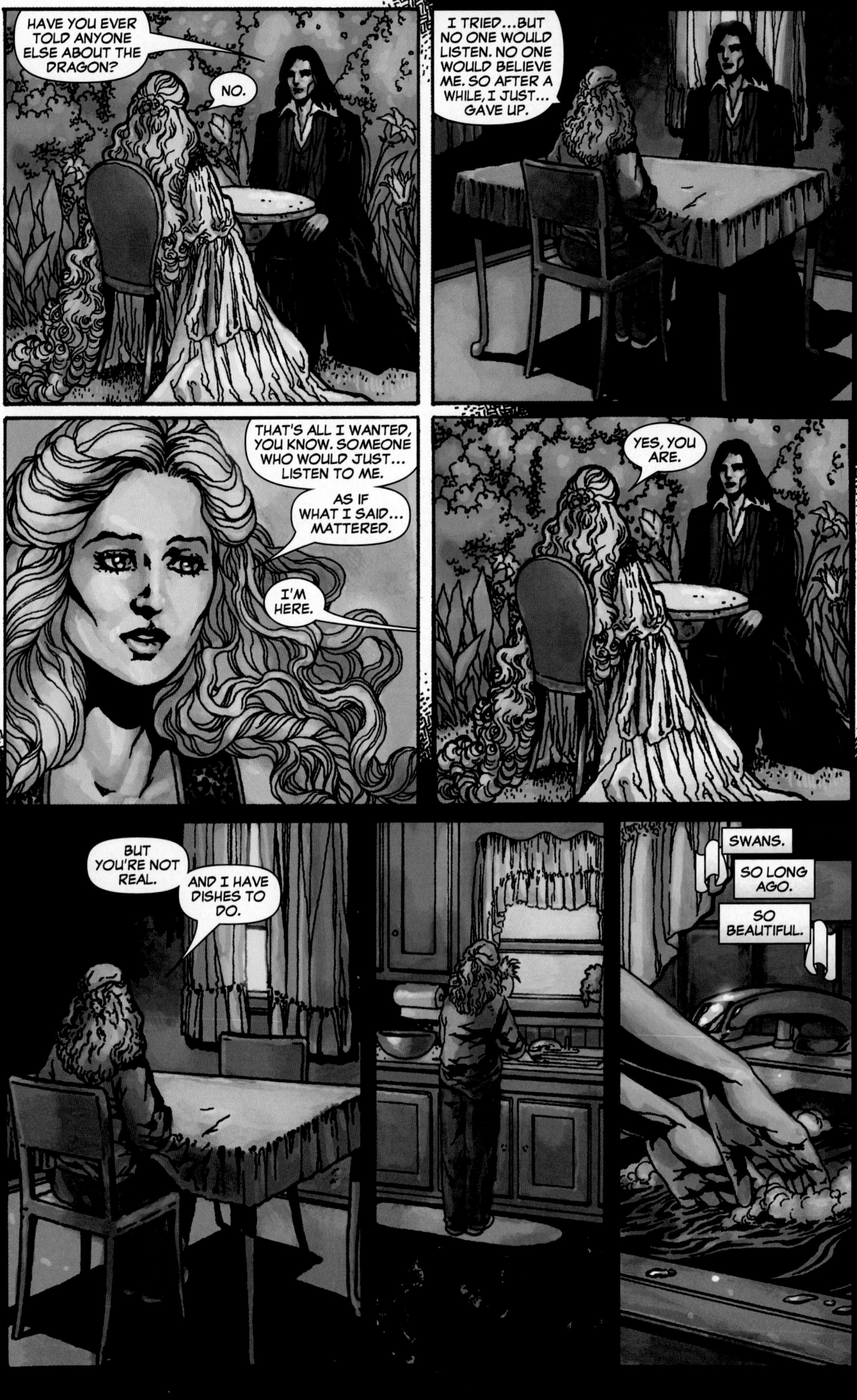
HAVE YOU EVER TOLD ANYONE ELSE ABOUT THE DRAGON?
NO.
I TRIED...BUT NO ONE WOULD LISTEN. NO ONE WOULD BELIEVE ME. SO AFTER A WHILE, I JUST... GAVE UP.
THAT'S ALL I WANTED, YOU KNOW. SOMEONE WHO WOULD JUST... LISTEN TO ME.
AS IF WHAT I SAID... MATTERED.
I'M HERE.
YES, YOU ARE.
BUT YOU'RE NOT REAL.
AND I HAVE DISHES TO DO.
SWANS.
SO LONG AGO.
SO BEAUTIFUL.

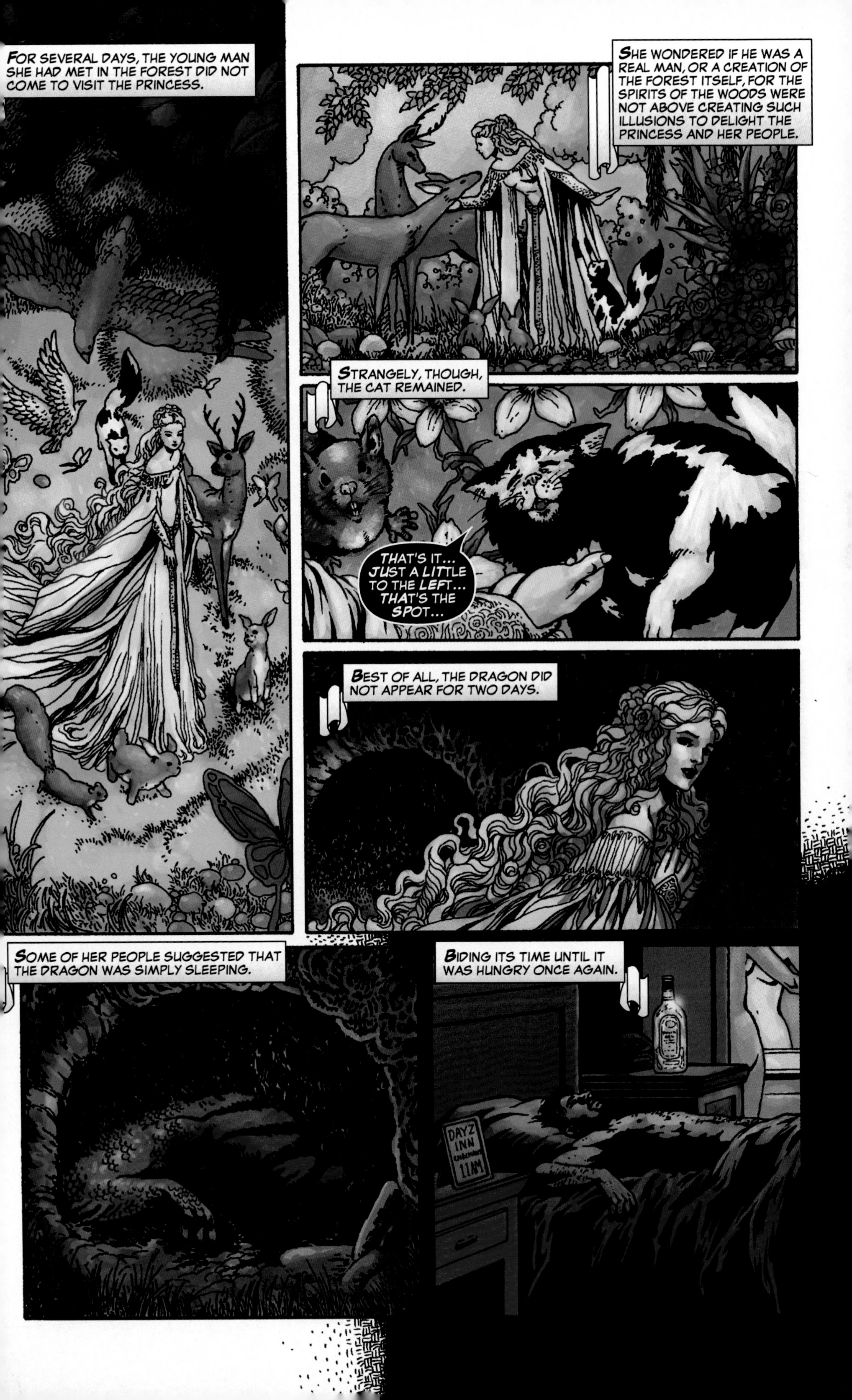
FOR SEVERAL DAYS, THE YOUNG MAN SHE HAD MET IN THE FOREST DID NOT COME TO VISIT THE PRINCESS.
SHE WONDERED IF HE WAS A REAL MAN, OR A CREATION OF THE FOREST ITSELF, FOR THE SPIRITS OF THE WOODS WERE NOT ABOVE CREATING SUCH ILLUSIONS TO DELIGHT THE PRINCESS AND HER PEOPLE.
STRANGELY, THOUGH, THE CAT REMAINED.
THAT'S IT... JUST A LITTLE TO THE LEFT... THAT'S THE SPOT...
BEST OF ALL, THE DRAGON DID NOT APPEAR FOR TWO DAYS.
SOME OF HER PEOPLE SUGGESTED THAT THE DRAGON WAS SIMPLY SLEEPING.
BIDING ITS TIME UNTIL IT WAS HUNGRY ONCE AGAIN.
DAYZ INN
11AM

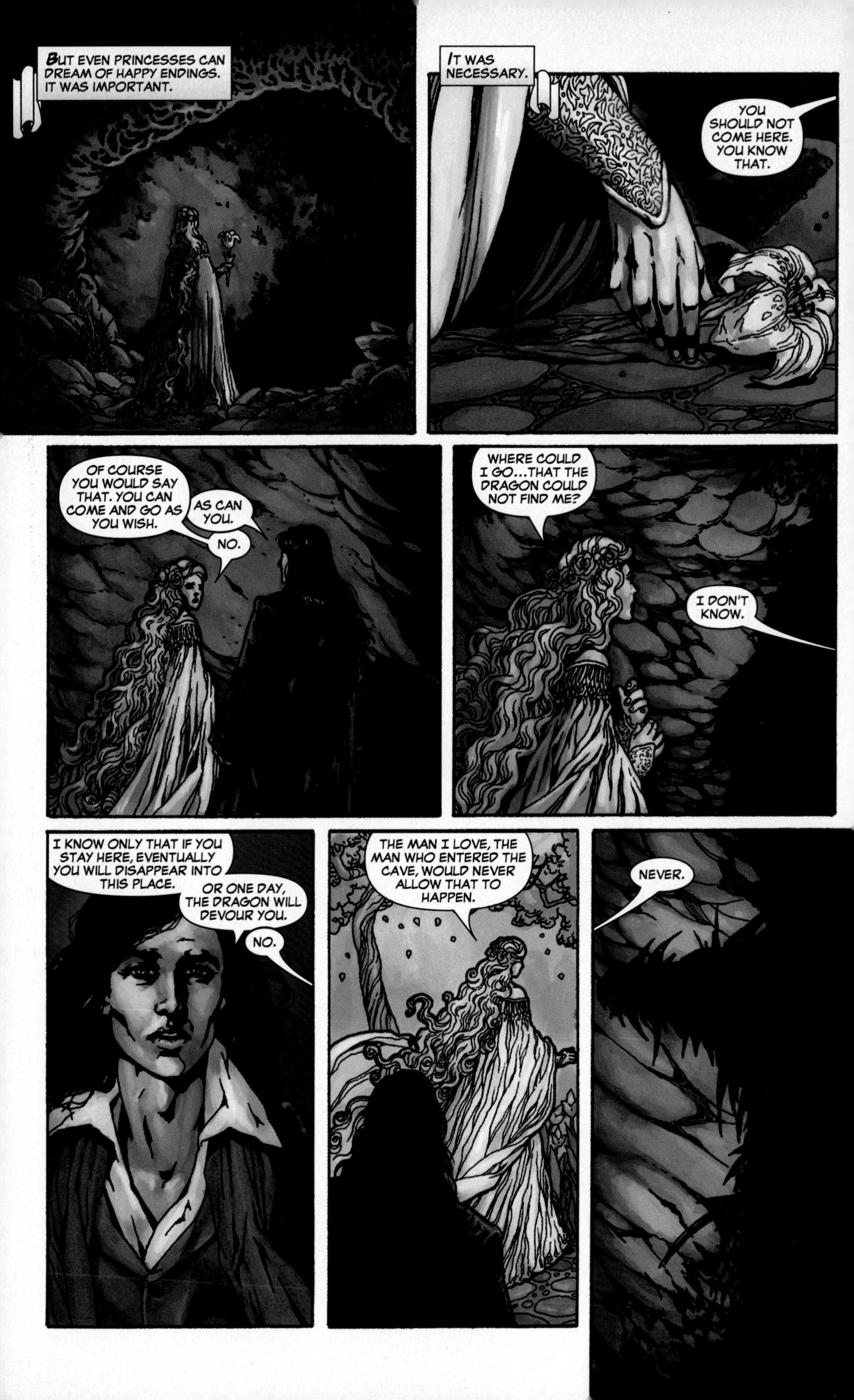
BUT EVEN PRINCESSES CAN DREAM OF HAPPY ENDINGS. IT WAS IMPORTANT.
IT WAS NECESSARY.
YOU SHOULD NOT COME HERE. YOU KNOW THAT.
OF COURSE YOU WOULD SAY THAT. YOU CAN COME AND GO AS YOU WISH.
AS CAN YOU.
NO.
WHERE COULD I GO...THAT THE DRAGON COULD NOT FIND ME?
I DON'T KNOW.
I KNOW ONLY THAT IF YOU STAY HERE, EVENTUALLY YOU WILL DISAPPEAR INTO THIS PLACE.
OR ONE DAY, THE DRAGON WILL DEVOUR YOU.
NO.
THE MAN I LOVE, THE MAN WHO ENTERED THE CAVE, WOULD NEVER ALLOW THAT TO HAPPEN.
NEVER.

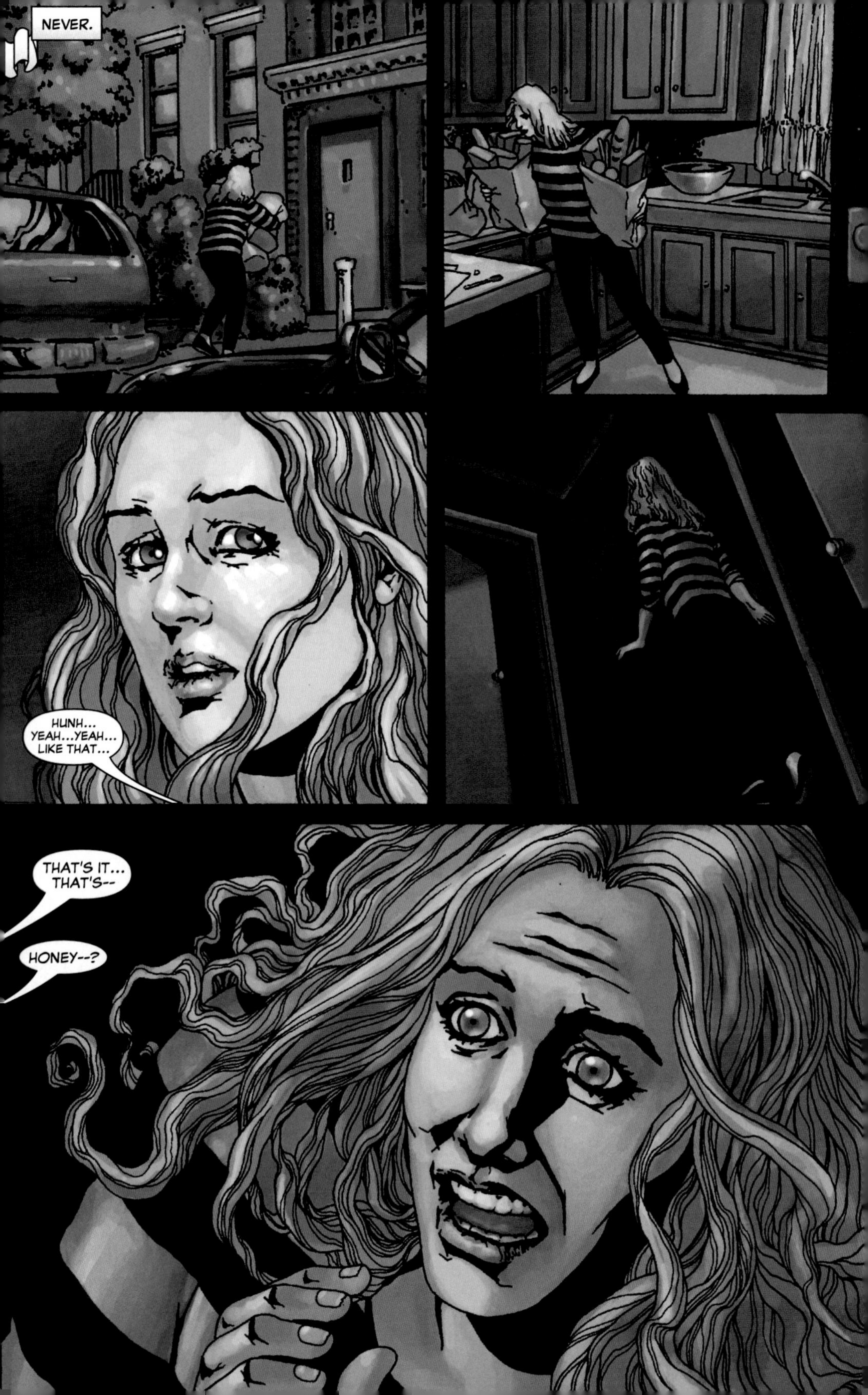
NEVER.
HUNH... YEAH...YEAH... LIKE THAT...
THAT'S IT... THAT'S--
HONEY--?

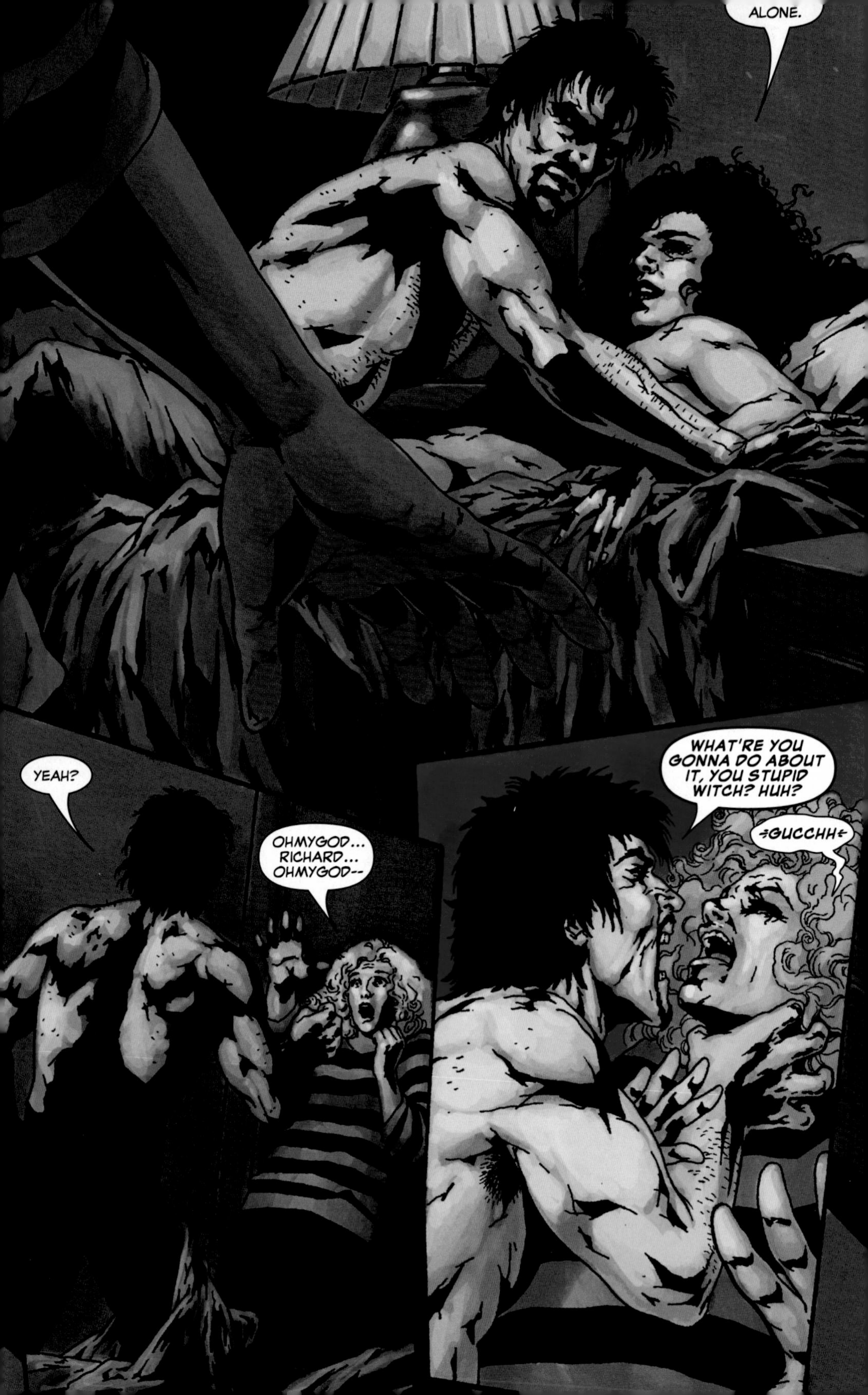
ALONE.
YEAH?
OHMYGOD... RICHARD... OHMYGOD--
WHAT'RE YOU GONNA DO ABOUT IT, YOU STUPID WITCH? HUH?
GUCCHH

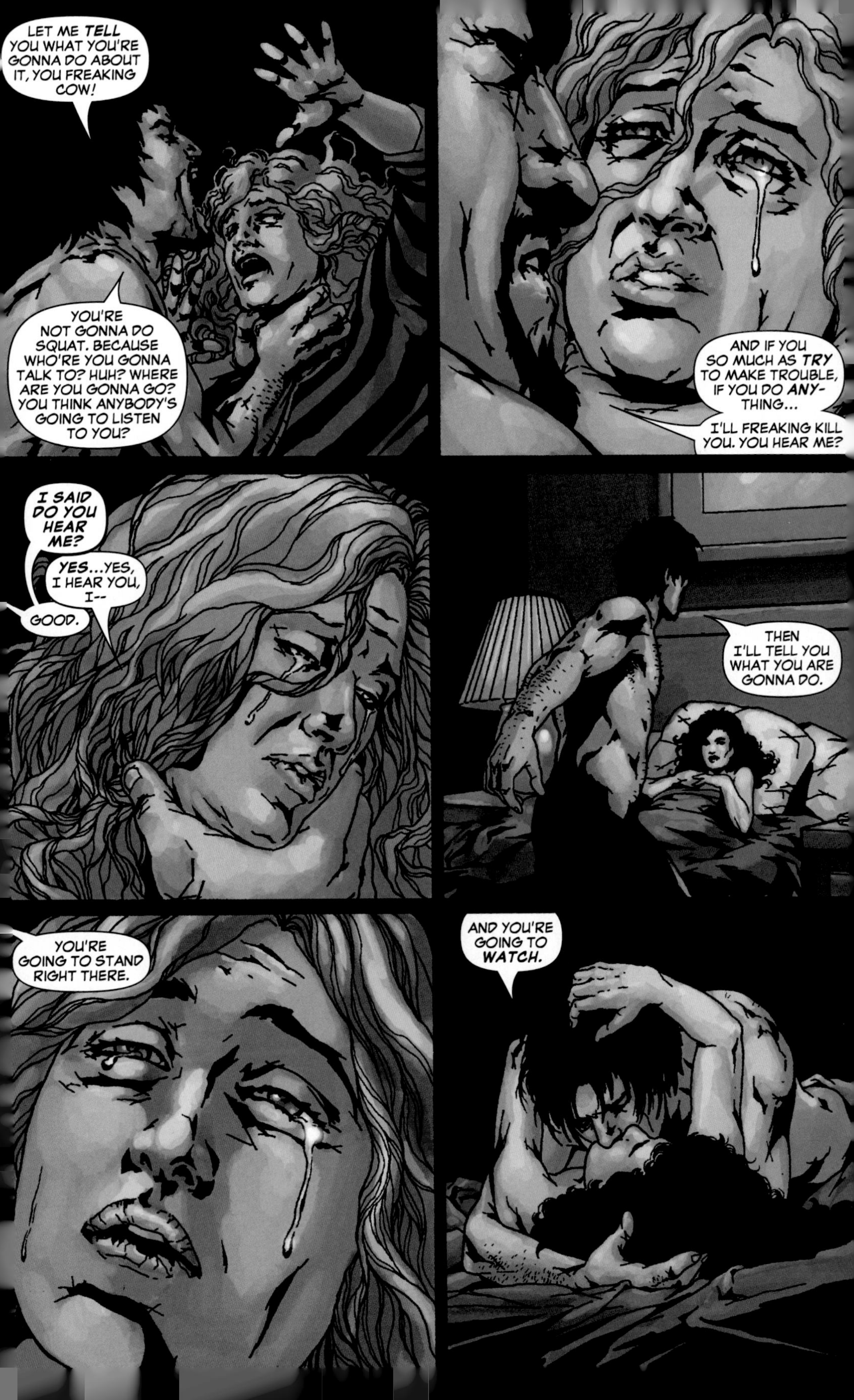
LET ME TELL YOU WHAT YOU'RE GONNA DO ABOUT IT, YOU FREAKING COW!
YOU'RE NOT GONNA DO SQUAT. BECAUSE WHO'RE YOU GONNA TALK TO? HUH? WHERE ARE YOU GONNA GO? YOU THINK ANYBODY'S GOING TO LISTEN TO YOU?
AND IF YOU SO MUCH AS TRY TO MAKE TROUBLE, IF YOU DO ANY- THING...
I'LL FREAKING KILL YOU. YOU HEAR ME?
I SAID DO YOU HEAR ME?
YES...YES, I HEAR YOU, I--
GOOD.
THEN I'LL TELL YOU WHAT YOU ARE GONNA DO.
YOU'RE GOING TO STAND RIGHT THERE.
AND YOU'RE GOING TO WATCH.

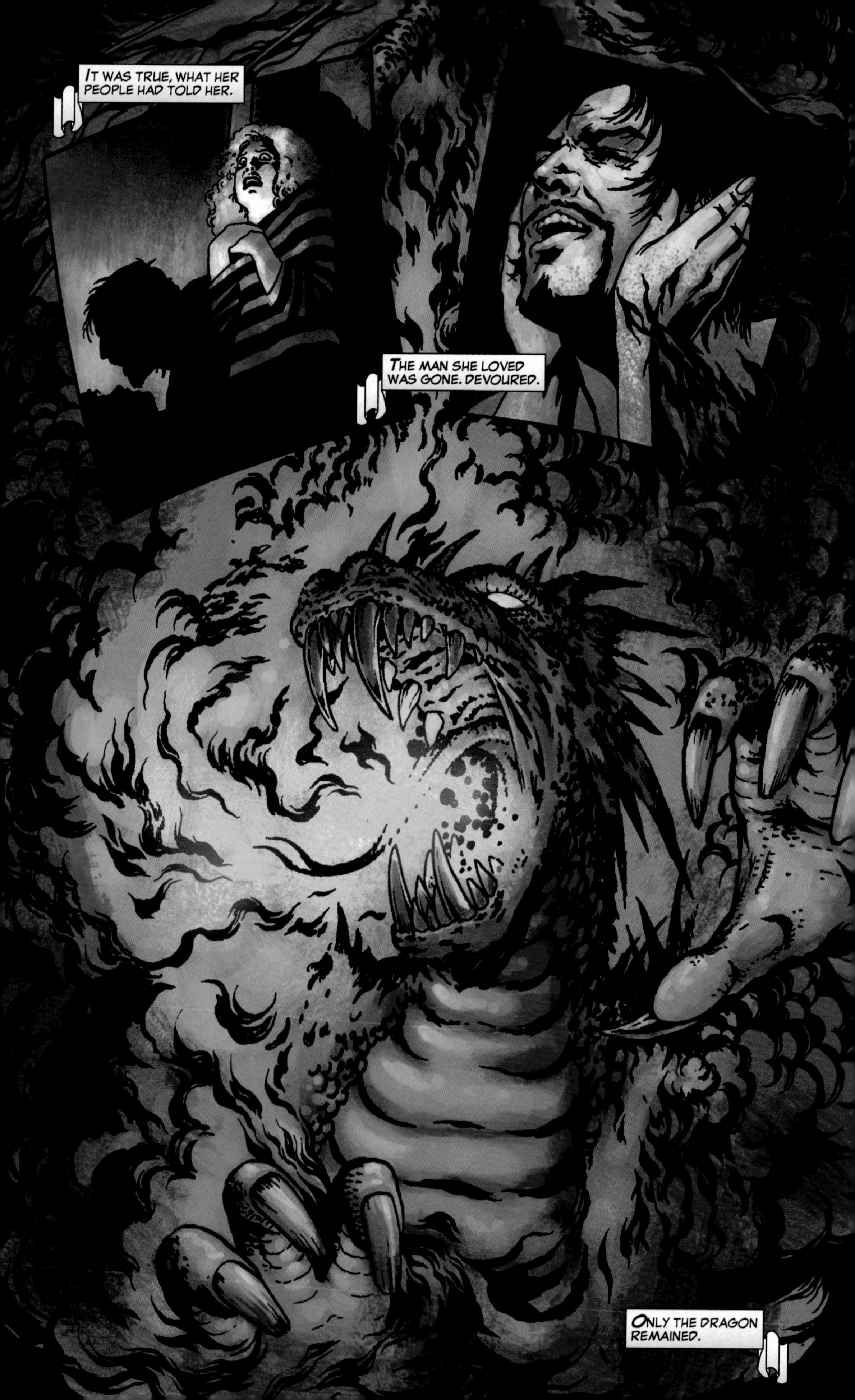
IT WAS TRUE, WHAT HER PEOPLE HAD TOLD HER.
THE MAN SHE LOVED WAS GONE. DEVOURED.
ONLY THE DRAGON REMAINED.

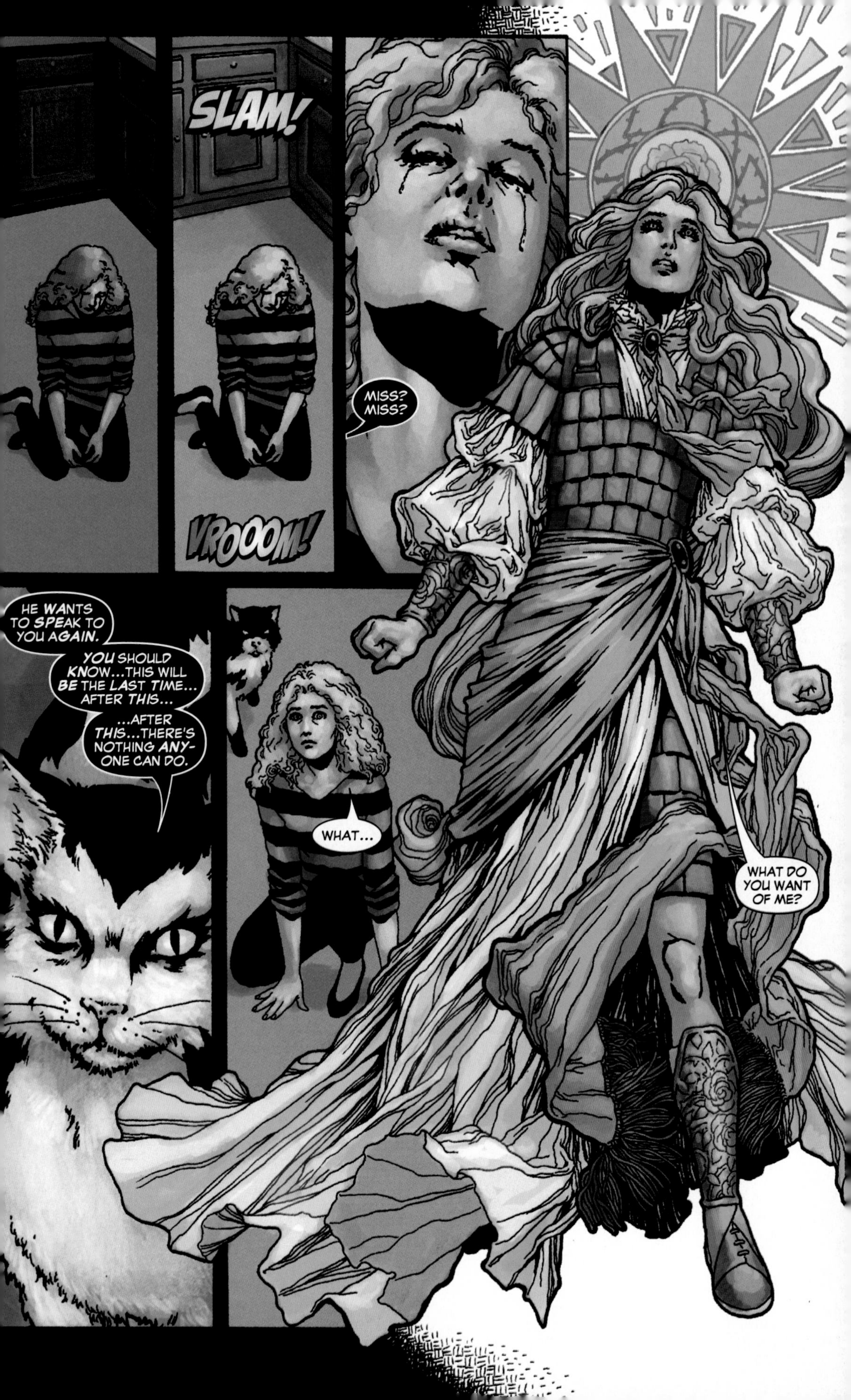
SLAM!
VROOOM!
MISS? MISS?
HE WANTS TO SPEAK TO YOU AGAIN.
YOU SHOULD KNOW...THIS WILL BE THE LAST TIME... AFTER THIS...
...AFTER THIS...THERE'S NOTHING ANY-ONE CAN DO.
WHAT...
WHAT DO YOU WANT OF ME?

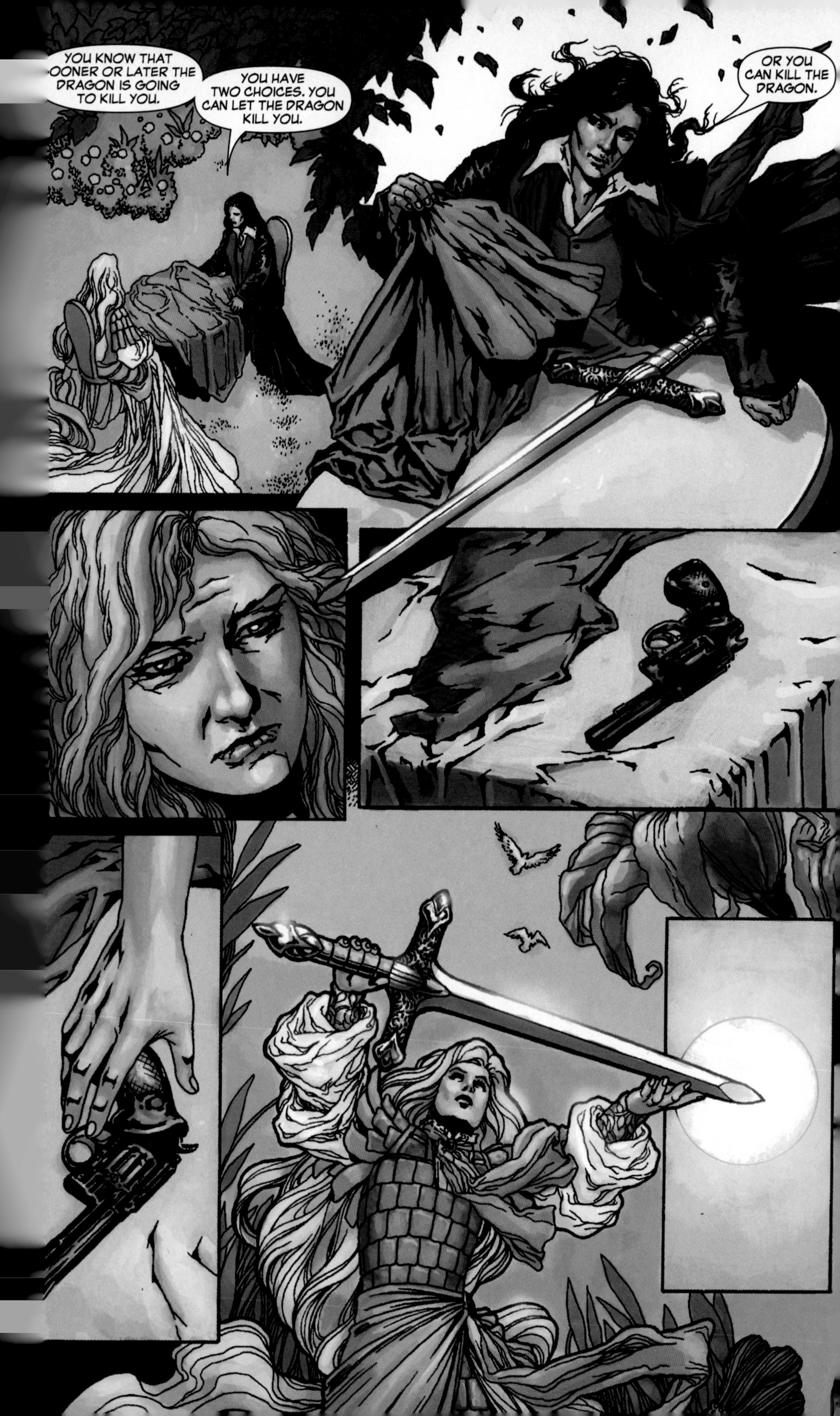
YOU KNOW THAT
OONER OR LATER THE DRAGON IS GOING TO KILL YOU.
YOU HAVE TWO CHOICES. YOU CAN LET THE DRAGON KILL YOU.
OR YOU CAN KILL THE DRAGON.

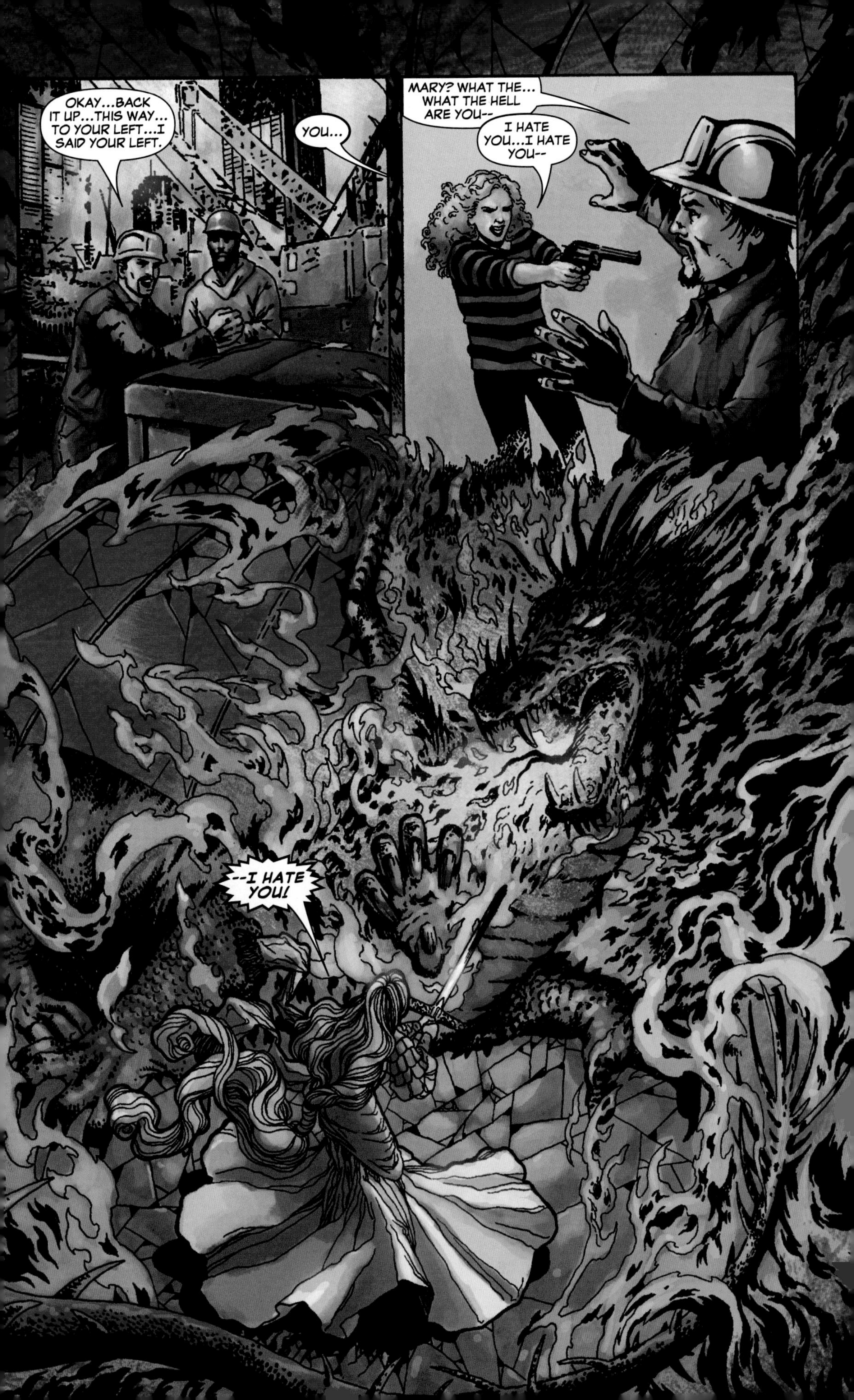
OKAY...BACK IT UP...THIS WAY... TO YOUR LEFT...I SAID YOUR LEFT.
YOU...
MARY? WHAT THE... WHAT THE HELL ARE YOU--
I HATE YOU...I HATE YOU--
--I HATE YOU!

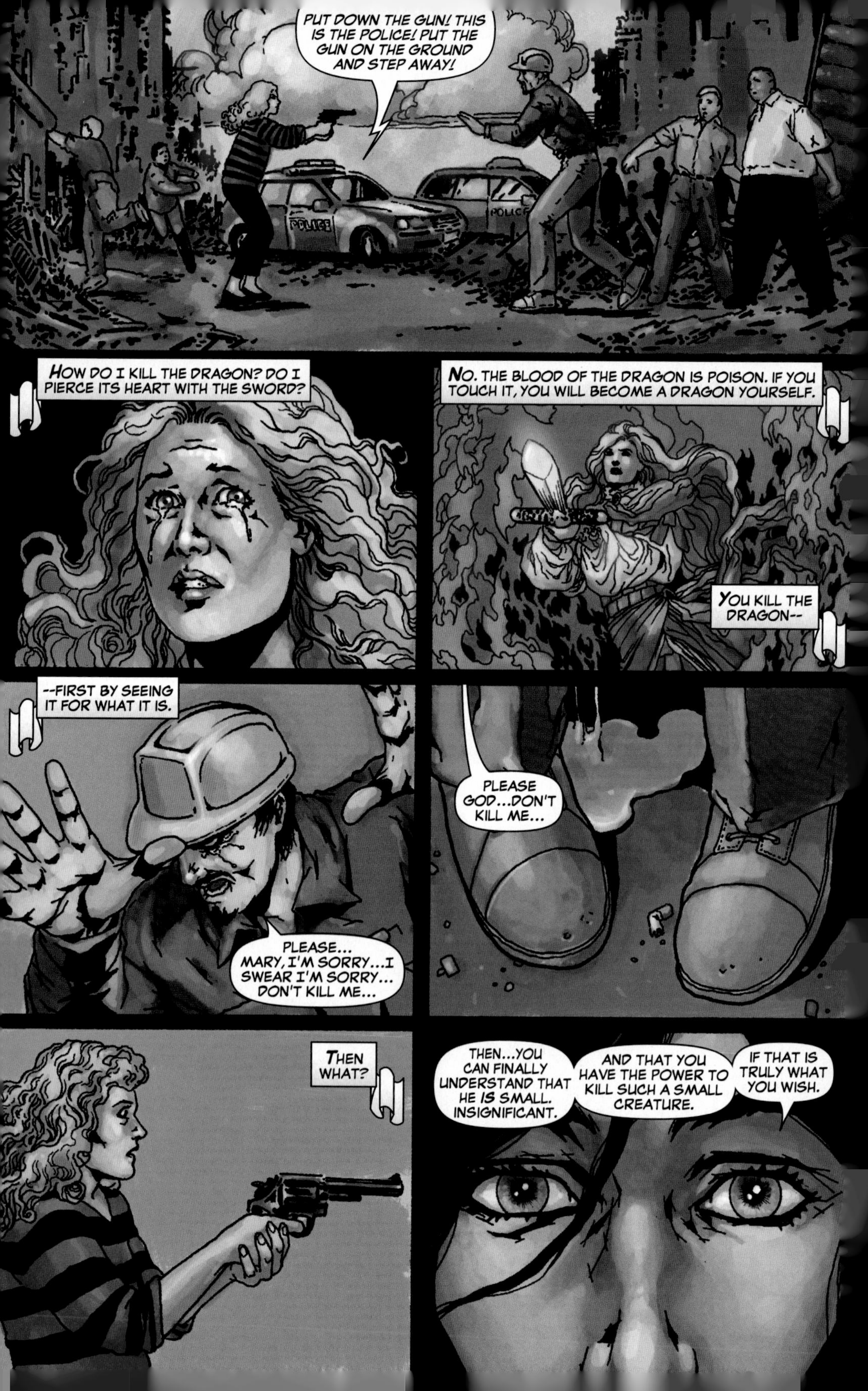
PUT DOWN THE GUN! THIS IS THE POLICE! PUT THE GUN ON THE GROUND AND STEP AWAY!
HOW DO I KILL THE DRAGON? DO I PIERCE ITS HEART WITH THE SWORD?
NO. THE BLOOD OF THE DRAGON IS POISON. IF YOU TOUCH IT, YOU WILL BECOME A DRAGON YOURSELF.
YOU KILL THE DRAGON--
--FIRST BY SEEING IT FOR WHAT IT IS.
PLEASE... MARY, I'M SORRY...I SWEAR I'M SORRY... DON'T KILL ME...
PLEASE GOD...DON'T KILL ME...
THEN WHAT?
THEN...YOU CAN FINALLY UNDERSTAND THAT HE IS SMALL. INSIGNIFICANT.
AND THAT YOU HAVE THE POWER TO KILL SUCH A SMALL CREATURE.
IF THAT IS TRULY WHAT YOU WISH.

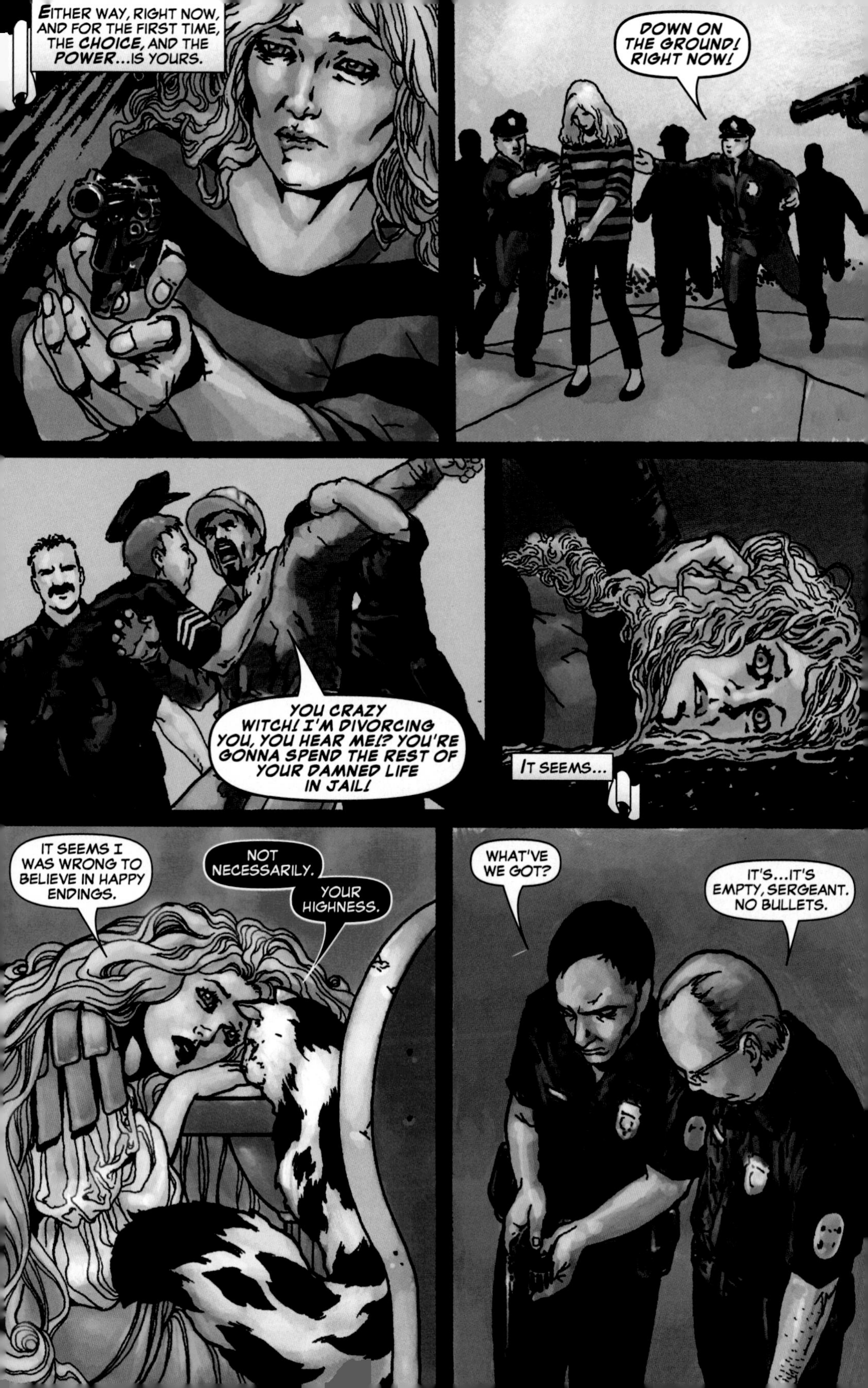
EITHER WAY, RIGHT NOW, AND FOR THE FIRST TIME, THE CHOICE, AND THE POWER...IS YOURS.
DOWN ON THE GROUND! RIGHT NOW!
YOU CRAZY WITCH! I'M DIVORCING YOU, YOU HEAR ME!? YOU'RE GONNA SPEND THE REST OF YOUR DAMNED LIFE IN JAIL!
IT SEEMS...
IT SEEMS I WAS WRONG TO BELIEVE IN HAPPY ENDINGS.
NOT NECESSARILY.
YOUR HIGHNESS.
WHAT'VE WE GOT?
IT'S...IT'S EMPTY, SERGEANT. NO BULLETS.

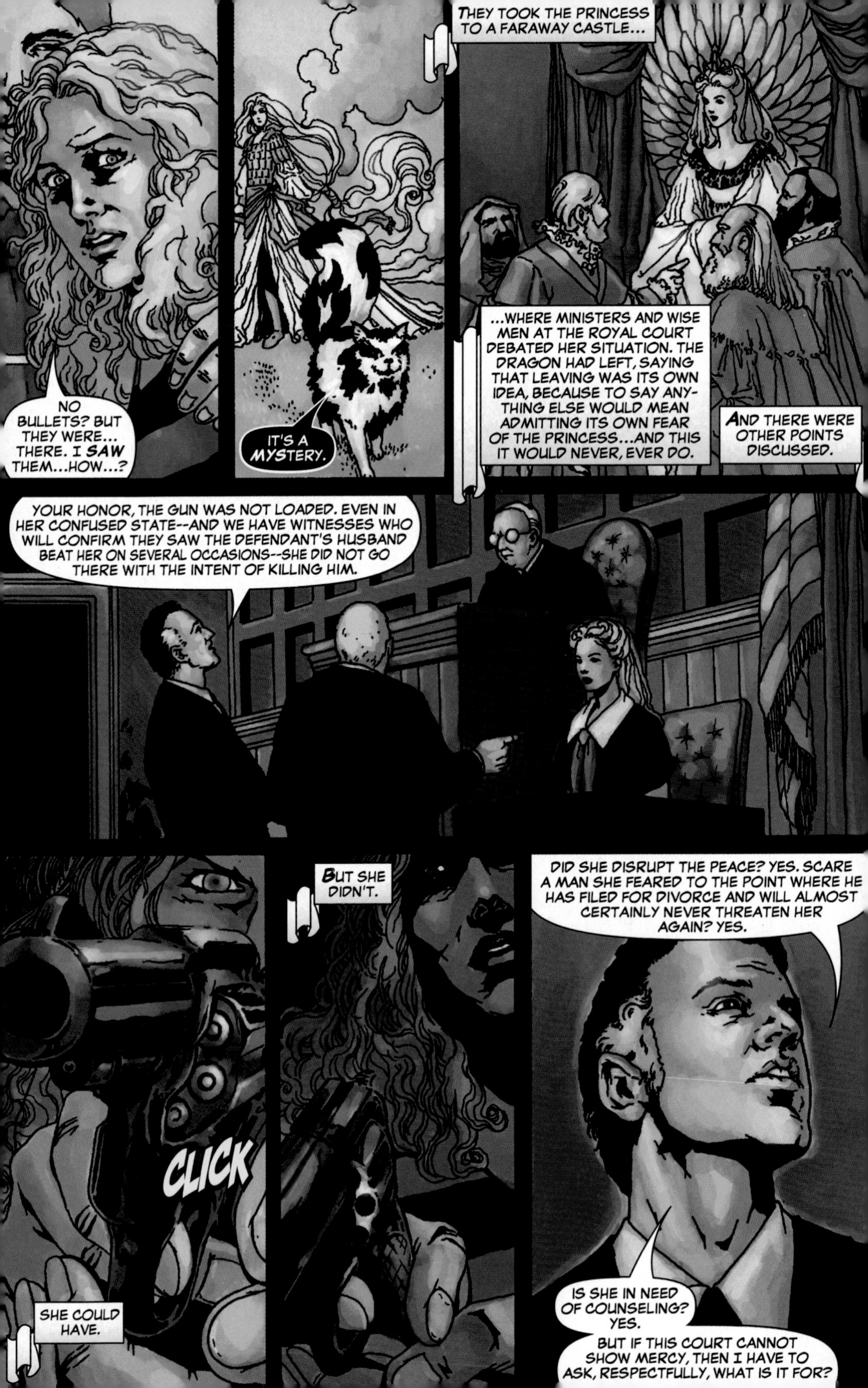
NO BULLETS? BUT THEY WERE... THERE. I SAW THEM...HOW...?
IT'S A MYSTERY.
THEY TOOK THE PRINCESS TO A FARAWAY CASTLE...
...WHERE MINISTERS AND WISE MEN AT THE ROYAL COURT DEBATED HER SITUATION. THE DRAGON HAD LEFT, SAYING THAT LEAVING WAS ITS OWN IDEA, BECAUSE TO SAY ANYTHING ELSE WOULD MEAN ADMITTING ITS OWN FEAR OF THE PRINCESS...AND THIS IT WOULD NEVER, EVER DO.
AND THERE WERE OTHER POINTS DISCUSSED.
YOUR HONOR, THE GUN WAS NOT LOADED. EVEN IN HER CONFUSED STATE--AND WE HAVE WITNESSES WHO WILL CONFIRM THEY SAW THE DEFENDANT'S HUSBAND BEAT HER ON SEVERAL OCCASIONS--SHE DID NOT GO THERE WITH THE INTENT OF KILLING HIM.
CLICK
SHE COULD HAVE.
BUT SHE DIDN'T.
DID SHE DISRUPT THE PEACE? YES. SCARE A MAN SHE FEARED TO THE POINT WHERE HE HAS FILED FOR DIVORCE AND WILL ALMOST CERTAINLY NEVER THREATEN HER AGAIN? YES.
IS SHE IN NEED OF COUNSELING? YES.
BUT IF THIS COURT CANNOT SHOW MERCY, THEN I HAVE TO ASK, RESPECTFULLY, WHAT IS IT FOR?

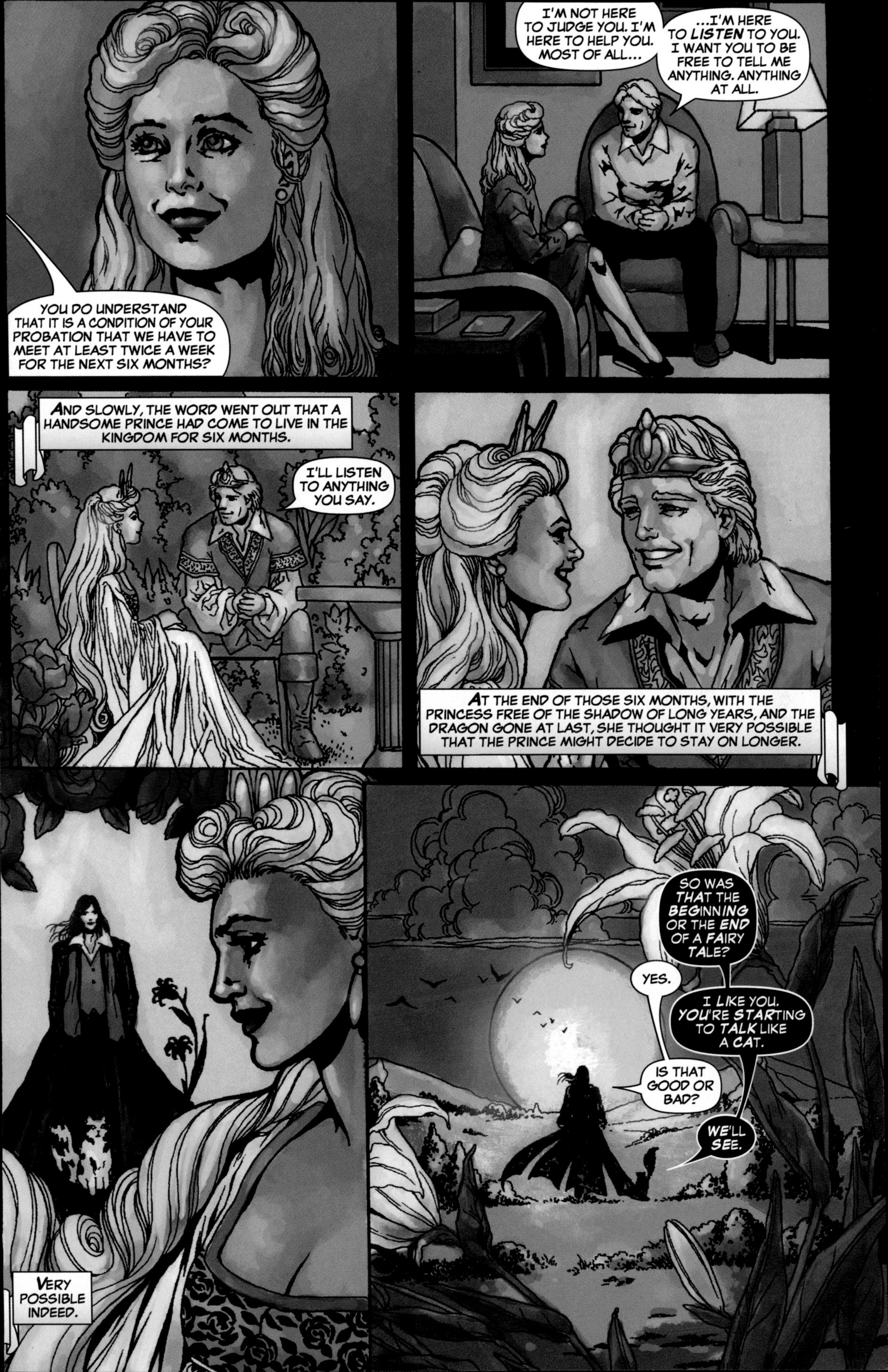
YOU DO UNDERSTAND THAT IT IS A CONDITION OF YOUR PROBATION THAT WE HAVE TO MEET AT LEAST TWICE A WEEK FOR THE NEXT SIX MONTHS?
I'M NOT HERE TO JUDGE YOU. I'M HERE TO HELP YOU. MOST OF ALL...
...I'M HERE TO LISTEN TO YOU. I WANT YOU TO BE FREE TO TELL ME ANYTHING. ANYTHING AT ALL.
AND SLOWLY, THE WORD WENT OUT THAT A HANDSOME PRINCE HAD COME TO LIVE IN THE KINGDOM FOR SIX MONTHS.
I'LL LISTEN TO ANYTHING YOU SAY.
AT THE END OF THOSE SIX MONTHS, WITH THE PRINCESS FREE OF THE SHADOW OF LONG YEARS, AND THE DRAGON GONE AT LAST, SHE THOUGHT IT VERY POSSIBLE THAT THE PRINCE MIGHT DECIDE TO STAY ON LONGER.
VERY POSSIBLE INDEED.
SO WAS THAT THE BEGINNING OR THE END OF A FAIRY TALE?
YES.
I LIKE YOU. YOU'RE STARTING TO TALK LIKE A CAT.
IS THAT GOOD OR BAD?
WE'LL SEE.

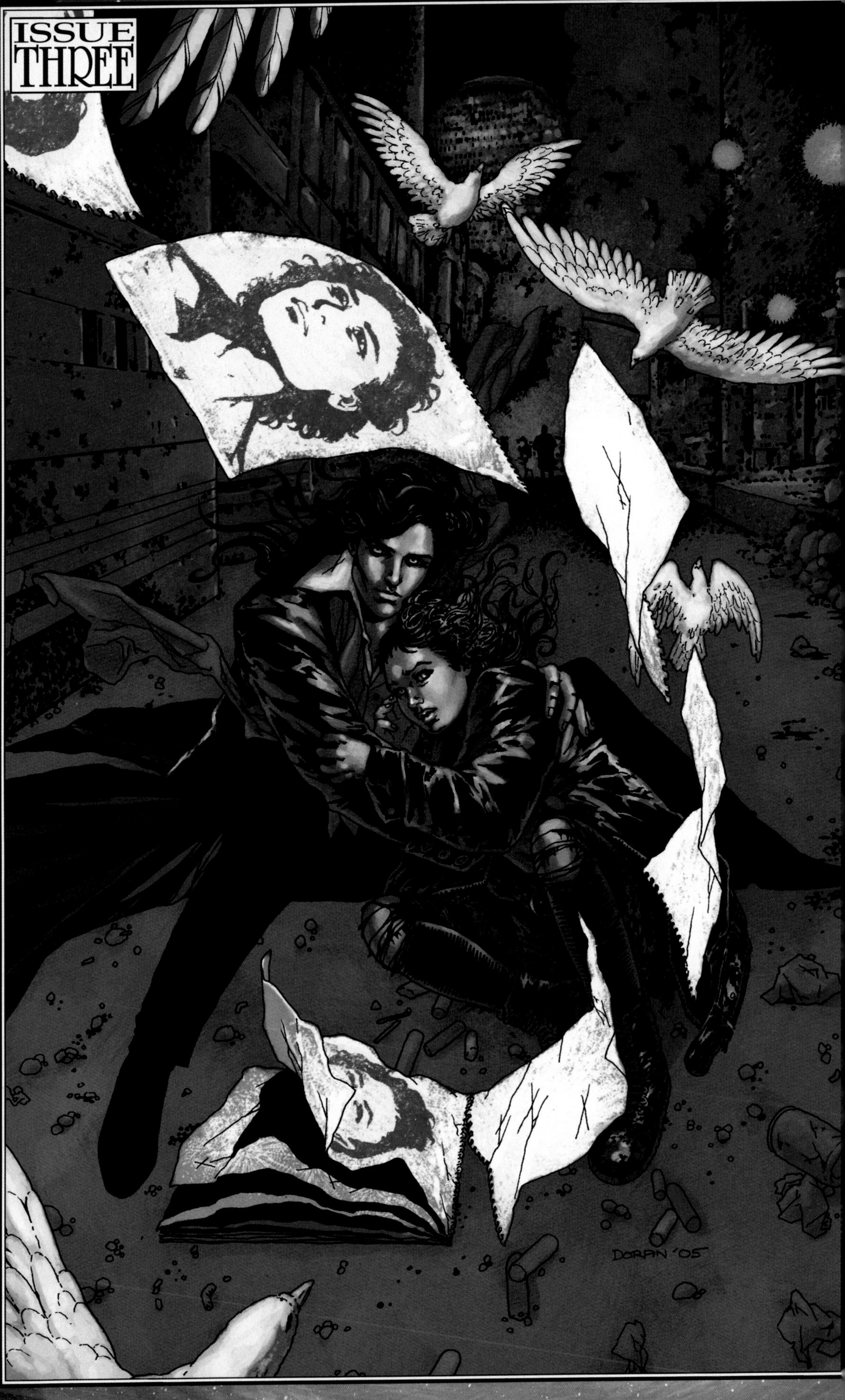
ISSUE THREE
DORAN '05

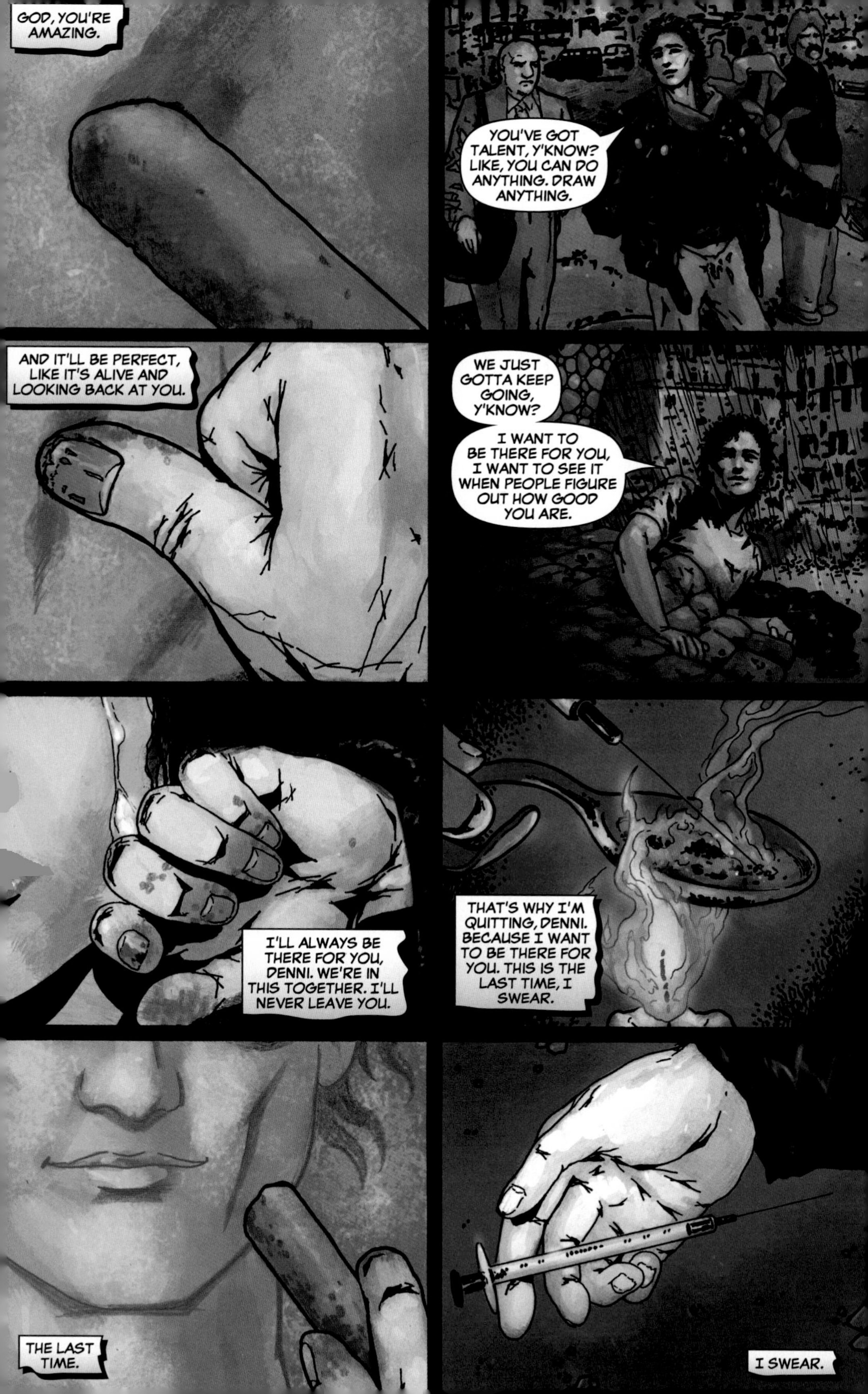
GOD, YOU'RE AMAZING.
YOU'VE GOT TALENT, Y'KNOW? LIKE, YOU CAN DO ANYTHING. DRAW ANYTHING.
AND IT'LL BE PERFECT, LIKE IT'S ALIVE AND LOOKING BACK AT YOU.
WE JUST GOTTA KEEP GOING, Y'KNOW?
I WANT TO BE THERE FOR YOU, I WANT TO SEE IT WHEN PEOPLE FIGURE OUT HOW GOOD YOU ARE.
I'LL ALWAYS BE THERE FOR YOU, DENNI. WE'RE IN THIS TOGETHER. I'LL NEVER LEAVE YOU.
THAT'S WHY I'M QUITTING, DENNI. BECAUSE I WANT TO BE THERE FOR YOU. THIS IS THE LAST TIME, I SWEAR.
THE LAST TIME.
I SWEAR.

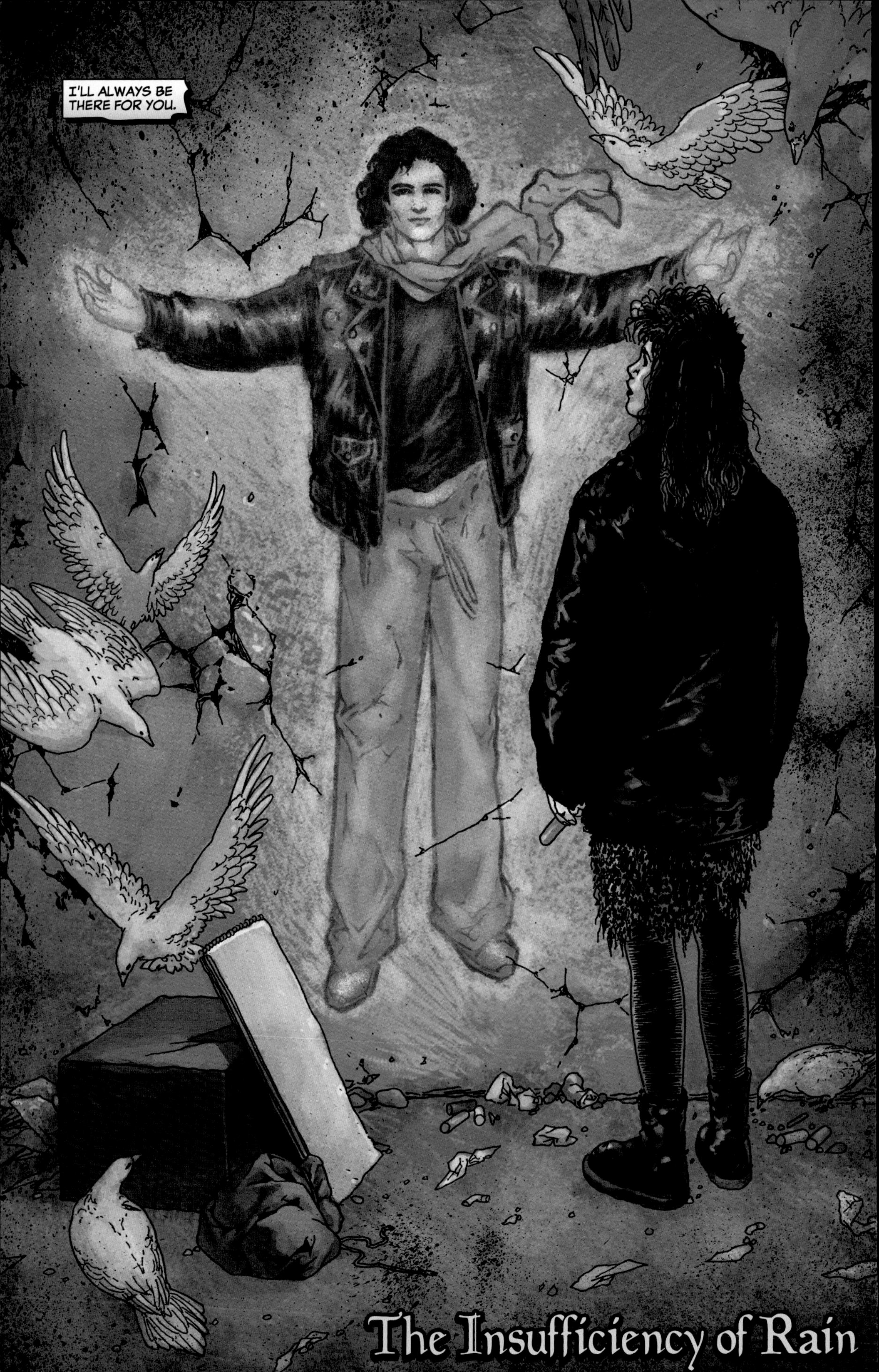
I'LL ALWAYS BE THERE FOR YOU.
The Insufficiency of Rain

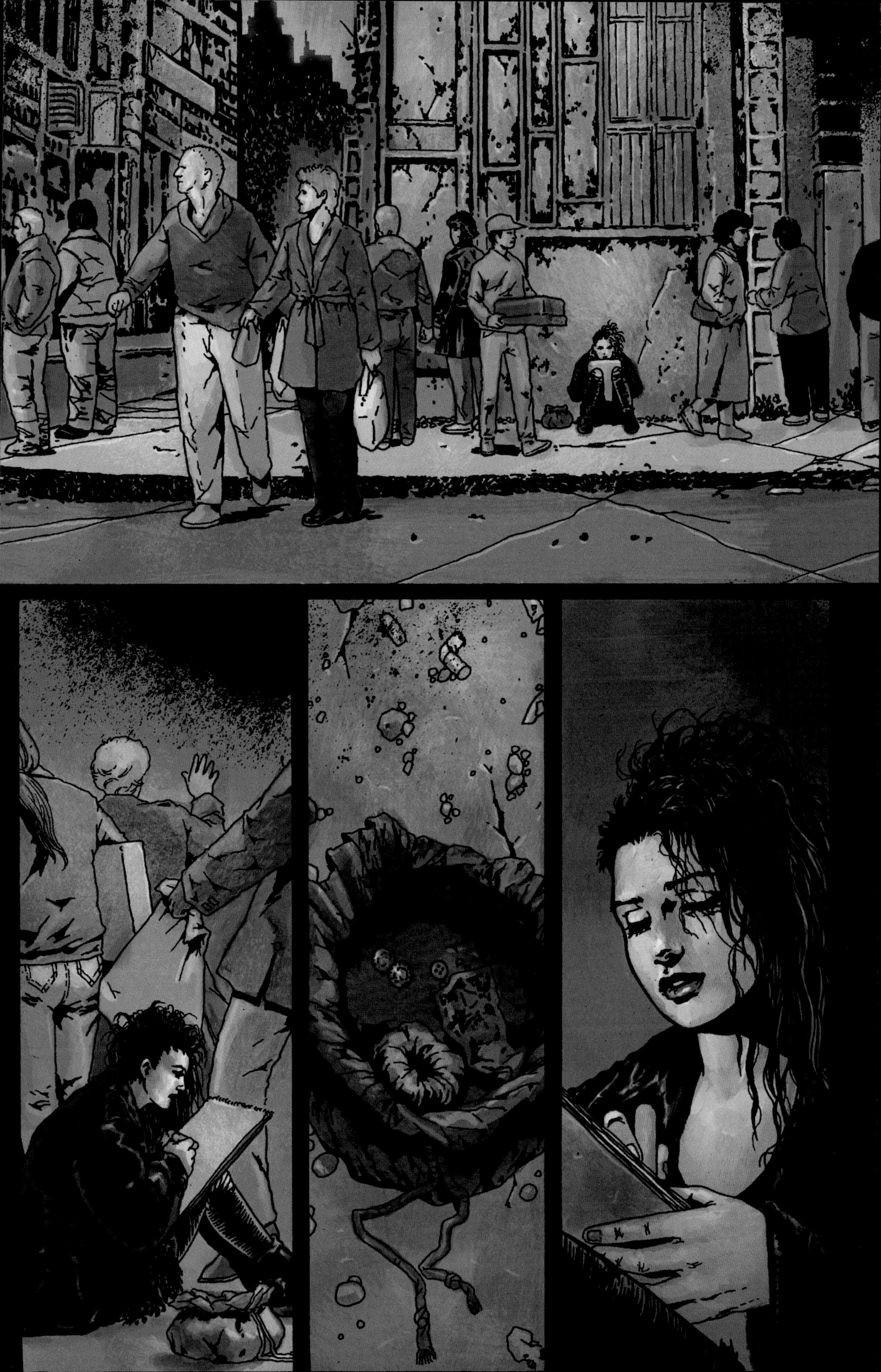

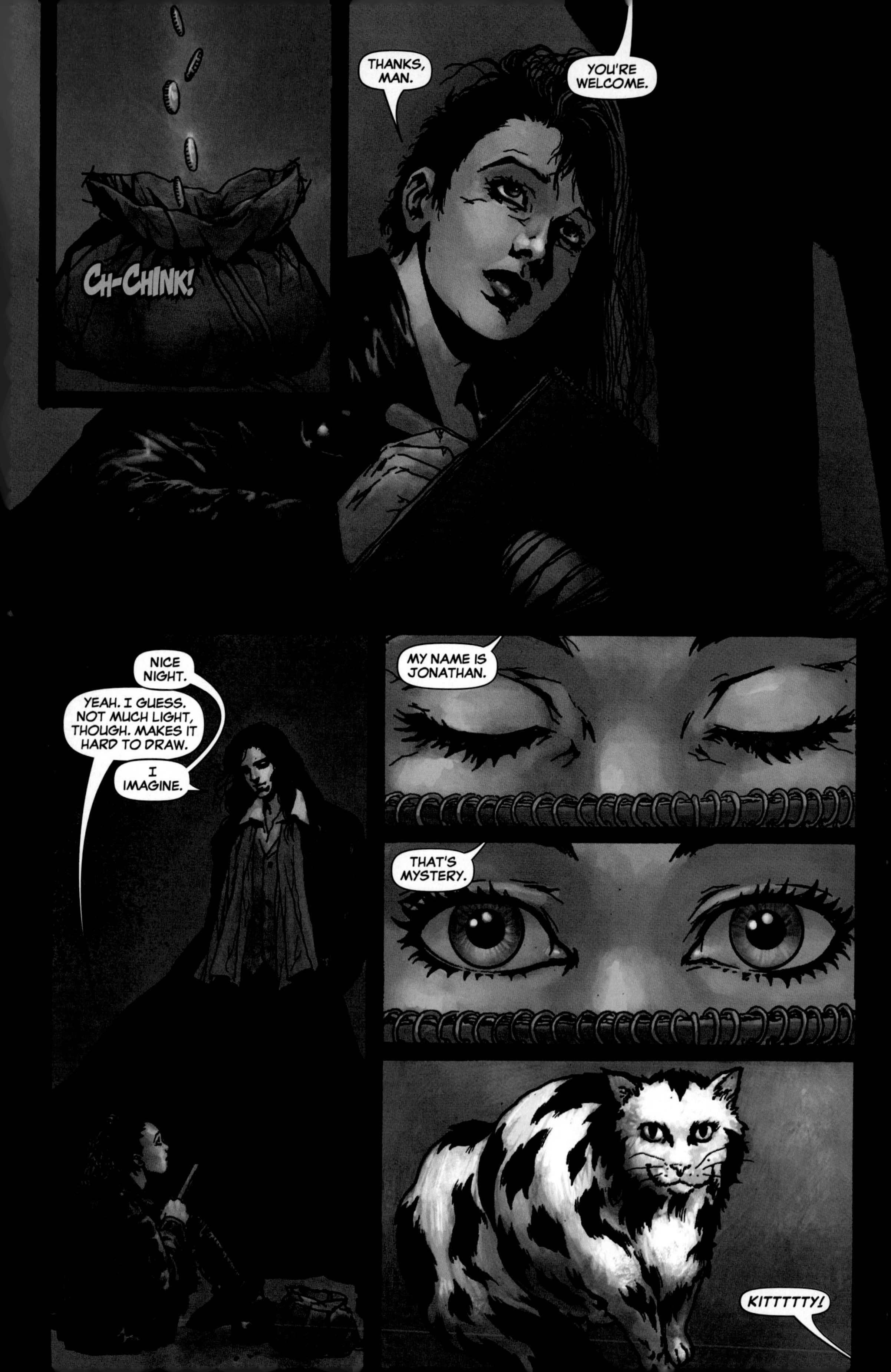

CH-CHINK!
THANKS, MAN.
YOU'RE WELCOME.
NICE NIGHT.
YEAH. I GUESS. NOT MUCH LIGHT, THOUGH. MAKES IT HARD TO DRAW.
I IMAGINE.
MY NAME IS JONATHAN.
THAT'S MYSTERY.
KITTTTTY!

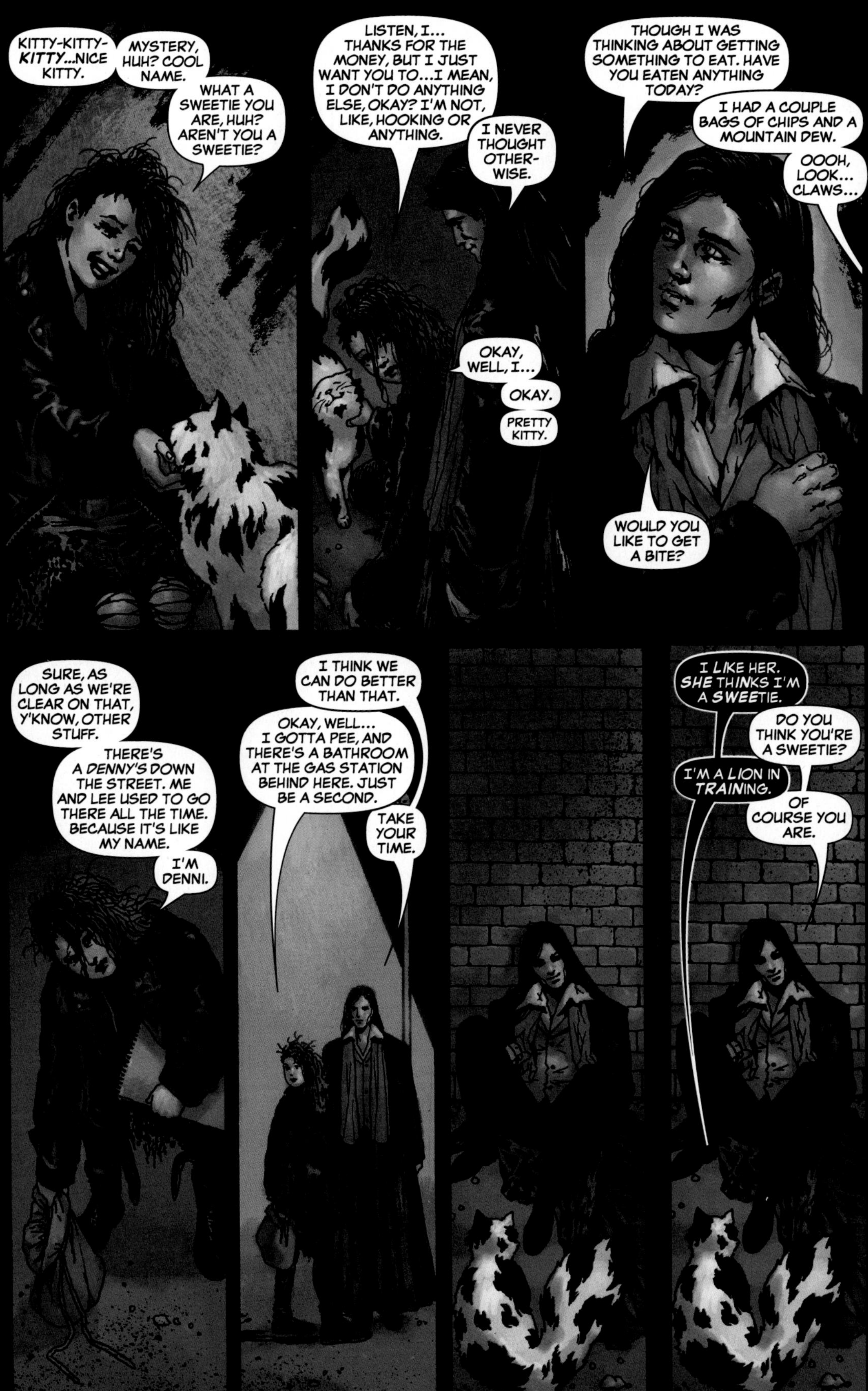
KITTY-KITTY-KITTY...NICE KITTY.
MYSTERY, HUH? COOL NAME.
WHAT A SWEETIE YOU ARE, HUH? AREN'T YOU A SWEETIE?
LISTEN, I... THANKS FOR THE MONEY, BUT I JUST WANT YOU TO...I MEAN, I DON'T DO ANYTHING ELSE, OKAY? I'M NOT, LIKE, HOOKING OR ANYTHING.
I NEVER THOUGHT OTHERWISE.
OKAY, WELL, I...
OKAY.
PRETTY KITTY.
THOUGH I WAS THINKING ABOUT GETTING SOMETHING TO EAT. HAVE YOU EATEN ANYTHING TODAY?
I HAD A COUPLE BAGS OF CHIPS AND A MOUNTAIN DEW.
OOOH, LOOK... CLAWS...
WOULD YOU LIKE TO GET A BITE?
SURE, AS LONG AS WE'RE CLEAR ON THAT, Y'KNOW, OTHER STUFF.
THERE'S A DENNY'S DOWN THE STREET. ME AND LEE USED TO GO THERE ALL THE TIME. BECAUSE IT'S LIKE MY NAME.
I'M DENNI.
I THINK WE CAN DO BETTER THAN THAT.
OKAY, WELL... I GOTTA PEE, AND THERE'S A BATHROOM AT THE GAS STATION BEHIND HERE. JUST BE A SECOND.
TAKE YOUR TIME.
I LIKE HER. SHE THINKS I'M A SWEETIE.
DO YOU THINK YOU'RE A SWEETIE?
I'M A LION IN TRAINING.
OF COURSE YOU ARE.

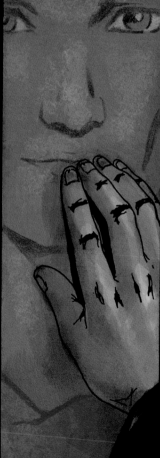

"YOU SURE YOU
DON'T WANT TO
DO THE DENNY'S
INSTEAD?"

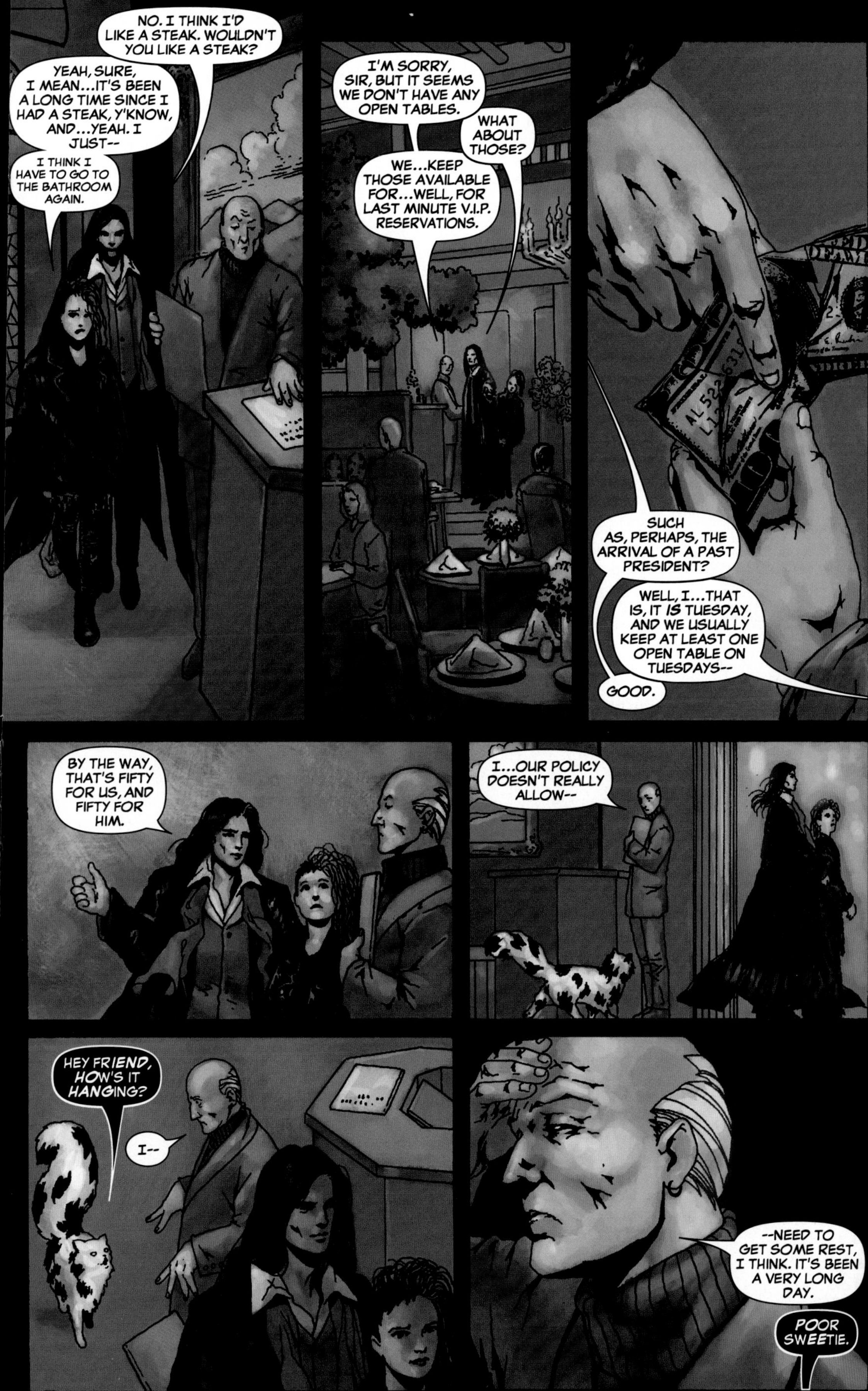
NO. I THINK I'D LIKE A STEAK. WOULDN'T YOU LIKE A STEAK?
YEAH, SURE, I MEAN...IT'S BEEN A LONG TIME SINCE I HAD A STEAK, Y'KNOW, AND...YEAH. I JUST--
I THINK I HAVE TO GO TO THE BATHROOM AGAIN.
I'M SORRY, SIR, BUT IT SEEMS WE DON'T HAVE ANY OPEN TABLES.
WHAT ABOUT THOSE?
WE...KEEP THOSE AVAILABLE FOR...WELL, FOR LAST MINUTE V.I.P. RESERVATIONS.
SUCH AS, PERHAPS, THE ARRIVAL OF A PAST PRESIDENT?
WELL, I...THAT IS, IT IS TUESDAY, AND WE USUALLY KEEP AT LEAST ONE OPEN TABLE ON TUESDAYS--
GOOD.
BY THE WAY, THAT'S FIFTY FOR US, AND FIFTY FOR HIM.
I...OUR POLICY DOESN'T REALLY ALLOW--
HEY FRIEND, HOW'S IT HANGING?
I--
--NEED TO GET SOME REST, I THINK. IT'S BEEN A VERY LONG DAY.
POOR SWEETIE.

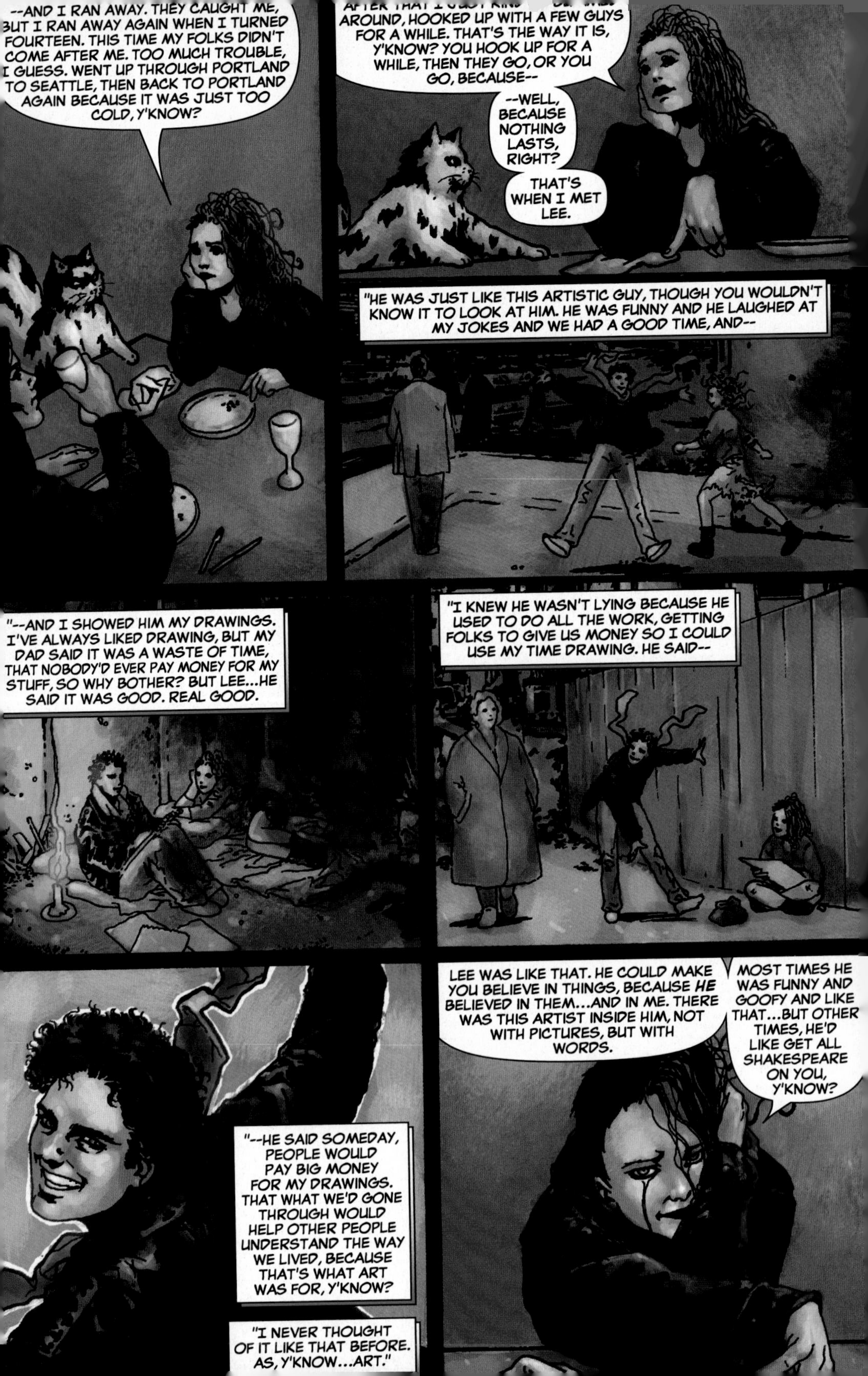
--AND I RAN AWAY. THEY CAUGHT ME, BUT I RAN AWAY AGAIN WHEN I TURNED FOURTEEN. THIS TIME MY FOLKS DIDN'T COME AFTER ME. TOO MUCH TROUBLE, I GUESS. WENT UP THROUGH PORTLAND TO SEATTLE, THEN BACK TO PORTLAND AGAIN BECAUSE IT WAS JUST TOO COLD, Y'KNOW?
AROUND, HOOKED UP WITH A FEW GUYS FOR A WHILE. THAT'S THE WAY IT IS, Y'KNOW? YOU HOOK UP FOR A WHILE, THEN THEY GO, OR YOU GO, BECAUSE--
--WELL, BECAUSE NOTHING LASTS, RIGHT?
THAT'S WHEN I MET LEE.
"HE WAS JUST LIKE THIS ARTISTIC GUY, THOUGH YOU WOULDN'T KNOW IT TO LOOK AT HIM. HE WAS FUNNY AND HE LAUGHED AT MY JOKES AND WE HAD A GOOD TIME, AND--
"--AND I SHOWED HIM MY DRAWINGS. I'VE ALWAYS LIKED DRAWING, BUT MY DAD SAID IT WAS A WASTE OF TIME, THAT NOBODY'D EVER PAY MONEY FOR MY STUFF, SO WHY BOTHER? BUT LEE...HE SAID IT WAS GOOD. REAL GOOD.
"I KNEW HE WASN'T LYING BECAUSE HE USED TO DO ALL THE WORK, GETTING FOLKS TO GIVE US MONEY SO I COULD USE MY TIME DRAWING. HE SAID--
"--HE SAID SOMEDAY, PEOPLE WOULD PAY BIG MONEY FOR MY DRAWINGS. THAT WHAT WE'D GONE THROUGH WOULD HELP OTHER PEOPLE UNDERSTAND THE WAY WE LIVED, BECAUSE THAT'S WHAT ART WAS FOR, Y'KNOW?
"I NEVER THOUGHT OF IT LIKE THAT BEFORE. AS, Y'KNOW...ART."
LEE WAS LIKE THAT. HE COULD MAKE YOU BELIEVE IN THINGS, BECAUSE *HE* BELIEVED IN THEM...AND IN ME. THERE WAS THIS ARTIST INSIDE HIM, NOT WITH PICTURES, BUT WITH WORDS.
MOST TIMES HE WAS FUNNY AND GOOFY AND LIKE THAT...BUT OTHER TIMES, HE'D LIKE GET ALL SHAKESPEARE ON YOU, Y'KNOW?

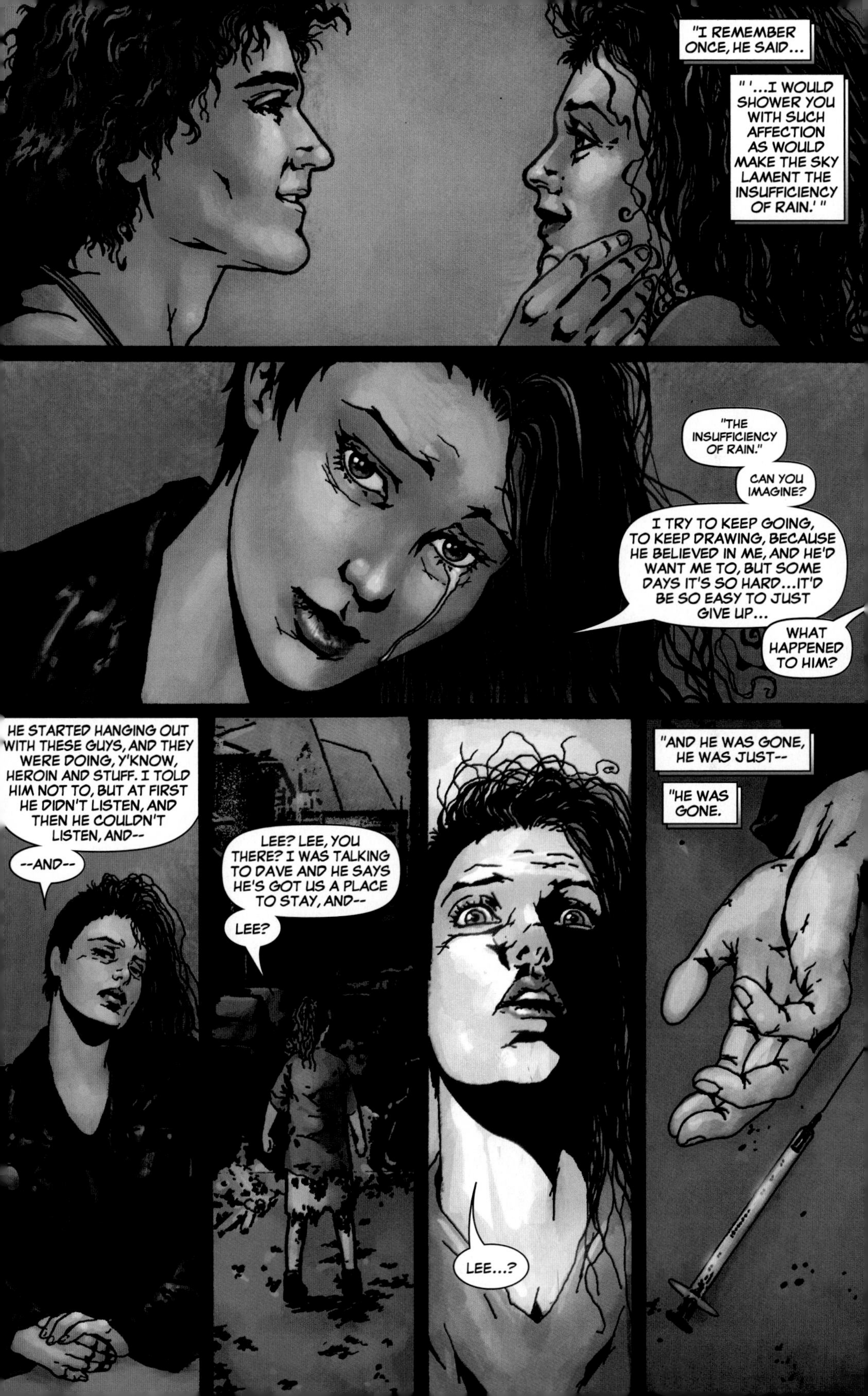
"I REMEMBER ONCE, HE SAID...
"'...I WOULD SHOWER YOU WITH SUCH AFFECTION AS WOULD MAKE THE SKY LAMENT THE INSUFFICIENCY OF RAIN.'"
"THE INSUFFICIENCY OF RAIN."
CAN YOU IMAGINE?
I TRY TO KEEP GOING, TO KEEP DRAWING, BECAUSE HE BELIEVED IN ME, AND HE'D WANT ME TO, BUT SOME DAYS IT'S SO HARD...IT'D BE SO EASY TO JUST GIVE UP...
WHAT HAPPENED TO HIM?
HE STARTED HANGING OUT WITH THESE GUYS, AND THEY WERE DOING, Y'KNOW, HEROIN AND STUFF. I TOLD HIM NOT TO, BUT AT FIRST HE DIDN'T LISTEN, AND THEN HE COULDN'T LISTEN, AND--
--AND--
LEE? LEE, YOU THERE? I WAS TALKING TO DAVE AND HE SAYS HE'S GOT US A PLACE TO STAY, AND--
LEE?
LEE...?
"AND HE WAS GONE, HE WAS JUST--
"HE WAS GONE.

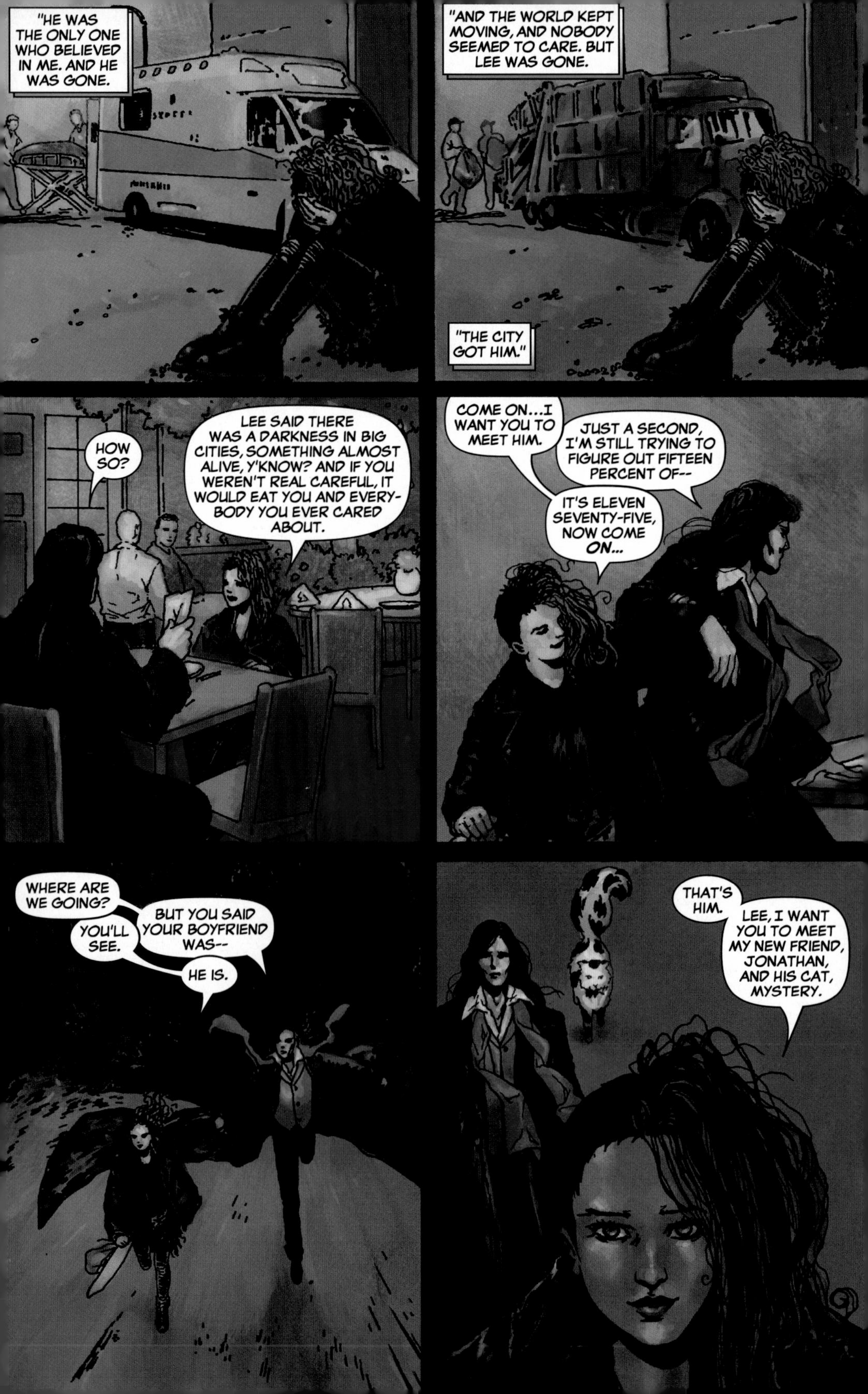
"HE WAS THE ONLY ONE WHO BELIEVED IN ME. AND HE WAS GONE.
"AND THE WORLD KEPT MOVING, AND NOBODY SEEMED TO CARE. BUT LEE WAS GONE.
"THE CITY GOT HIM."
HOW SO?
LEE SAID THERE WAS A DARKNESS IN BIG CITIES, SOMETHING ALMOST ALIVE, Y'KNOW? AND IF YOU WEREN'T REAL CAREFUL, IT WOULD EAT YOU AND EVERY-BODY YOU EVER CARED ABOUT.
COME ON...I WANT YOU TO MEET HIM.
JUST A SECOND, I'M STILL TRYING TO FIGURE OUT FIFTEEN PERCENT OF--
IT'S ELEVEN SEVENTY-FIVE, NOW COME ON...
WHERE ARE WE GOING?
YOU'LL SEE.
BUT YOU SAID YOUR BOYFRIEND WAS--
HE IS.
THAT'S HIM.
LEE, I WANT YOU TO MEET MY NEW FRIEND, JONATHAN, AND HIS CAT, MYSTERY.

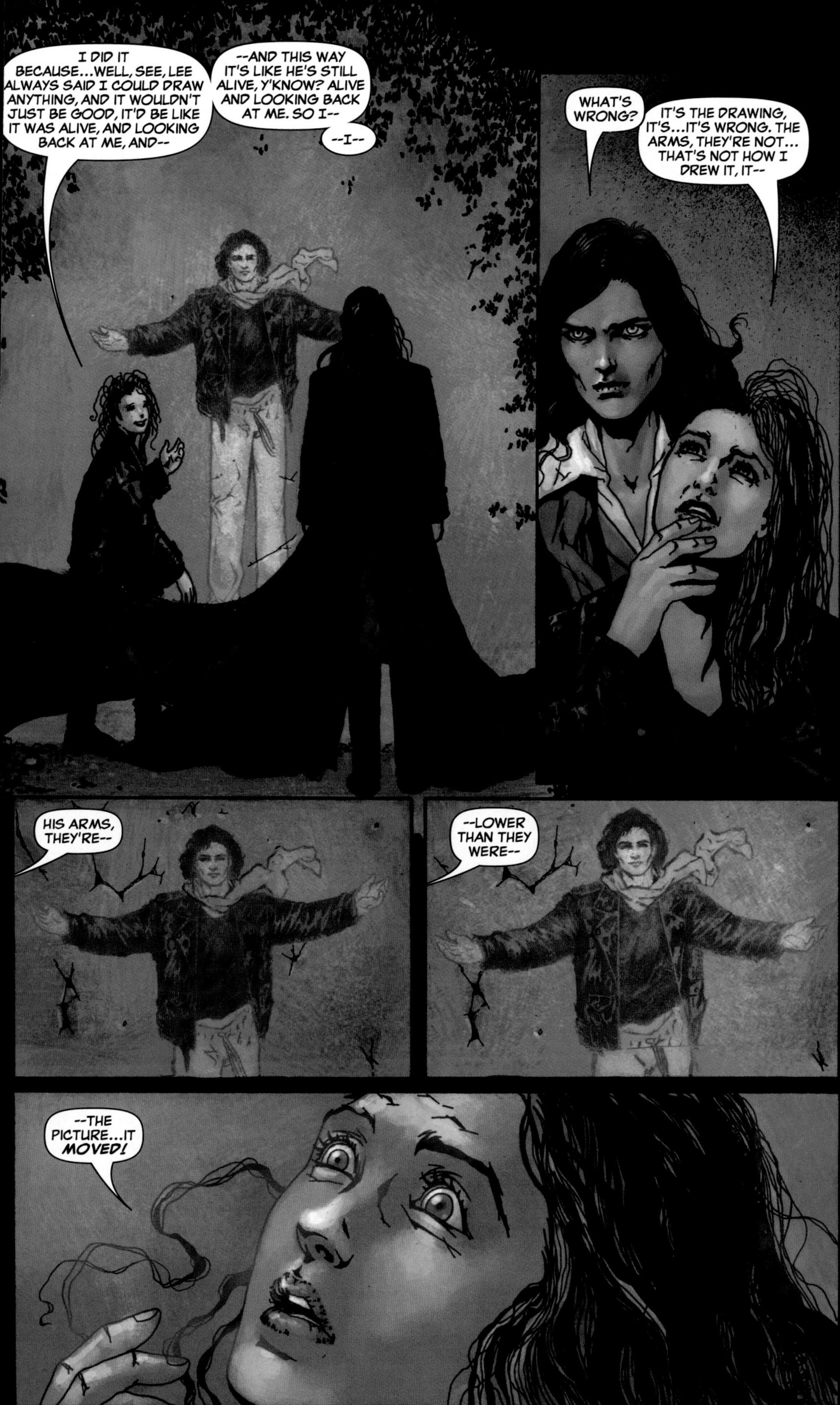
I DID IT BECAUSE...WELL, SEE, LEE ALWAYS SAID I COULD DRAW ANYTHING, AND IT WOULDN'T JUST BE GOOD, IT'D BE LIKE IT WAS ALIVE, AND LOOKING BACK AT ME, AND--
--AND THIS WAY IT'S LIKE HE'S STILL ALIVE, Y'KNOW? ALIVE AND LOOKING BACK AT ME. SO I--
--I--
WHAT'S WRONG?
IT'S THE DRAWING, IT'S...IT'S WRONG. THE ARMS, THEY'RE NOT... THAT'S NOT HOW I DREW IT, IT--
HIS ARMS, THEY'RE--
--LOWER THAN THEY WERE--
--THE PICTURE...IT MOVED!

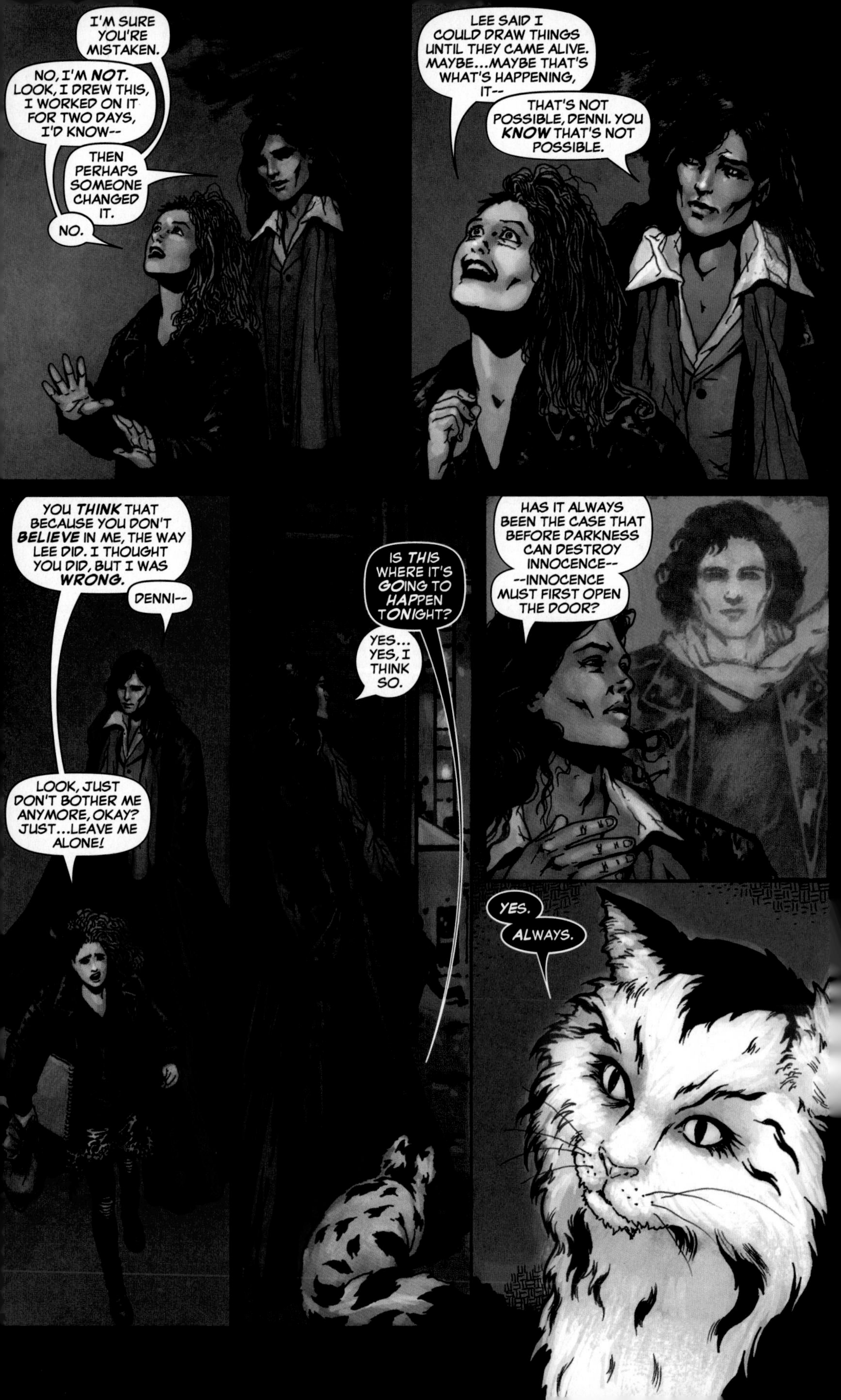
I'M SURE YOU'RE MISTAKEN.
NO, I'M NOT. LOOK, I DREW THIS, I WORKED ON IT FOR TWO DAYS, I'D KNOW--
THEN PERHAPS SOMEONE CHANGED IT.
NO.
LEE SAID I COULD DRAW THINGS UNTIL THEY CAME ALIVE. MAYBE...MAYBE THAT'S WHAT'S HAPPENING, IT--
THAT'S NOT POSSIBLE, DENNI. YOU KNOW THAT'S NOT POSSIBLE.
YOU THINK THAT BECAUSE YOU DON'T BELIEVE IN ME, THE WAY LEE DID. I THOUGHT YOU DID, BUT I WAS WRONG.
DENNI--
LOOK, JUST DON'T BOTHER ME ANYMORE, OKAY? JUST...LEAVE ME ALONE!
IS THIS WHERE IT'S GOING TO HAPPEN TONIGHT?
YES... YES, I THINK SO.
HAS IT ALWAYS BEEN THE CASE THAT BEFORE DARKNESS CAN DESTROY INNOCENCE--
--INNOCENCE MUST FIRST OPEN THE DOOR?
YES.
ALWAYS.

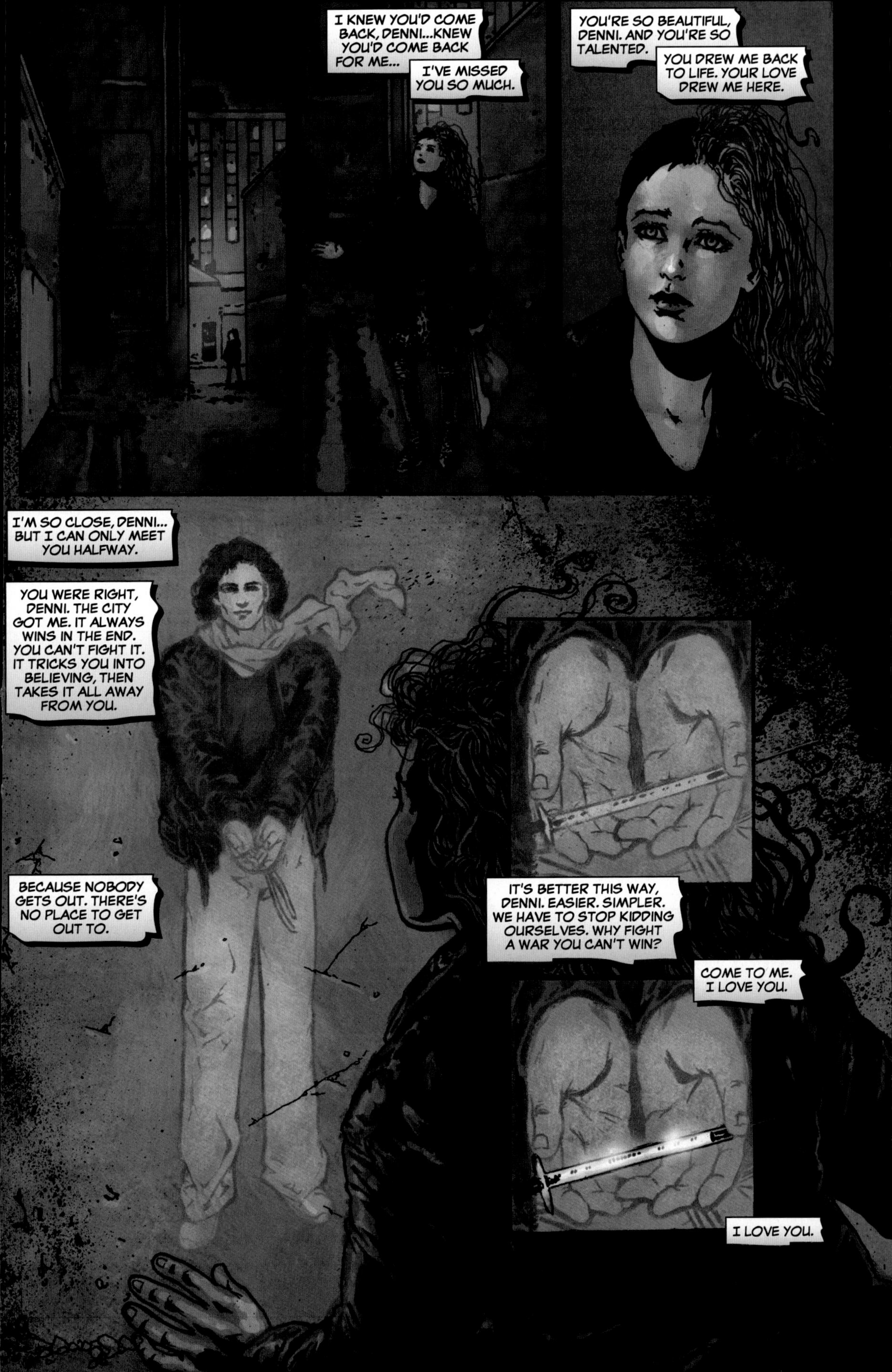

I KNEW YOU'D COME BACK, DENNI...KNEW YOU'D COME BACK FOR ME...
I'VE MISSED YOU SO MUCH.
YOU'RE SO BEAUTIFUL, DENNI. AND YOU'RE SO TALENTED.
YOU DREW ME BACK TO LIFE. YOUR LOVE DREW ME HERE.
I'M SO CLOSE, DENNI... BUT I CAN ONLY MEET YOU HALFWAY.
YOU WERE RIGHT, DENNI. THE CITY GOT ME. IT ALWAYS WINS IN THE END. YOU CAN'T FIGHT IT. IT TRICKS YOU INTO BELIEVING, THEN TAKES IT ALL AWAY FROM YOU.
BECAUSE NOBODY GETS OUT. THERE'S NO PLACE TO GET OUT TO.
IT'S BETTER THIS WAY, DENNI. EASIER. SIMPLER. WE HAVE TO STOP KIDDING OURSELVES. WHY FIGHT A WAR YOU CAN'T WIN?
COME TO ME. I LOVE YOU.
I LOVE YOU.

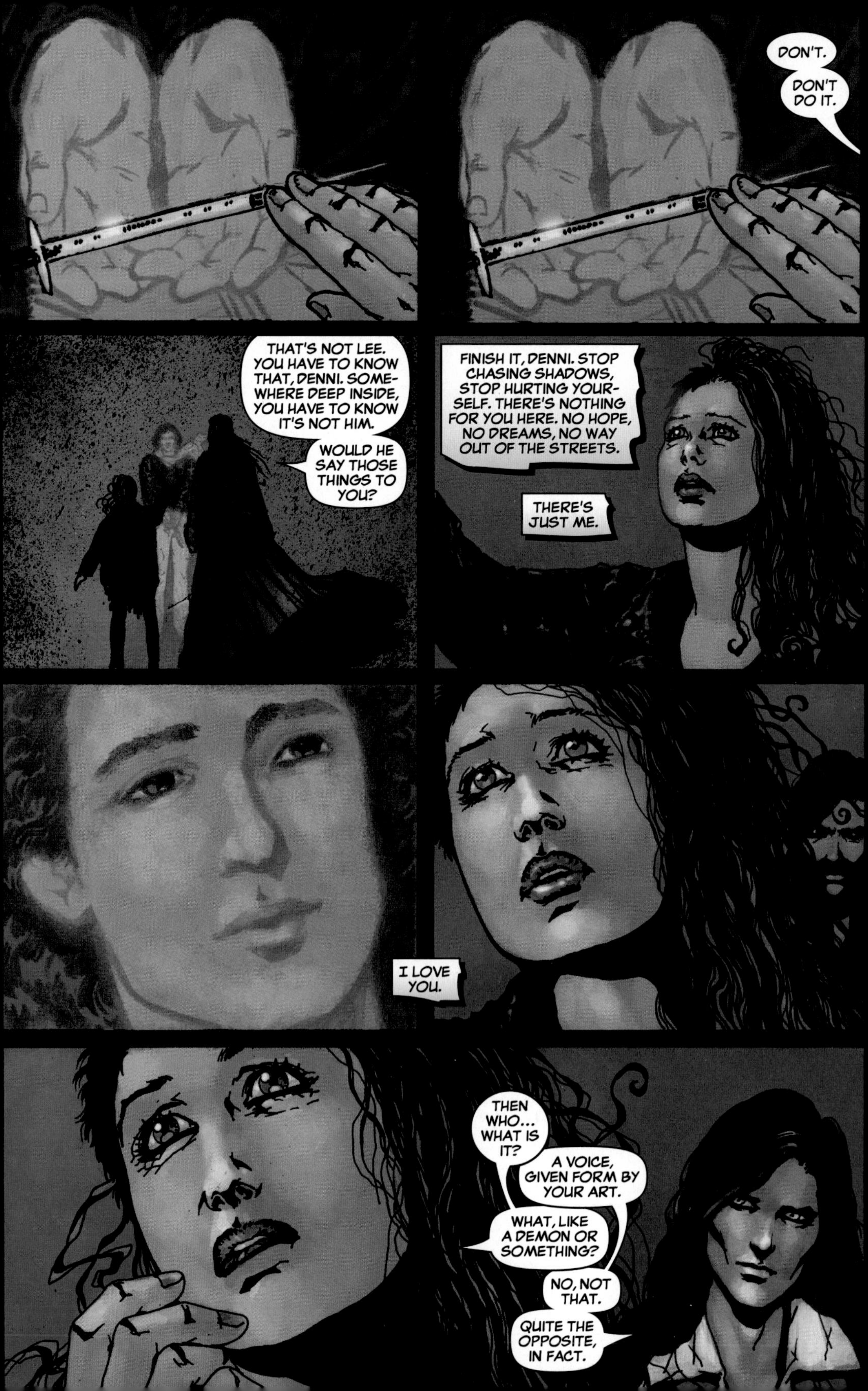
DON'T.
DON'T DO IT.
THAT'S NOT LEE. YOU HAVE TO KNOW THAT, DENNI. SOME-WHERE DEEP INSIDE, YOU HAVE TO KNOW IT'S NOT HIM.
WOULD HE SAY THOSE THINGS TO YOU?
FINISH IT, DENNI. STOP CHASING SHADOWS, STOP HURTING YOUR-SELF. THERE'S NOTHING FOR YOU HERE. NO HOPE, NO DREAMS, NO WAY OUT OF THE STREETS.
THERE'S JUST ME.
I LOVE YOU.
THEN WHO... WHAT IS IT?
A VOICE, GIVEN FORM BY YOUR ART.
WHAT, LIKE A DEMON OR SOMETHING?
NO, NOT THAT.
QUITE THE OPPOSITE, IN FACT.

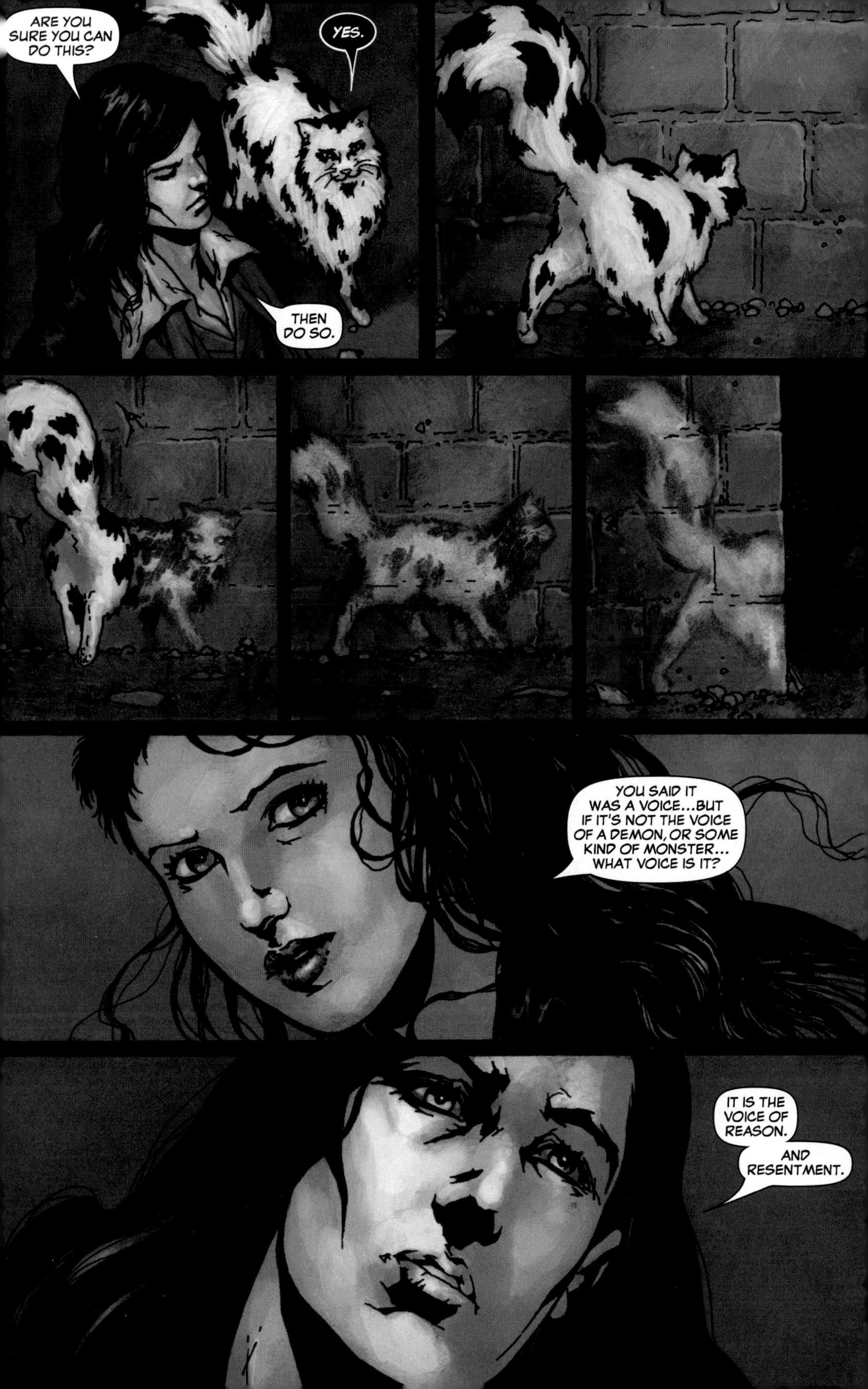
ARE YOU SURE YOU CAN DO THIS?
YES.
THEN DO SO.
YOU SAID IT WAS A VOICE...BUT IF IT'S NOT THE VOICE OF A DEMON, OR SOME KIND OF MONSTER... WHAT VOICE IS IT?
IT IS THE VOICE OF REASON.
AND RESENTMENT.

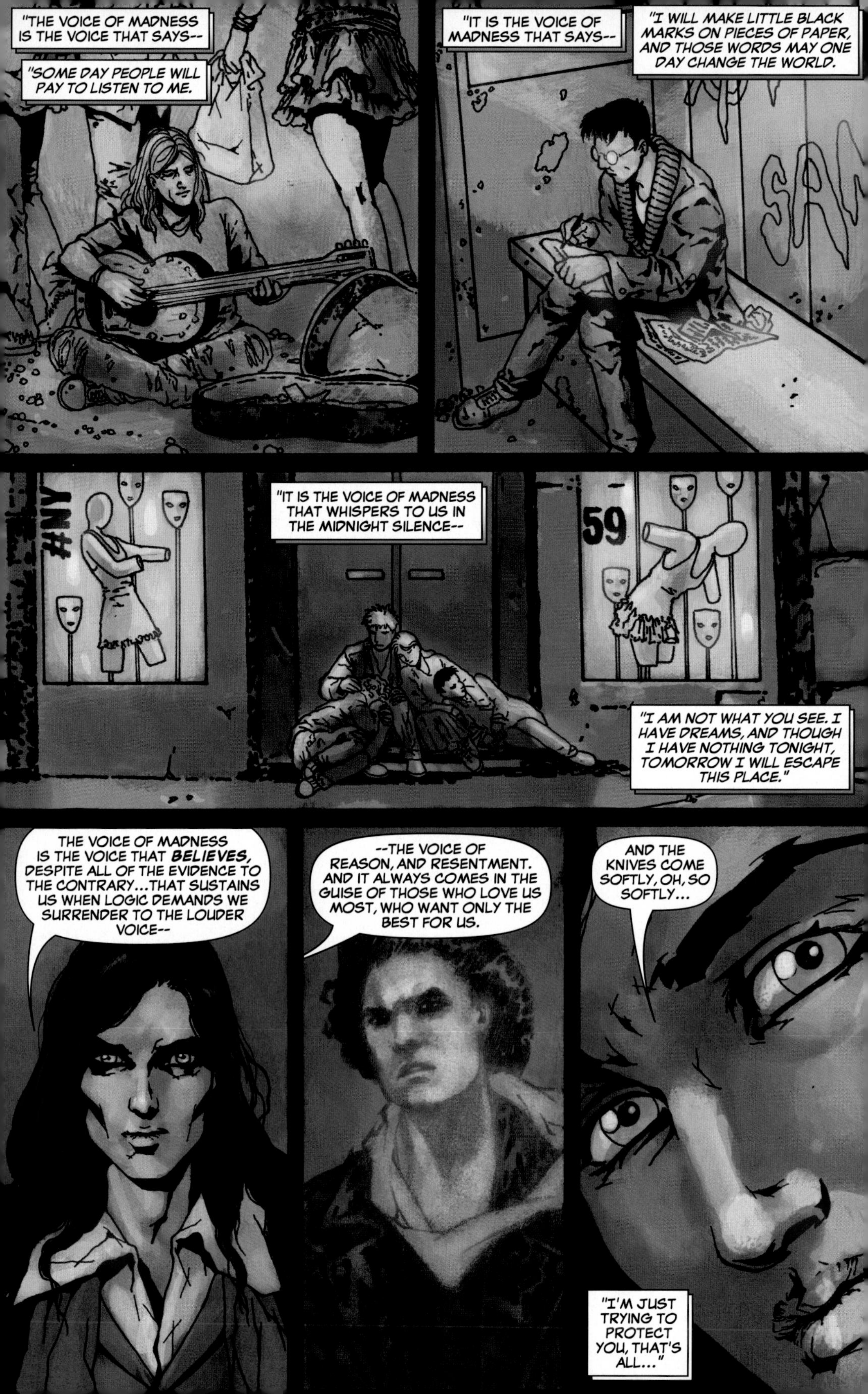
"THE VOICE OF MADNESS IS THE VOICE THAT SAYS--
"SOME DAY PEOPLE WILL PAY TO LISTEN TO ME.
"IT IS THE VOICE OF MADNESS THAT SAYS--
"I WILL MAKE LITTLE BLACK MARKS ON PIECES OF PAPER, AND THOSE WORDS MAY ONE DAY CHANGE THE WORLD.
#NY
"IT IS THE VOICE OF MADNESS THAT WHISPERS TO US IN THE MIDNIGHT SILENCE--
59
"I AM NOT WHAT YOU SEE. I HAVE DREAMS, AND THOUGH I HAVE NOTHING TONIGHT, TOMORROW I WILL ESCAPE THIS PLACE."
THE VOICE OF MADNESS IS THE VOICE THAT BELIEVES, DESPITE ALL OF THE EVIDENCE TO THE CONTRARY...THAT SUSTAINS US WHEN LOGIC DEMANDS WE SURRENDER TO THE LOUDER VOICE--
--THE VOICE OF REASON, AND RESENTMENT. AND IT ALWAYS COMES IN THE GUISE OF THOSE WHO LOVE US MOST, WHO WANT ONLY THE BEST FOR US.
AND THE KNIVES COME SOFTLY, OH, SO SOFTLY...
"I'M JUST TRYING TO PROTECT YOU, THAT'S ALL..."

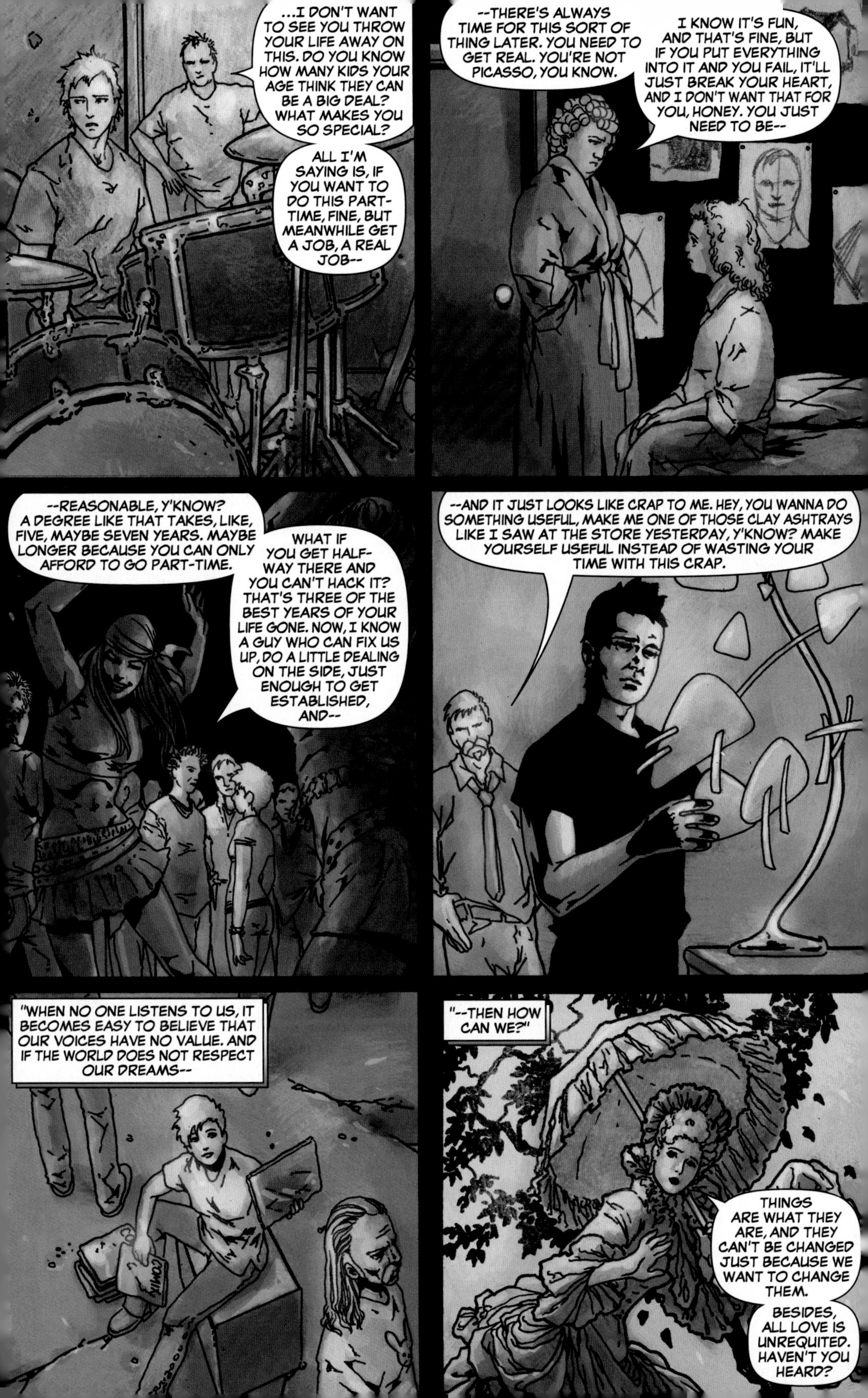
...I DON'T WANT TO SEE YOU THROW YOUR LIFE AWAY ON THIS. DO YOU KNOW HOW MANY KIDS YOUR AGE THINK THEY CAN BE A BIG DEAL? WHAT MAKES YOU SO SPECIAL?
ALL I'M SAYING IS, IF YOU WANT TO DO THIS PART-TIME, FINE, BUT MEANWHILE GET A JOB, A REAL JOB--
--THERE'S ALWAYS TIME FOR THIS SORT OF THING LATER. YOU NEED TO GET REAL. YOU'RE NOT PICASSO, YOU KNOW.
I KNOW IT'S FUN, AND THAT'S FINE, BUT IF YOU PUT EVERYTHING INTO IT AND YOU FAIL, IT'LL JUST BREAK YOUR HEART, AND I DON'T WANT THAT FOR YOU, HONEY. YOU JUST NEED TO BE--
--REASONABLE, Y'KNOW? A DEGREE LIKE THAT TAKES, LIKE, FIVE, MAYBE SEVEN YEARS. MAYBE LONGER BECAUSE YOU CAN ONLY AFFORD TO GO PART-TIME.
WHAT IF YOU GET HALF-WAY THERE AND YOU CAN'T HACK IT? THAT'S THREE OF THE BEST YEARS OF YOUR LIFE GONE. NOW, I KNOW A GUY WHO CAN FIX US UP, DO A LITTLE DEALING ON THE SIDE, JUST ENOUGH TO GET ESTABLISHED, AND--
--AND IT JUST LOOKS LIKE CRAP TO ME. HEY, YOU WANNA DO SOMETHING USEFUL, MAKE ME ONE OF THOSE CLAY ASHTRAYS LIKE I SAW AT THE STORE YESTERDAY, Y'KNOW? MAKE YOURSELF USEFUL INSTEAD OF WASTING YOUR TIME WITH THIS CRAP.
"WHEN NO ONE LISTENS TO US, IT BECOMES EASY TO BELIEVE THAT OUR VOICES HAVE NO VALUE. AND IF THE WORLD DOES NOT RESPECT OUR DREAMS--
COMIX
"--THEN HOW CAN WE?"
THINGS ARE WHAT THEY ARE, AND THEY CAN'T BE CHANGED JUST BECAUSE WE WANT TO CHANGE THEM.
BESIDES, ALL LOVE IS UNREQUITED. HAVEN'T YOU HEARD?

SOMETIMES THEIR MOTIVES ARE PURE, WISHING ONLY TO SAVE US FROM PAIN.

AND SOMETIMES THE PAIN THEY WISH TO SPARE IS THEIR OWN, BECAUSE IF YOU CAN BE CONVINCED TO SET ASIDE YOUR OWN DREAMS, THEY CAN REMAIN COMFORTABLE WITH THEIR DECISION TO DO THE SAME.

THE VOICE OF REASON IS THE VOICE THAT TELLS US THAT OUR DREAMS ARE FOOLISH, AND THE AGONY THAT FOLLOWS IS SO THICK IN SOME PLACES THAT IT SETTLES INTO WOOD AND STONE, INTO BRICK AND MORTAR--

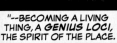

"--BECOMING A LIVING THING, A *GENIUS LOCI*, THE SPIRIT OF THE PLACE."

"AND THE SPIRIT OF THIS PLACE IS DESPAIR."

HE *TALKS* AND HE *TALKS*. I THINK I LIKED THE *OTHER* ONES *BETTER*.

"MYSTERY...ARE YOU THERE YET? DO YOU SEE IT?"

NO, I-- OH, WAIT...

OH YES, I'VE *FOUND* IT...

...FOUND... *HIM*.

WHAT DID HE FIND?

THERE ARE VOICES OF REASON, VOICES OF RESENTMENT, VOICES OF SANITY AND VOICES OF MADNESS.

BUT THERE ARE STILL OTHER VOICES, WAITING TO BE HEARD FROM.

THE VOICE OF TRUTH...

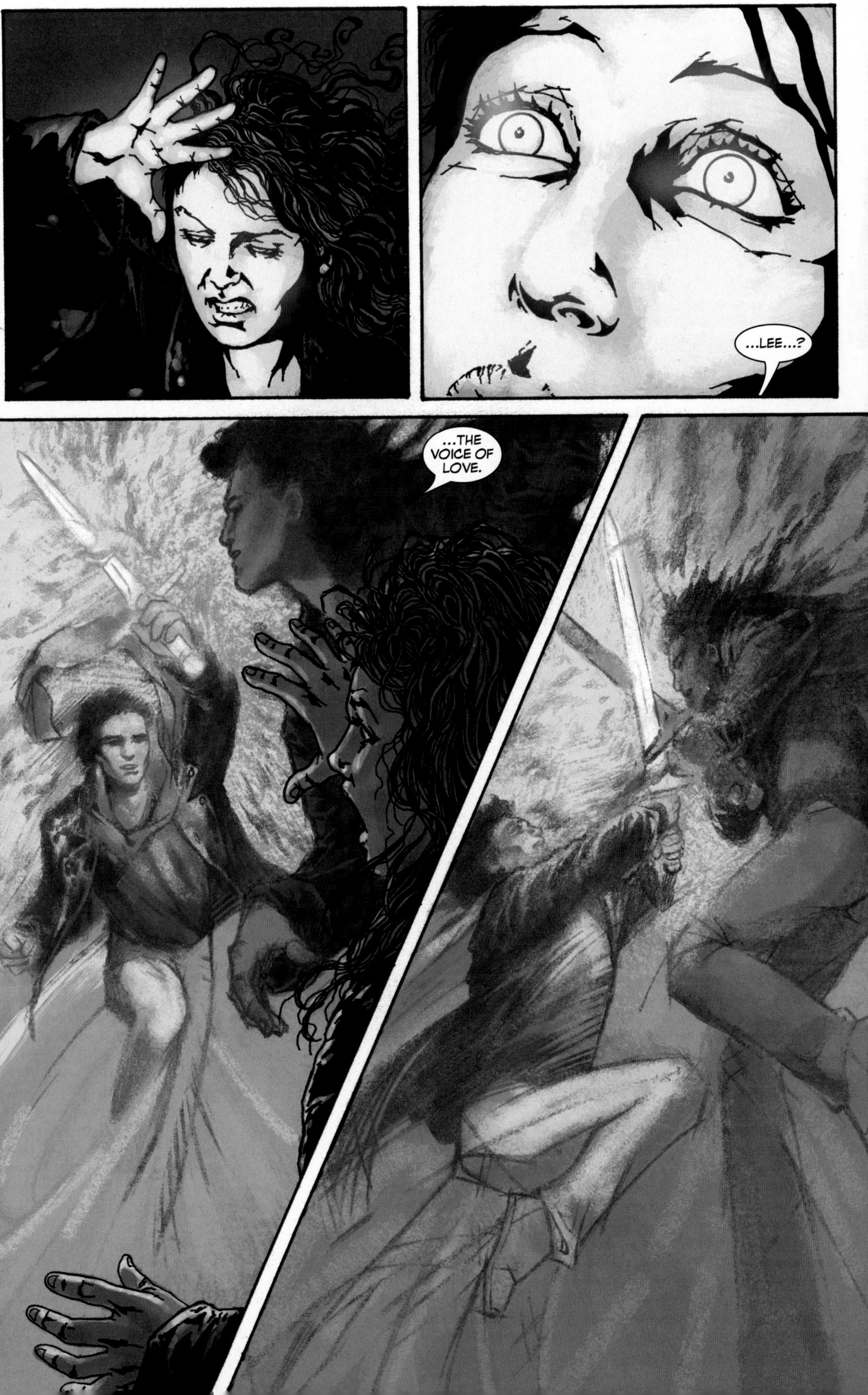
...LEE...?
...THE VOICE OF LOVE.

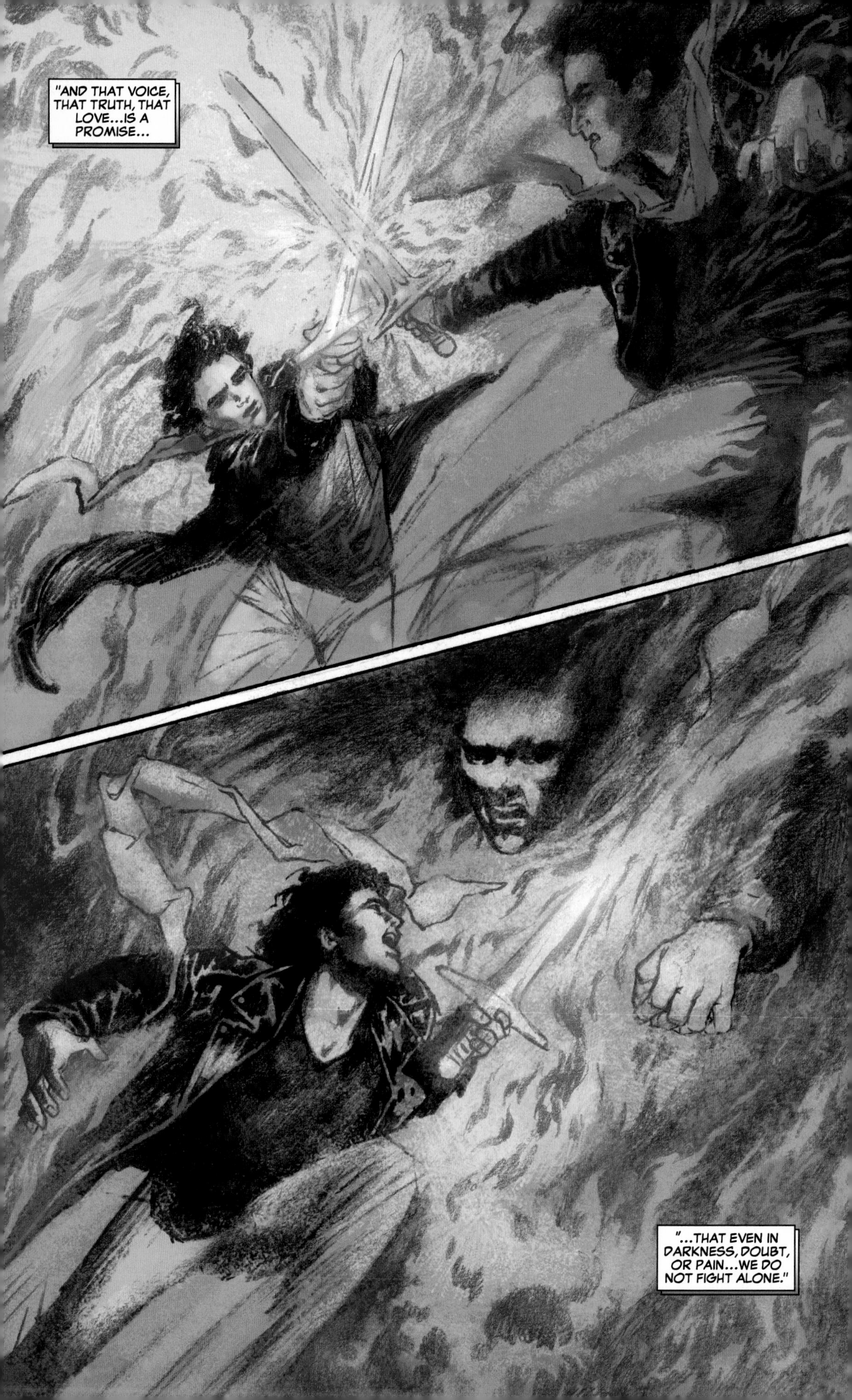
"AND THAT VOICE, THAT TRUTH, THAT LOVE...IS A PROMISE...
"...THAT EVEN IN DARKNESS, DOUBT, OR PAIN...WE DO NOT FIGHT ALONE."

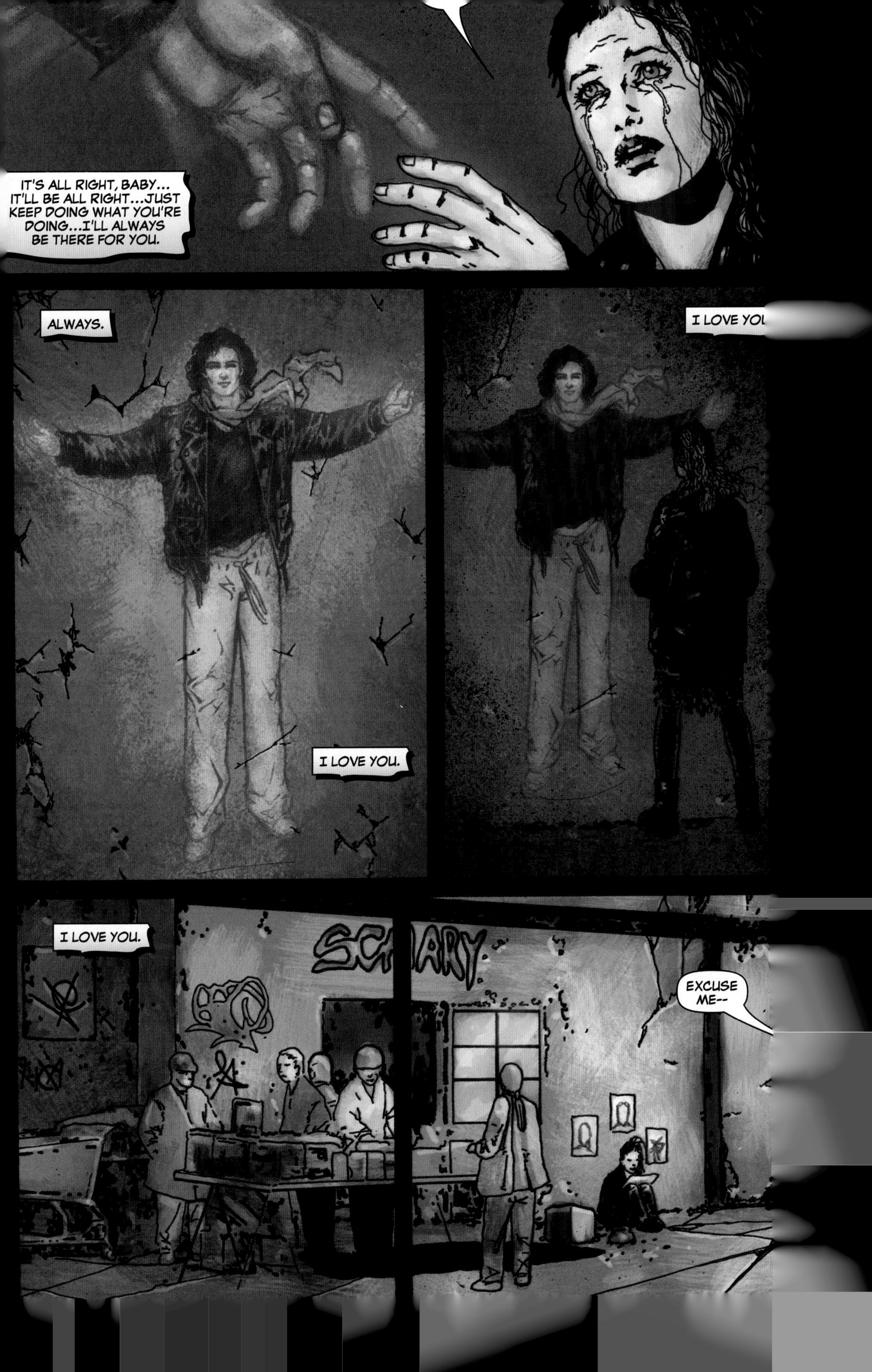
IT'S ALL RIGHT, BABY... IT'LL BE ALL RIGHT...JUST KEEP DOING WHAT YOU'RE DOING...I'LL ALWAYS BE THERE FOR YOU.
ALWAYS.
I LOVE YOU.
I LOVE YOU
I LOVE YOU.
SCHARY
EXCUSE ME--

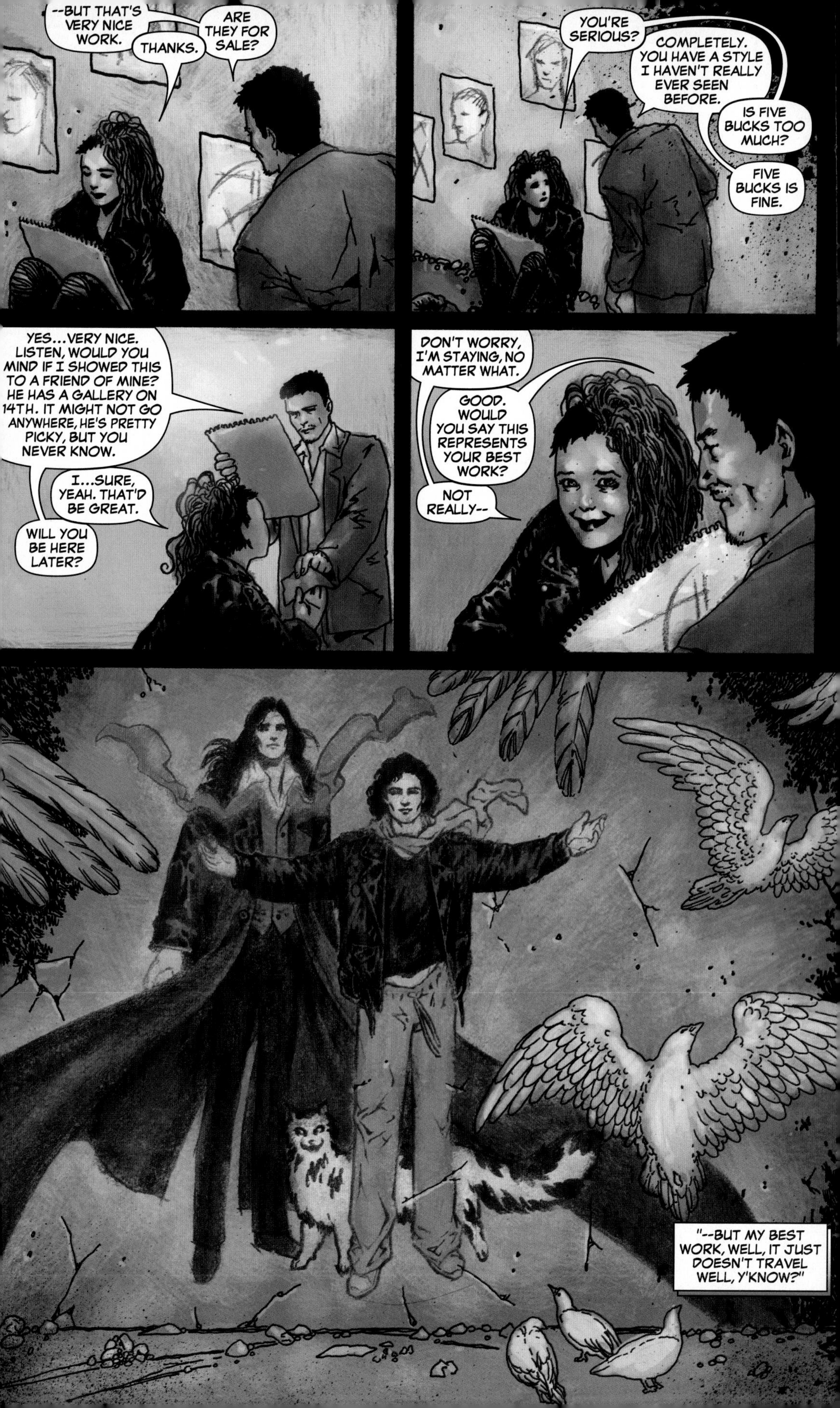
--BUT THAT'S VERY NICE WORK.
THANKS.
ARE THEY FOR SALE?
YOU'RE SERIOUS?
COMPLETELY. YOU HAVE A STYLE I HAVEN'T REALLY EVER SEEN BEFORE.
IS FIVE BUCKS TOO MUCH?
FIVE BUCKS IS FINE.
YES...VERY NICE. LISTEN, WOULD YOU MIND IF I SHOWED THIS TO A FRIEND OF MINE? HE HAS A GALLERY ON 14TH. IT MIGHT NOT GO ANYWHERE, HE'S PRETTY PICKY, BUT YOU NEVER KNOW.
I...SURE, YEAH. THAT'D BE GREAT.
WILL YOU BE HERE LATER?
DON'T WORRY, I'M STAYING, NO MATTER WHAT.
GOOD. WOULD YOU SAY THIS REPRESENTS YOUR BEST WORK?
NOT REALLY--
"--BUT MY BEST WORK, WELL, IT JUST DOESN'T TRAVEL WELL, Y'KNOW?"

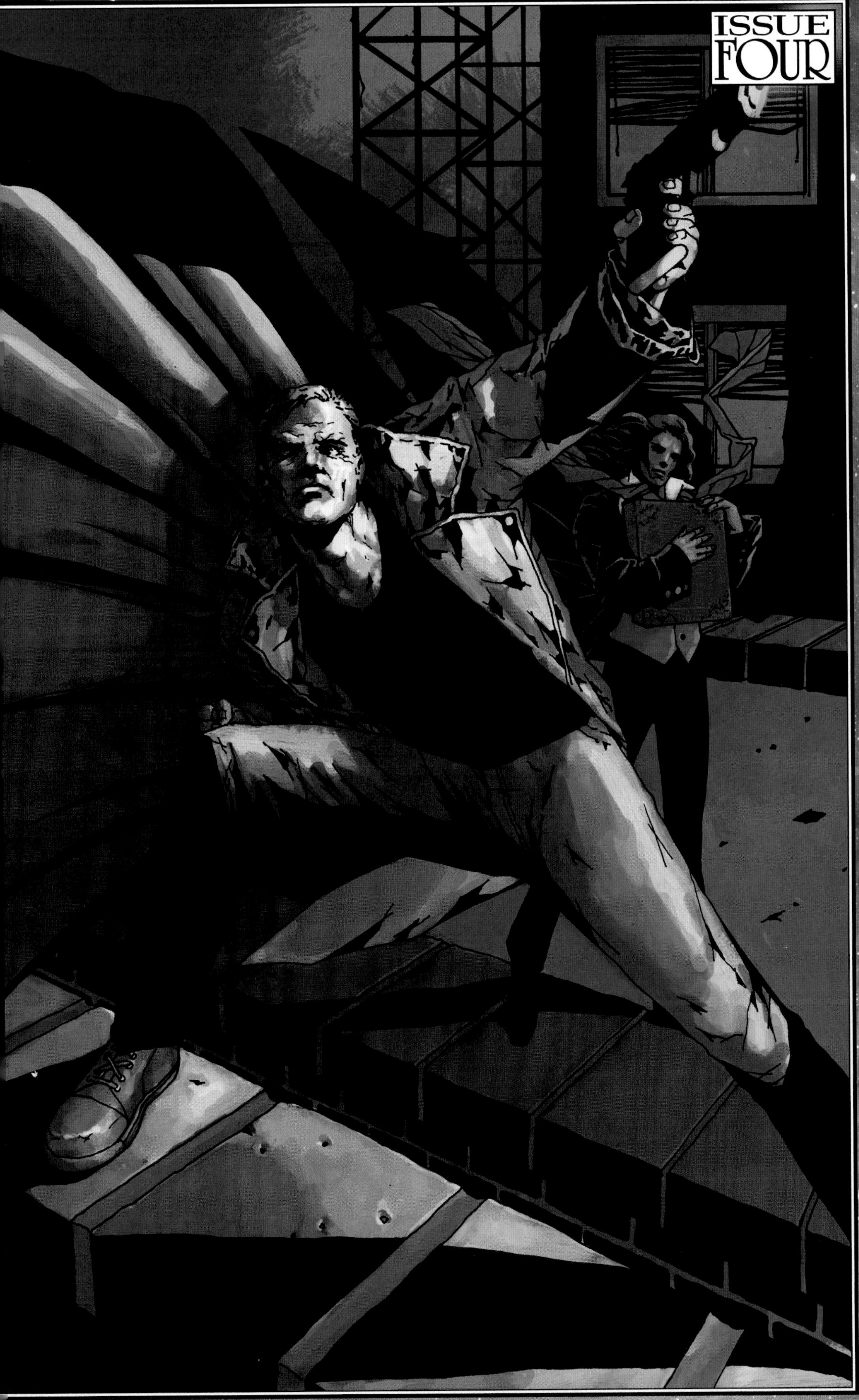
ISSUE
FOUR

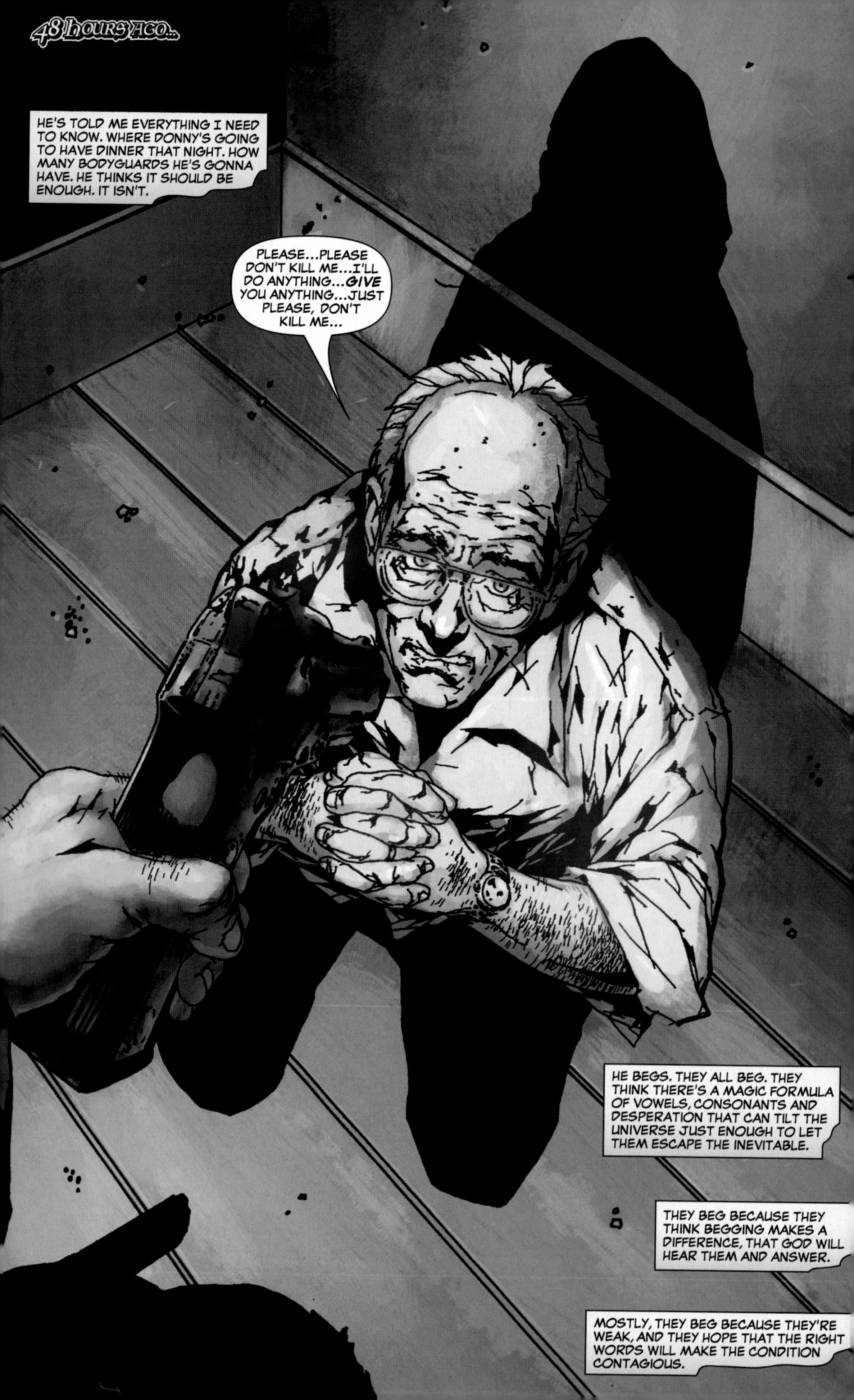
48 HOURS AGO...
HE'S TOLD ME EVERYTHING I NEED TO KNOW. WHERE DONNY'S GOING TO HAVE DINNER THAT NIGHT. HOW MANY BODYGUARDS HE'S GONNA HAVE. HE THINKS IT SHOULD BE ENOUGH. IT ISN'T.
PLEASE...PLEASE DON'T KILL ME...I'LL DO ANYTHING...GIVE YOU ANYTHING...JUST PLEASE, DON'T KILL ME...
HE BEGS. THEY ALL BEG. THEY THINK THERE'S A MAGIC FORMULA OF VOWELS, CONSONANTS AND DESPERATION THAT CAN TILT THE UNIVERSE JUST ENOUGH TO LET THEM ESCAPE THE INEVITABLE.
THEY BEG BECAUSE THEY THINK BEGGING MAKES A DIFFERENCE, THAT GOD WILL HEAR THEM AND ANSWER.
MOSTLY, THEY BEG BECAUSE THEY'RE WEAK, AND THEY HOPE THAT THE RIGHT WORDS WILL MAKE THE CONDITION CONTAGIOUS.

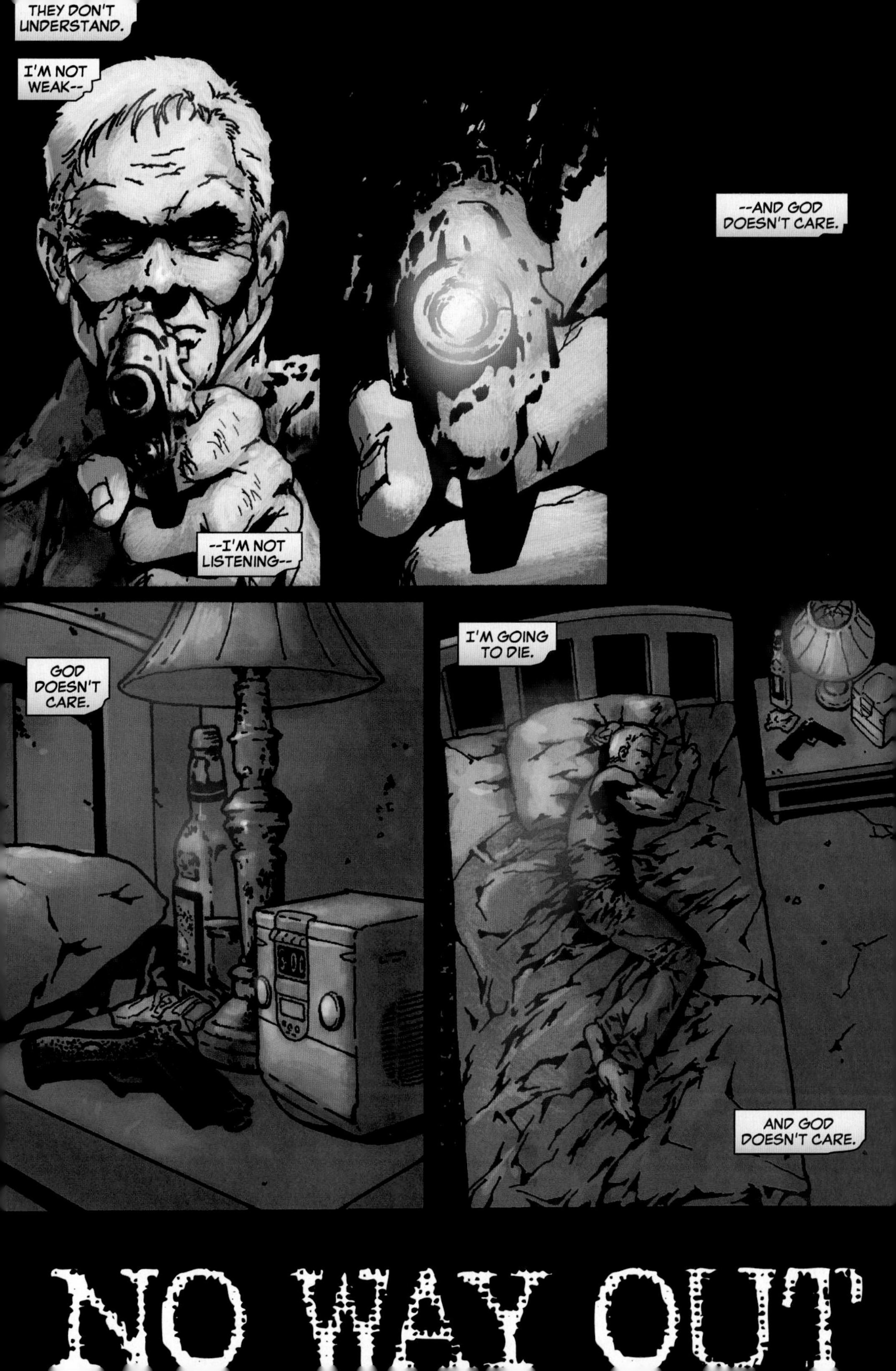
THEY DON'T UNDERSTAND.
I'M NOT WEAK--
--I'M NOT LISTENING--
--AND GOD DOESN'T CARE.
GOD DOESN'T CARE.
I'M GOING TO DIE.
AND GOD DOESN'T CARE.
NO WAY OUT

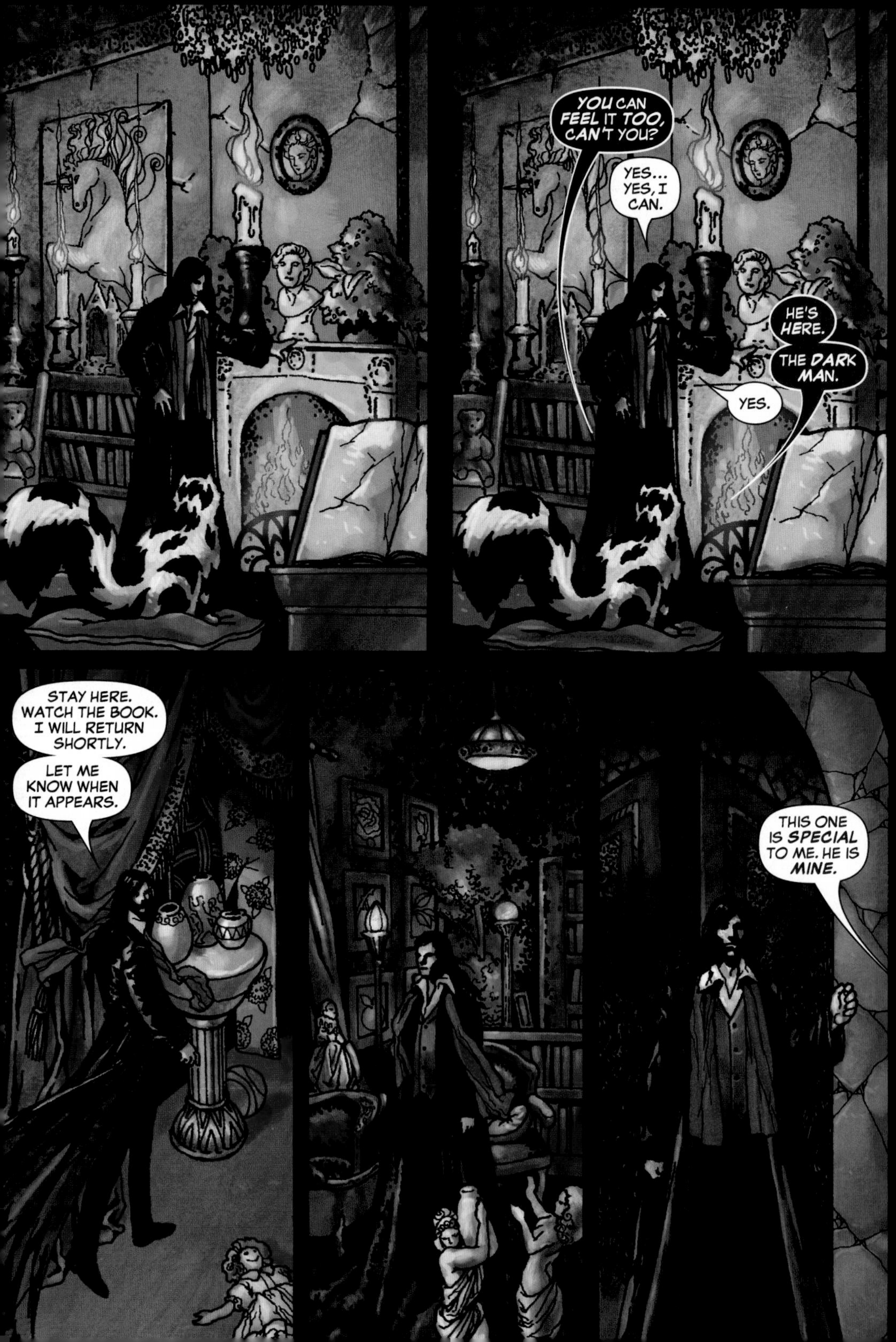
YOU CAN FEEL IT TOO, CAN'T YOU?
YES... YES, I CAN.
HE'S HERE.
THE DARK MAN.
YES.
STAY HERE. WATCH THE BOOK. I WILL RETURN SHORTLY.
LET ME KNOW WHEN IT APPEARS.
THIS ONE IS SPECIAL TO ME. HE IS MINE.

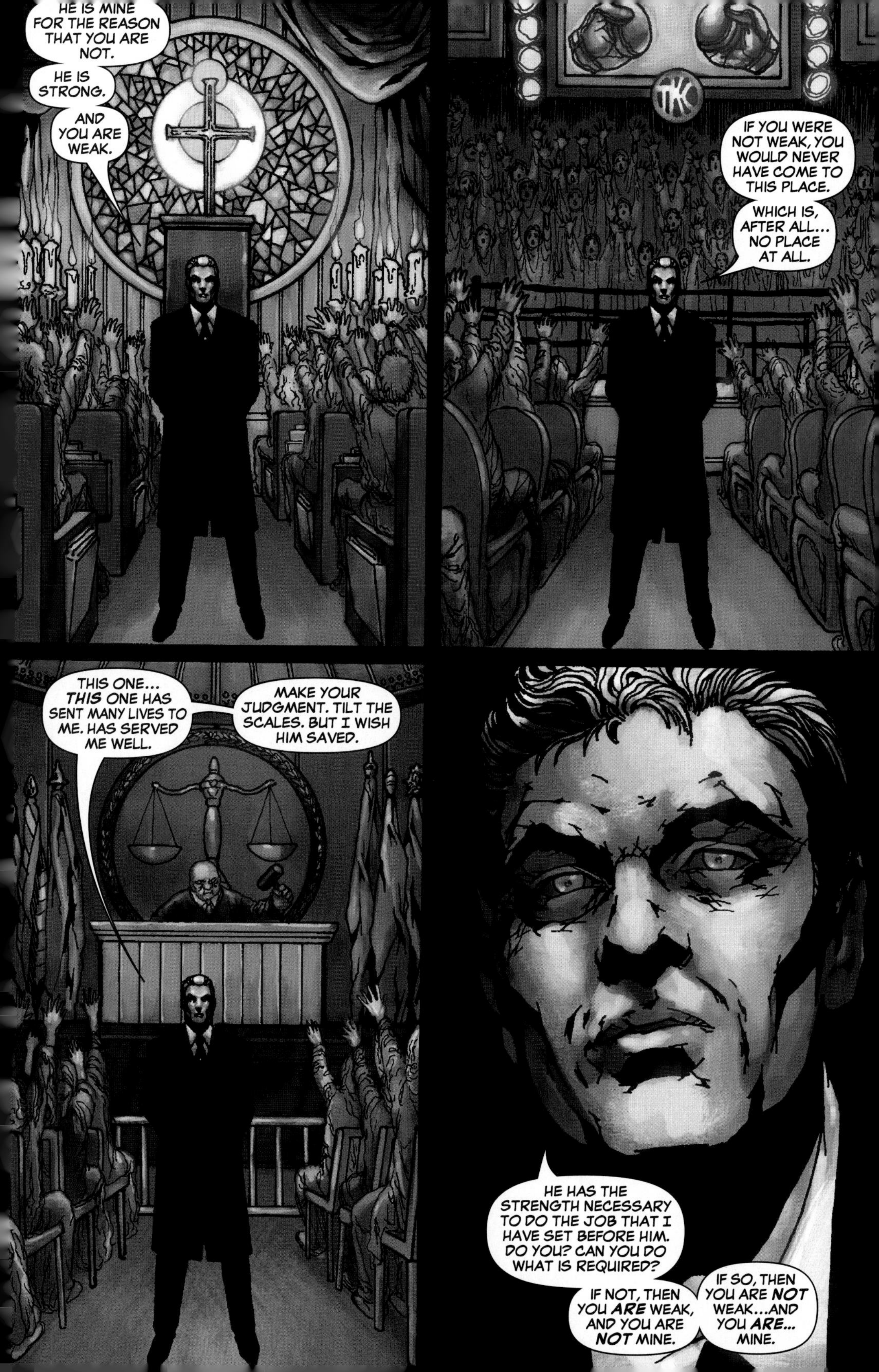
HE IS MINE FOR THE REASON THAT YOU ARE NOT.
HE IS STRONG.
AND YOU ARE WEAK.
IF YOU WERE NOT WEAK, YOU WOULD NEVER HAVE COME TO THIS PLACE.
WHICH IS, AFTER ALL... NO PLACE AT ALL.
THIS ONE... *THIS* ONE HAS SENT MANY LIVES TO ME. HAS SERVED ME WELL.
MAKE YOUR JUDGMENT. TILT THE SCALES. BUT I WISH HIM SAVED.
HE HAS THE STRENGTH NECESSARY TO DO THE JOB THAT I HAVE SET BEFORE HIM. DO YOU? CAN YOU DO WHAT IS REQUIRED?
IF NOT, THEN YOU *ARE* WEAK, AND YOU ARE *NOT* MINE.
IF SO, THEN YOU ARE *NOT* WEAK...AND YOU *ARE*... MINE.

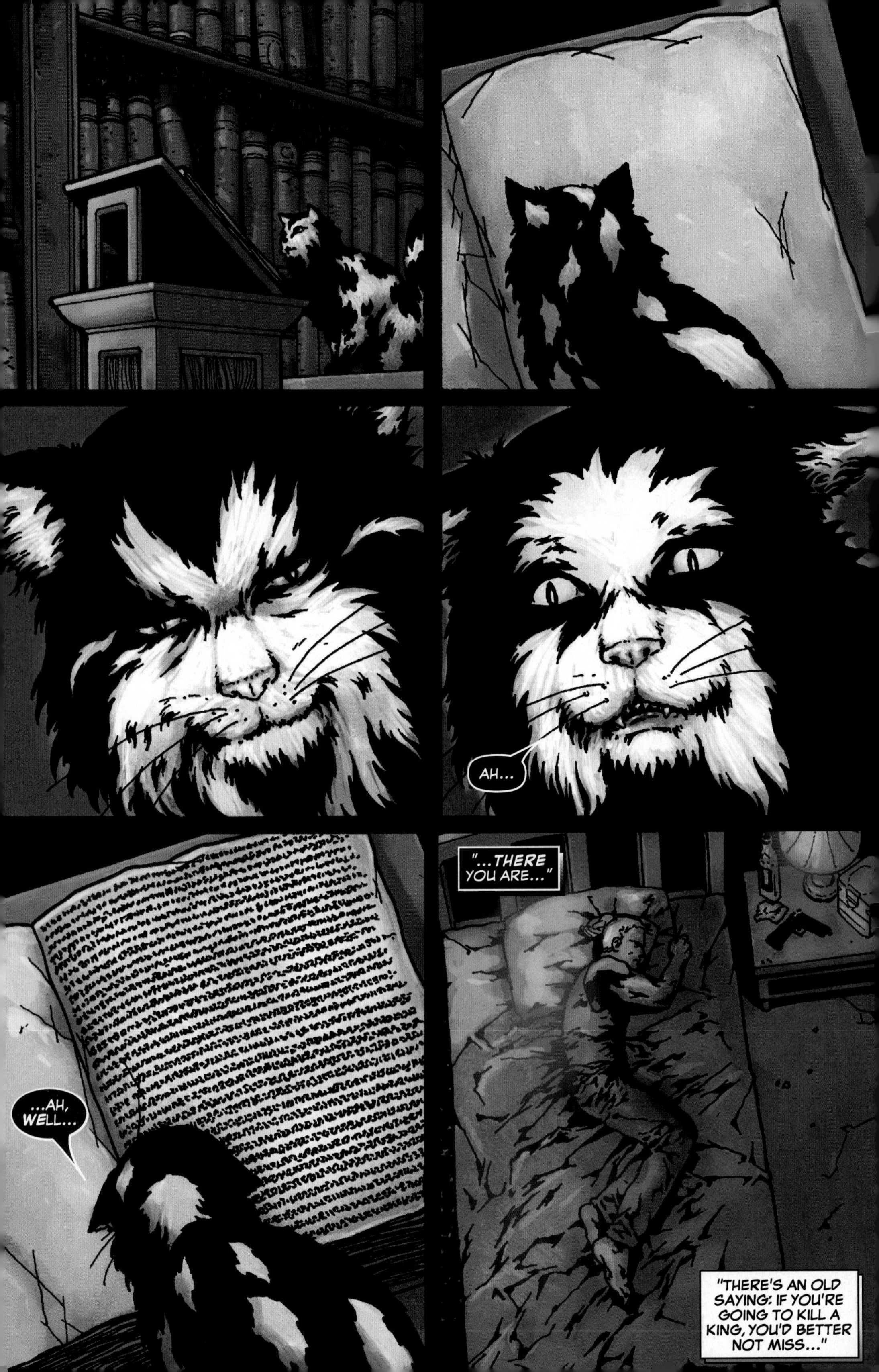
AH...
...AH, WELL...
"...THERE YOU ARE..."
"THERE'S AN OLD SAYING: IF YOU'RE GOING TO KILL A KING, YOU'D BETTER NOT MISS..."

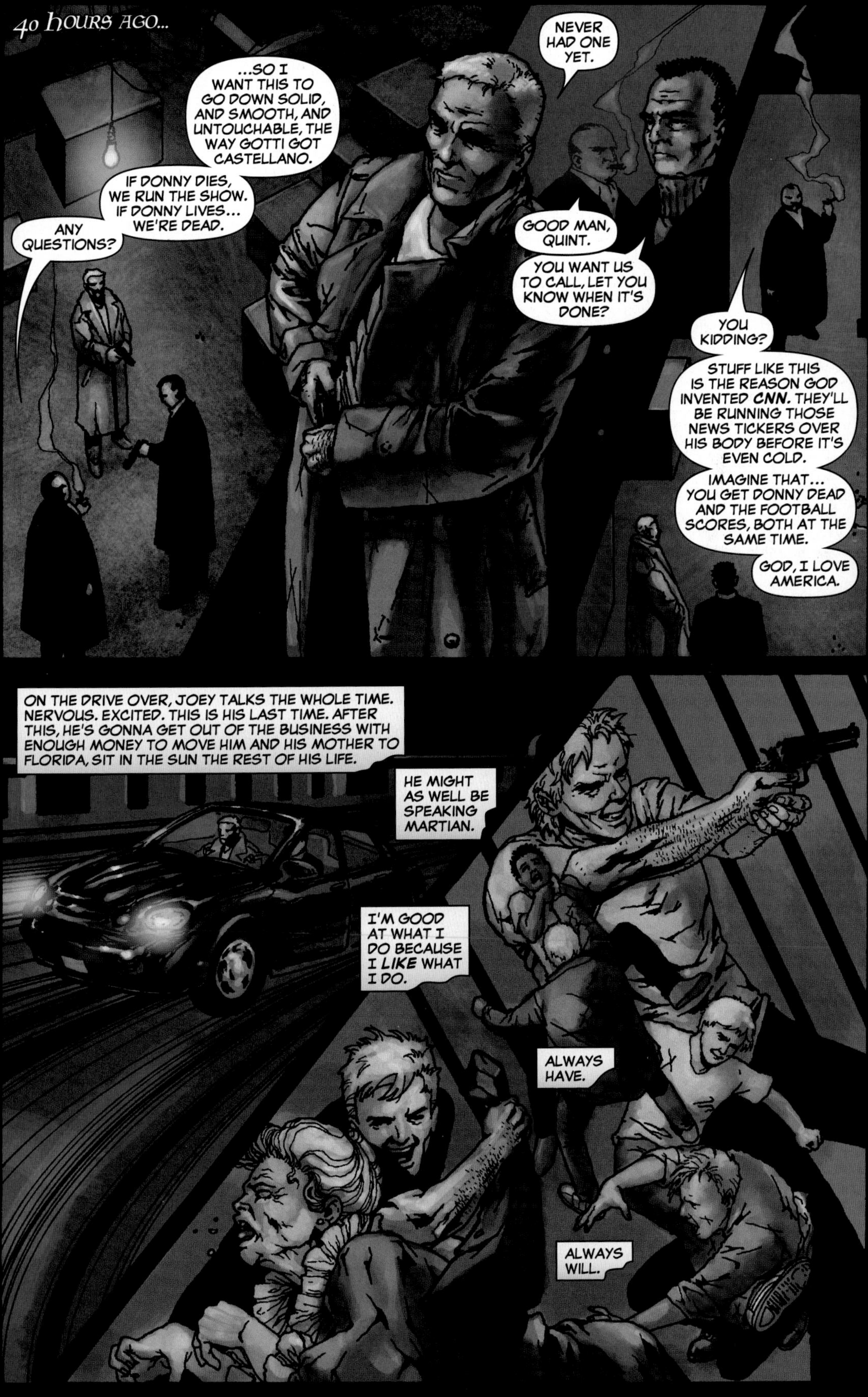
40 HOURS AGO...
...SO I WANT THIS TO GO DOWN SOLID, AND SMOOTH, AND UNTOUCHABLE, THE WAY GOTTI GOT CASTELLANO.
IF DONNY DIES, WE RUN THE SHOW. IF DONNY LIVES... WE'RE DEAD.
ANY QUESTIONS?
NEVER HAD ONE YET.
GOOD MAN, QUINT.
YOU WANT US TO CALL, LET YOU KNOW WHEN IT'S DONE?
YOU KIDDING?
STUFF LIKE THIS IS THE REASON GOD INVENTED CNN. THEY'LL BE RUNNING THOSE NEWS TICKERS OVER HIS BODY BEFORE IT'S EVEN COLD.
IMAGINE THAT... YOU GET DONNY DEAD AND THE FOOTBALL SCORES, BOTH AT THE SAME TIME.
GOD, I LOVE AMERICA.
ON THE DRIVE OVER, JOEY TALKS THE WHOLE TIME. NERVOUS. EXCITED. THIS IS HIS LAST TIME. AFTER THIS, HE'S GONNA GET OUT OF THE BUSINESS WITH ENOUGH MONEY TO MOVE HIM AND HIS MOTHER TO FLORIDA, SIT IN THE SUN THE REST OF HIS LIFE.
HE MIGHT AS WELL BE SPEAKING MARTIAN.
I'M GOOD AT WHAT I DO BECAUSE I LIKE WHAT I DO.
ALWAYS HAVE.
ALWAYS WILL.

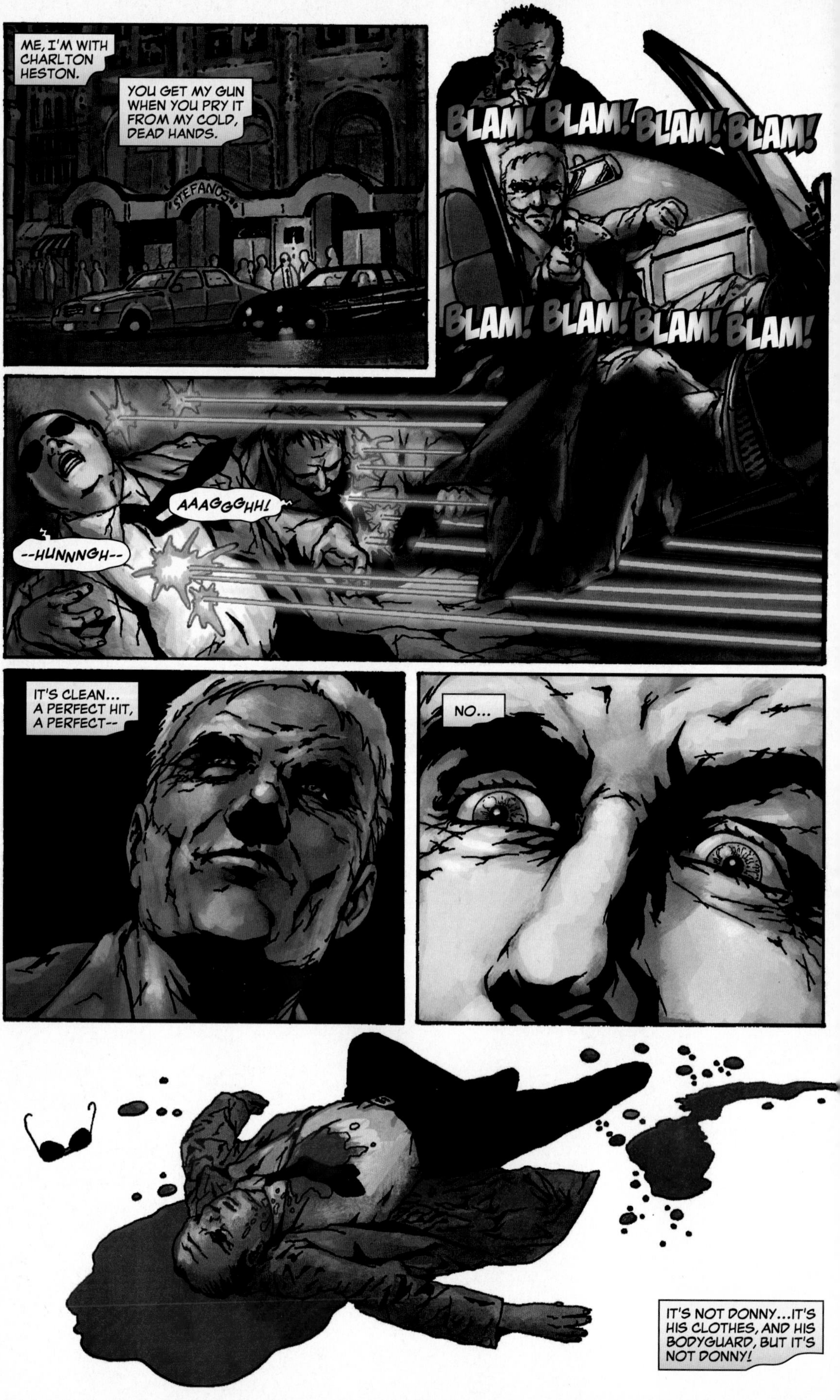
ME, I'M WITH CHARLTON HESTON.
YOU GET MY GUN WHEN YOU PRY IT FROM MY COLD, DEAD HANDS.
STEFANOS
BLAM! BLAM! BLAM! BLAM!
BLAM! BLAM! BLAM! BLAM!
AAAGGGHH!
--HUNNNGH--
IT'S CLEAN... A PERFECT HIT, A PERFECT--
NO...
IT'S NOT DONNY...IT'S HIS CLOTHES, AND HIS BODYGUARD, BUT IT'S NOT DONNY!

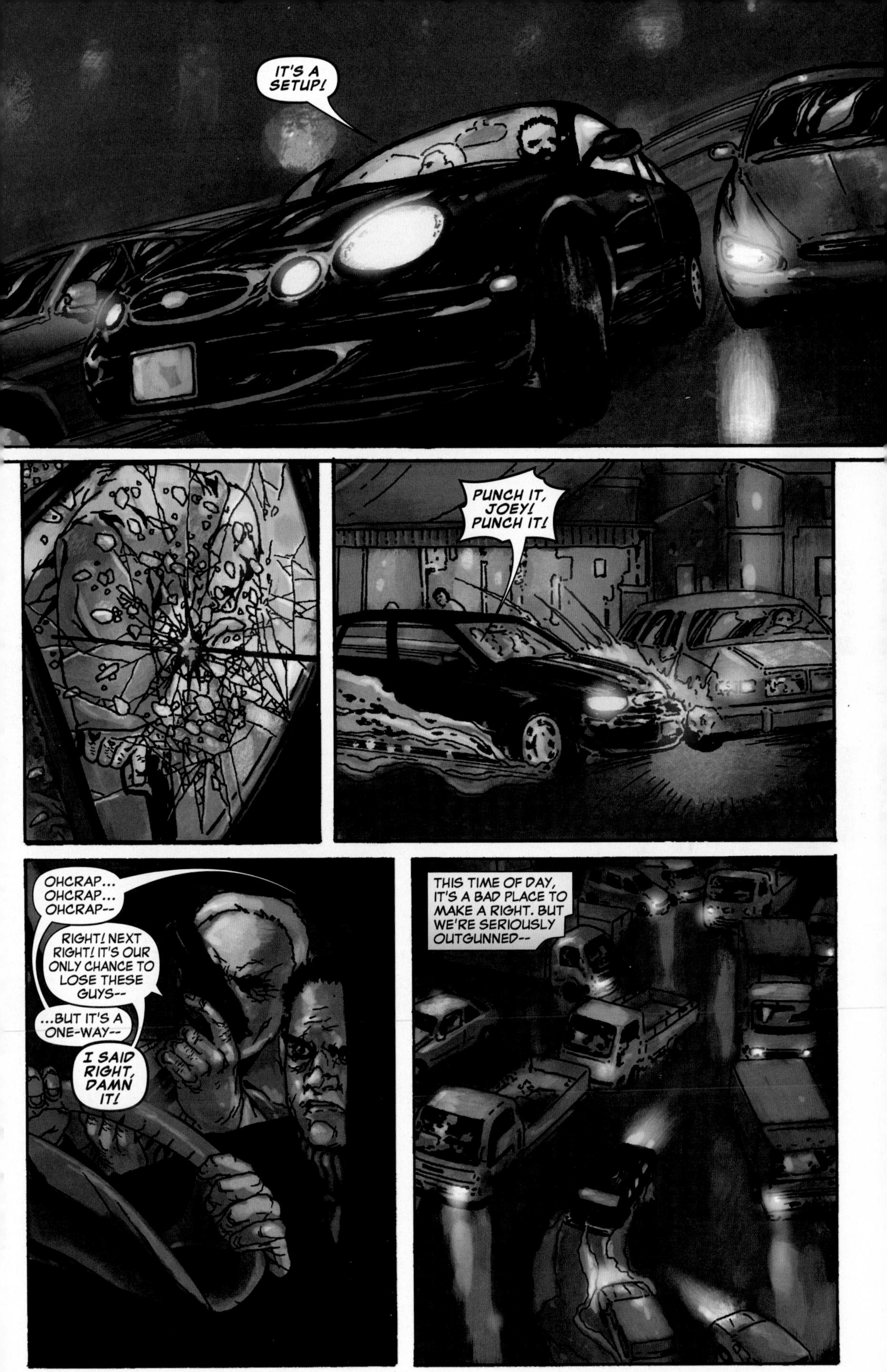
IT'S A SETUP!
PUNCH IT, JOEY! PUNCH IT!
OHCRAP... OHCRAP... OHCRAP--
RIGHT! NEXT RIGHT! IT'S OUR ONLY CHANCE TO LOSE THESE GUYS--
...BUT IT'S A ONE-WAY--
I SAID RIGHT, DAMN IT!
THIS TIME OF DAY, IT'S A BAD PLACE TO MAKE A RIGHT. BUT WE'RE SERIOUSLY OUTGUNNED--

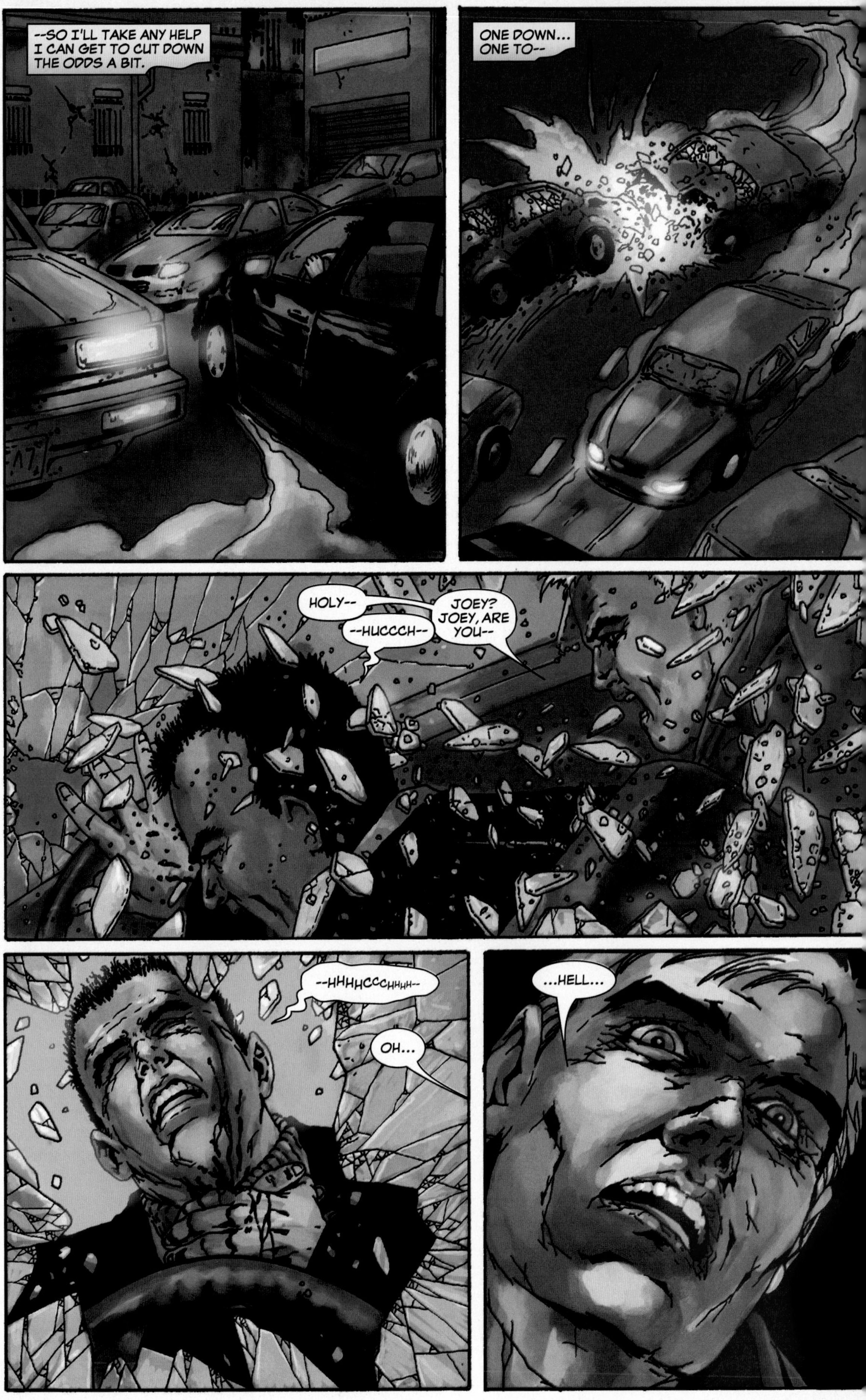
--SO I'LL TAKE ANY HELP I CAN GET TO CUT DOWN THE ODDS A BIT.
ONE DOWN... ONE TO--
HOLY--
--HUCCCH--
JOEY? JOEY, ARE YOU--
--HHHHCCCHHHH--
OH...
...HELL...

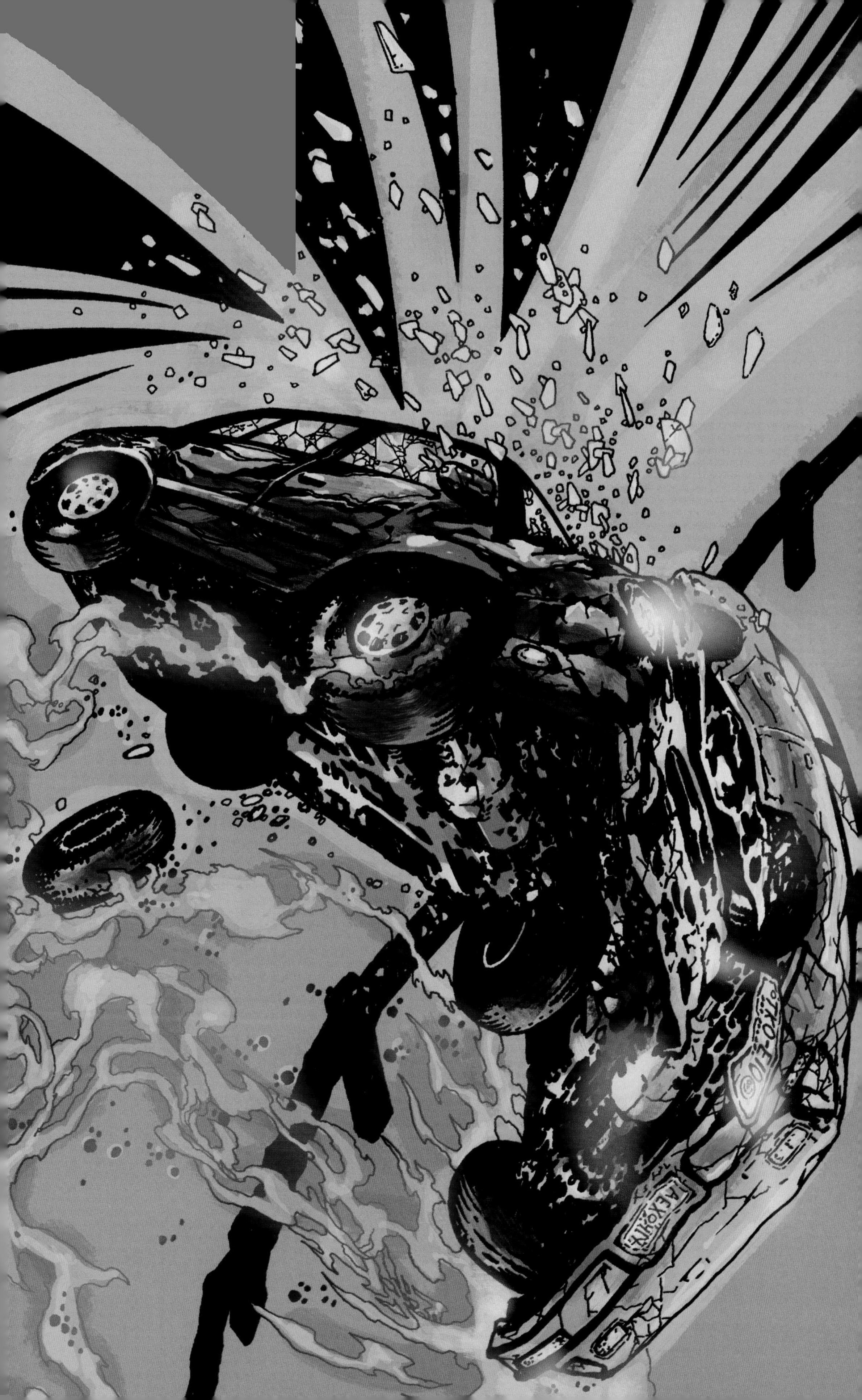

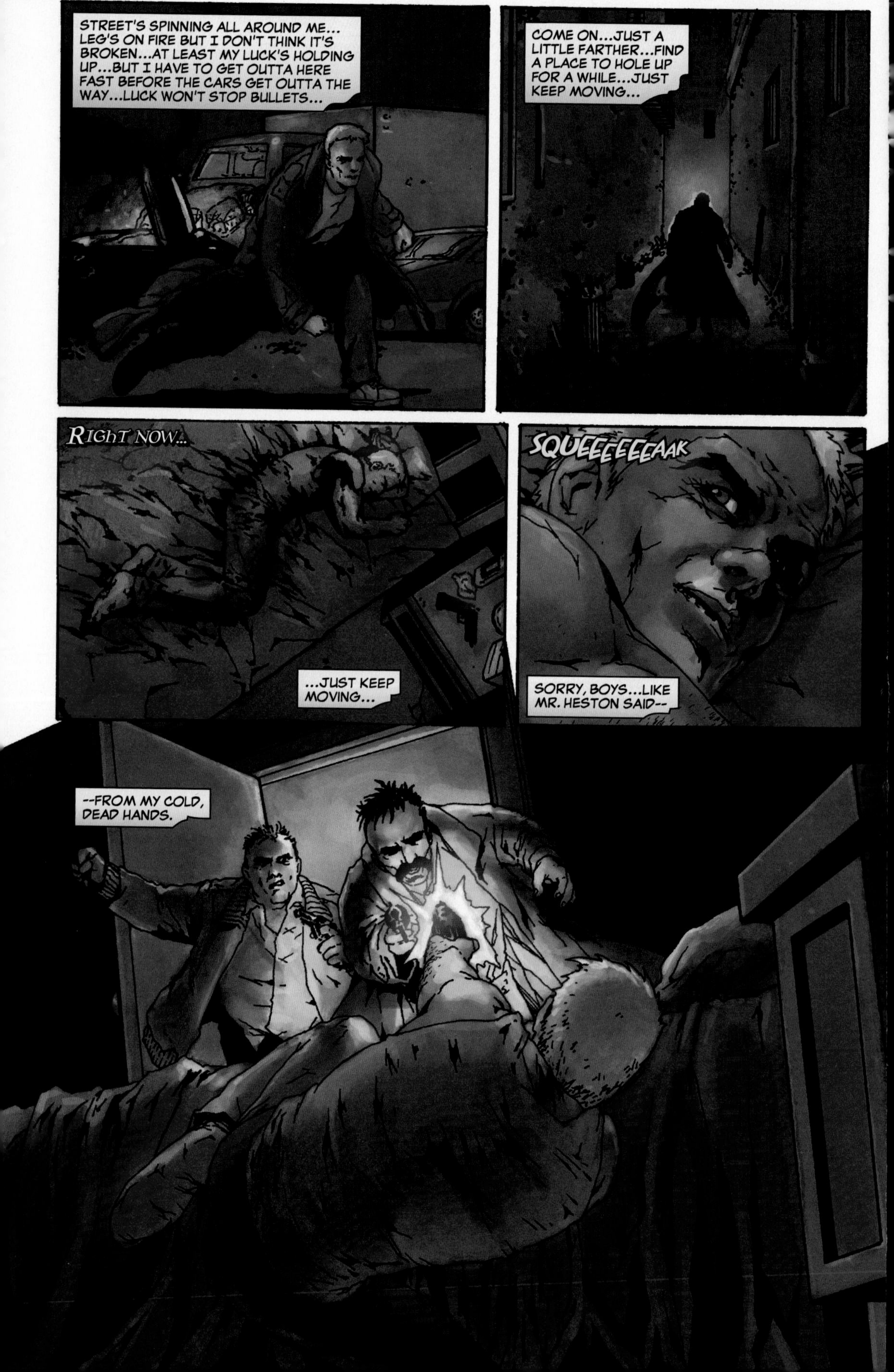
STREET'S SPINNING ALL AROUND ME... LEG'S ON FIRE BUT I DON'T THINK IT'S BROKEN...AT LEAST MY LUCK'S HOLDING UP...BUT I HAVE TO GET OUTTA HERE FAST BEFORE THE CARS GET OUTTA THE WAY...LUCK WON'T STOP BULLETS...
COME ON...JUST A LITTLE FARTHER...FIND A PLACE TO HOLE UP FOR A WHILE...JUST KEEP MOVING...
RIGHT NOW...
...JUST KEEP MOVING...
SQUEEEEEEEAAK
SORRY, BOYS...LIKE MR. HESTON SAID--
--FROM MY COLD, DEAD HANDS.

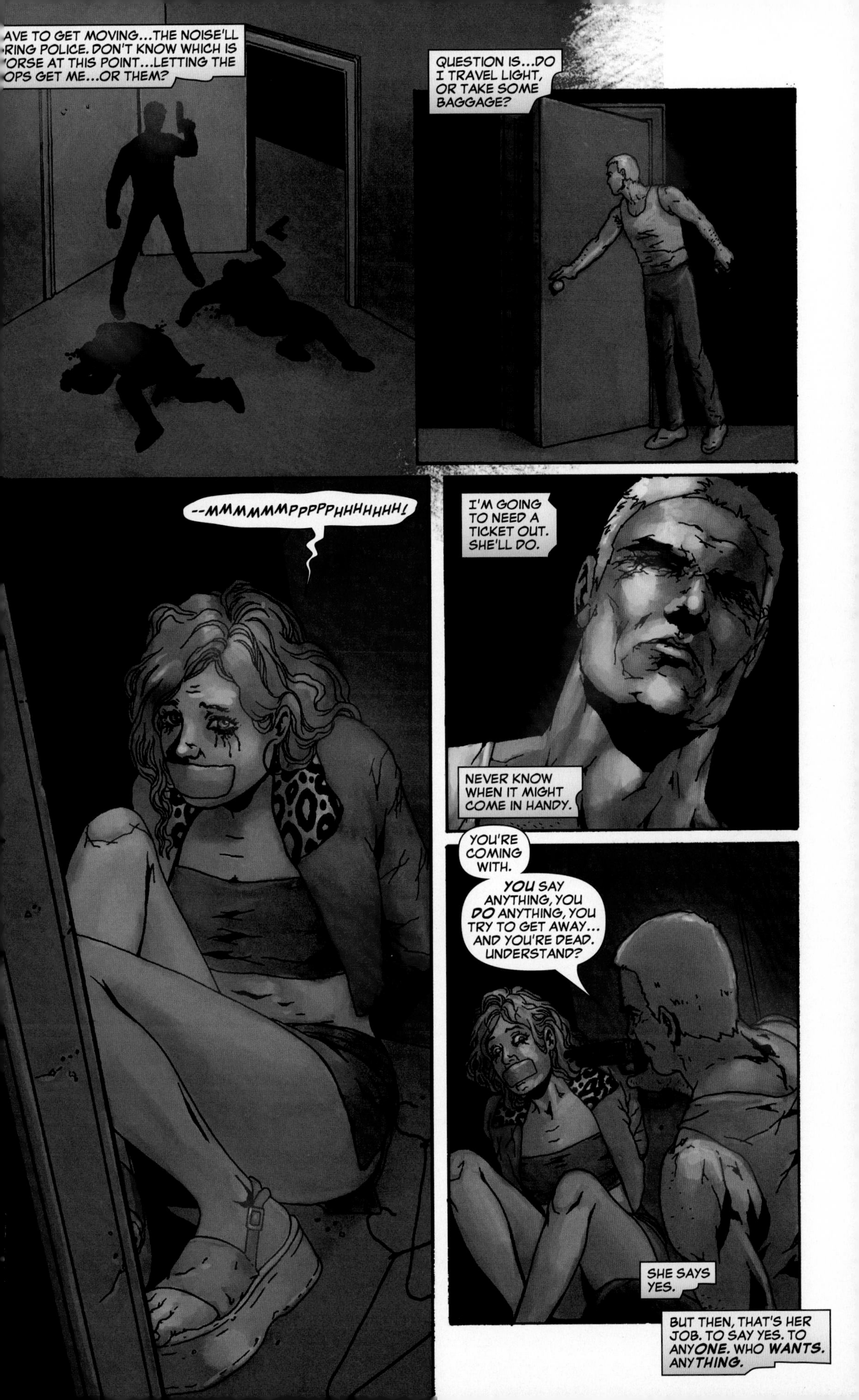
AVE TO GET MOVING...THE NOISE'LL
RING POLICE. DON'T KNOW WHICH IS
ORSE AT THIS POINT...LETTING THE
OPS GET ME...OR THEM?
QUESTION IS...DO I TRAVEL LIGHT, OR TAKE SOME BAGGAGE?
--MMMMMMPPPPPHHHHHHH!
I'M GOING TO NEED A TICKET OUT. SHE'LL DO.
NEVER KNOW WHEN IT MIGHT COME IN HANDY.
YOU'RE COMING WITH.
YOU SAY ANYTHING, YOU DO ANYTHING, YOU TRY TO GET AWAY... AND YOU'RE DEAD. UNDERSTAND?
SHE SAYS YES.
BUT THEN, THAT'S HER JOB. TO SAY YES. TO ANYONE. WHO WANTS. ANYTHING.

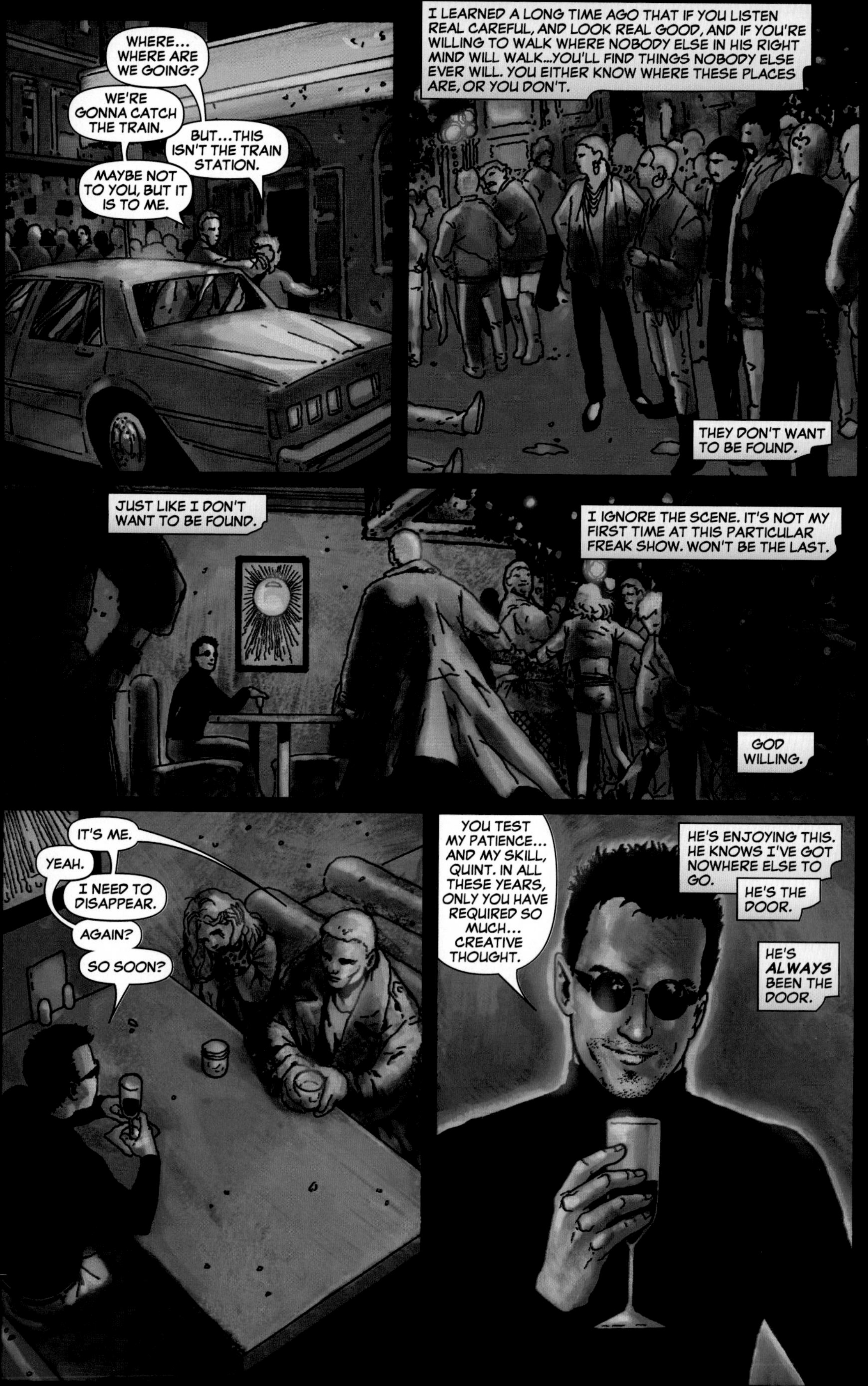
WHERE... WHERE ARE WE GOING?
WE'RE GONNA CATCH THE TRAIN.
BUT...THIS ISN'T THE TRAIN STATION.
MAYBE NOT TO YOU, BUT IT IS TO ME.
I LEARNED A LONG TIME AGO THAT IF YOU LISTEN REAL CAREFUL, AND LOOK REAL GOOD, AND IF YOU'RE WILLING TO WALK WHERE NOBODY ELSE IN HIS RIGHT MIND WILL WALK...YOU'LL FIND THINGS NOBODY ELSE EVER WILL. YOU EITHER KNOW WHERE THESE PLACES ARE, OR YOU DON'T.
THEY DON'T WANT TO BE FOUND.
JUST LIKE I DON'T WANT TO BE FOUND.
I IGNORE THE SCENE. IT'S NOT MY FIRST TIME AT THIS PARTICULAR FREAK SHOW. WON'T BE THE LAST.
GOD WILLING.
IT'S ME.
YEAH.
I NEED TO DISAPPEAR.
AGAIN?
SO SOON?
YOU TEST MY PATIENCE... AND MY SKILL, QUINT. IN ALL THESE YEARS, ONLY YOU HAVE REQUIRED SO MUCH... CREATIVE THOUGHT.
HE'S ENJOYING THIS. HE KNOWS I'VE GOT NOWHERE ELSE TO GO.
HE'S THE DOOR.
HE'S **ALWAYS** BEEN THE DOOR.

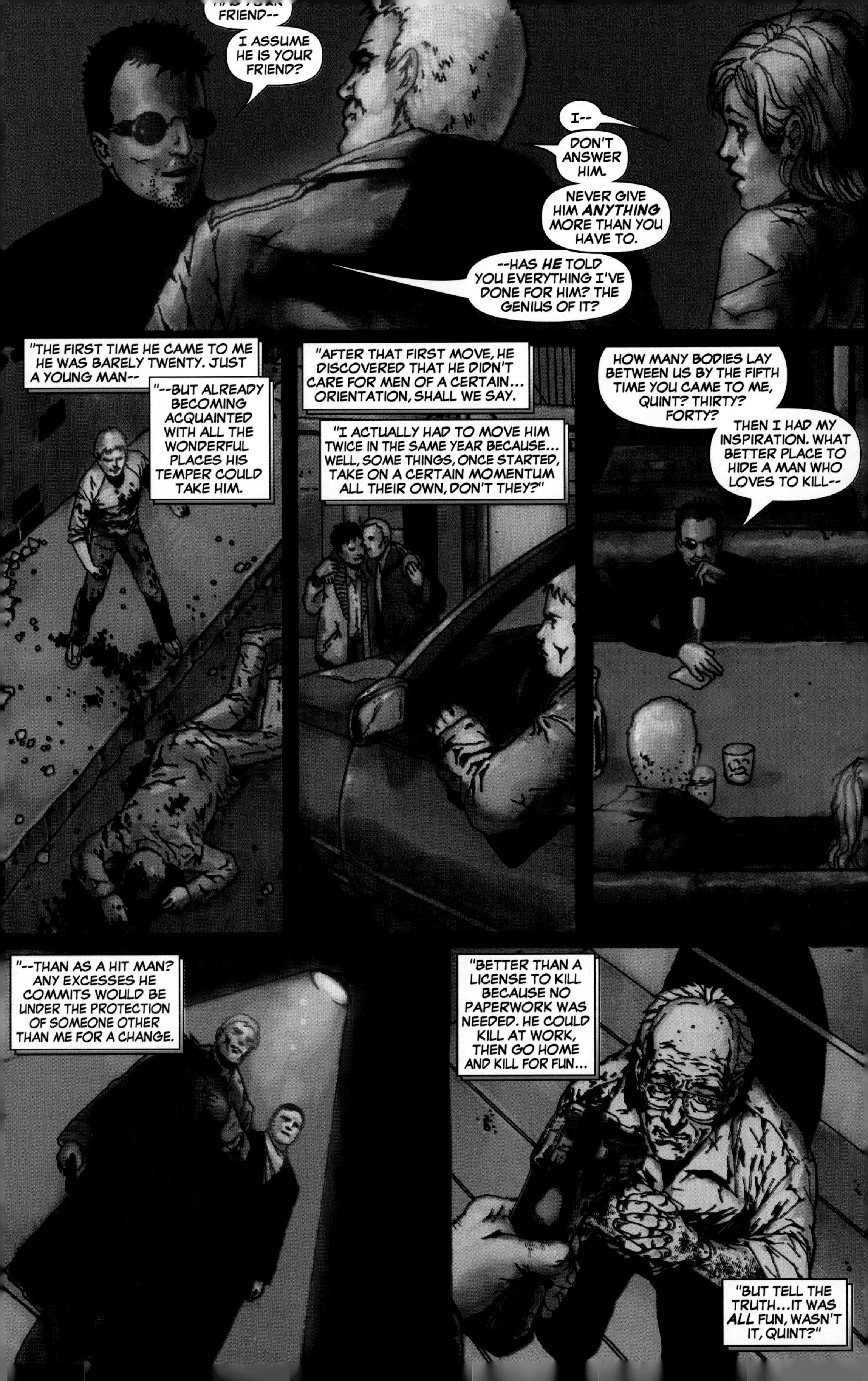

FRIEND--
I ASSUME HE IS YOUR FRIEND?
I--
DON'T ANSWER HIM.
NEVER GIVE HIM ANYTHING MORE THAN YOU HAVE TO.
--HAS HE TOLD YOU EVERYTHING I'VE DONE FOR HIM? THE GENIUS OF IT?
"THE FIRST TIME HE CAME TO ME HE WAS BARELY TWENTY. JUST A YOUNG MAN--
"--BUT ALREADY BECOMING ACQUAINTED WITH ALL THE WONDERFUL PLACES HIS TEMPER COULD TAKE HIM.
"AFTER THAT FIRST MOVE, HE DISCOVERED THAT HE DIDN'T CARE FOR MEN OF A CERTAIN... ORIENTATION, SHALL WE SAY.
"I ACTUALLY HAD TO MOVE HIM TWICE IN THE SAME YEAR BECAUSE... WELL, SOME THINGS, ONCE STARTED, TAKE ON A CERTAIN MOMENTUM ALL THEIR OWN, DON'T THEY?"
HOW MANY BODIES LAY BETWEEN US BY THE FIFTH TIME YOU CAME TO ME, QUINT? THIRTY? FORTY?
THEN I HAD MY INSPIRATION. WHAT BETTER PLACE TO HIDE A MAN WHO LOVES TO KILL--
"--THAN AS A HIT MAN? ANY EXCESSES HE COMMITS WOULD BE UNDER THE PROTECTION OF SOMEONE OTHER THAN ME FOR A CHANGE.
"BETTER THAN A LICENSE TO KILL BECAUSE NO PAPERWORK WAS NEEDED. HE COULD KILL AT WORK, THEN GO HOME AND KILL FOR FUN...
"BUT TELL THE TRUTH...IT WAS ALL FUN, WASN'T IT, QUINT?"

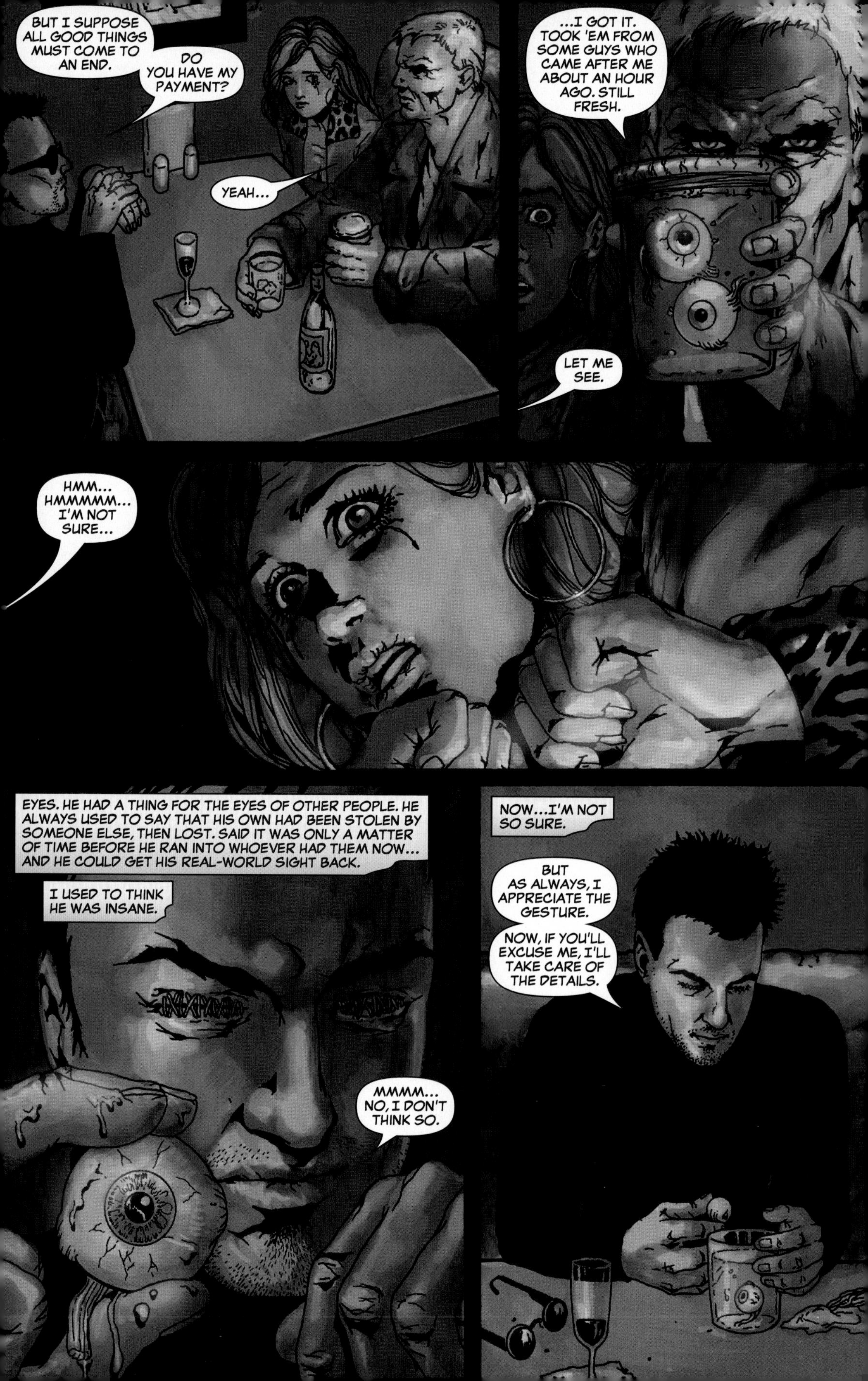

BUT I SUPPOSE ALL GOOD THINGS MUST COME TO AN END.
DO YOU HAVE MY PAYMENT?
YEAH...
...I GOT IT. TOOK 'EM FROM SOME GUYS WHO CAME AFTER ME ABOUT AN HOUR AGO. STILL FRESH.
LET ME SEE.
HMM... HMMMMM... I'M NOT SURE...
EYES. HE HAD A THING FOR THE EYES OF OTHER PEOPLE. HE ALWAYS USED TO SAY THAT HIS OWN HAD BEEN STOLEN BY SOMEONE ELSE, THEN LOST. SAID IT WAS ONLY A MATTER OF TIME BEFORE HE RAN INTO WHOEVER HAD THEM NOW... AND HE COULD GET HIS REAL-WORLD SIGHT BACK.
I USED TO THINK HE WAS INSANE.
MMMM... NO, I DON'T THINK SO.
NOW...I'M NOT SO SURE.
BUT AS ALWAYS, I APPRECIATE THE GESTURE.
NOW, IF YOU'LL EXCUSE ME, I'LL TAKE CARE OF THE DETAILS.

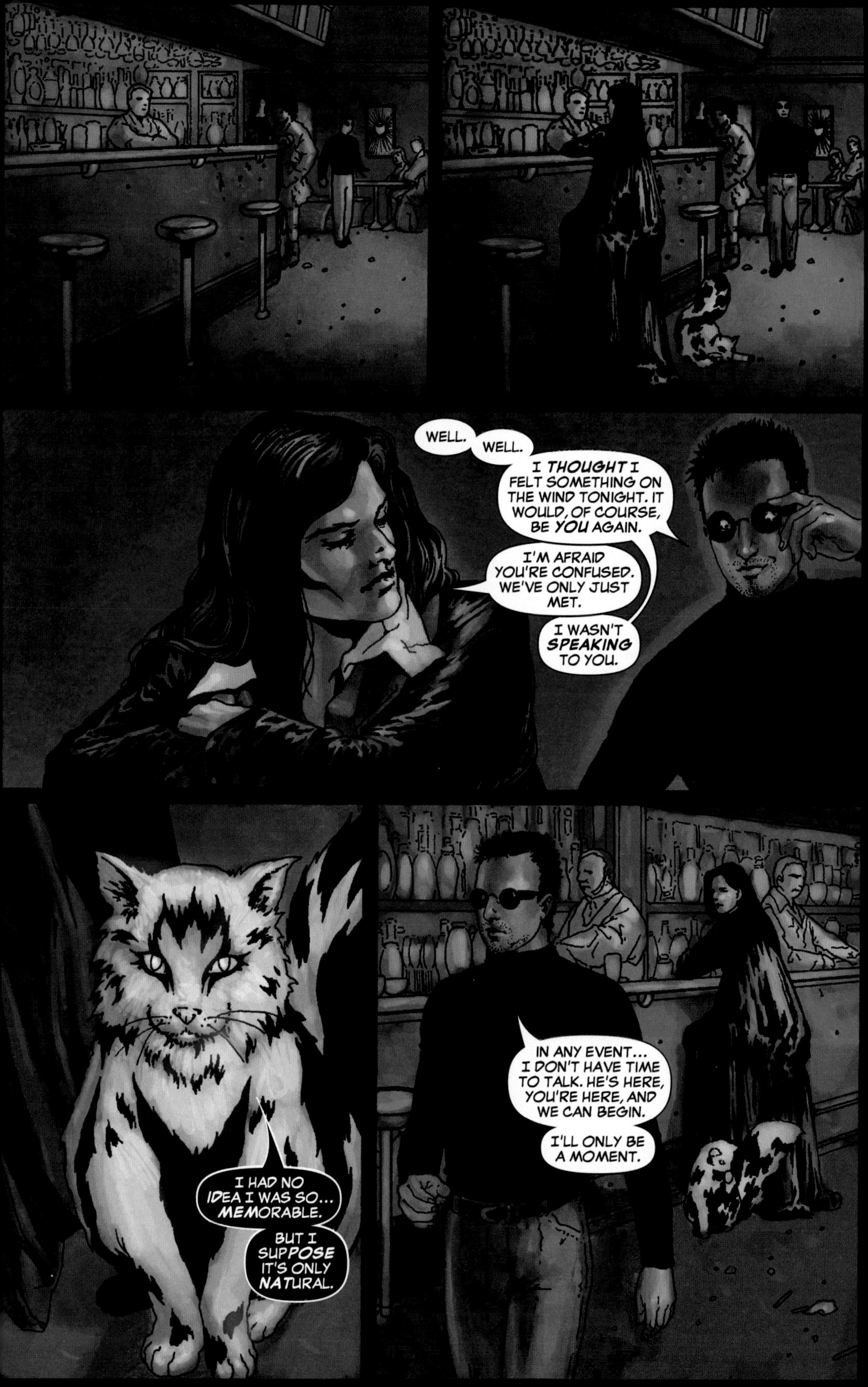
WELL.
WELL.
I THOUGHT I FELT SOMETHING ON THE WIND TONIGHT. IT WOULD, OF COURSE, BE YOU AGAIN.
I'M AFRAID YOU'RE CONFUSED. WE'VE ONLY JUST MET.
I WASN'T SPEAKING TO YOU.
I HAD NO IDEA I WAS SO... MEMORABLE.
BUT I SUPPOSE IT'S ONLY NATURAL.
IN ANY EVENT... I DON'T HAVE TIME TO TALK. HE'S HERE, YOU'RE HERE, AND WE CAN BEGIN.
I'LL ONLY BE A MOMENT.

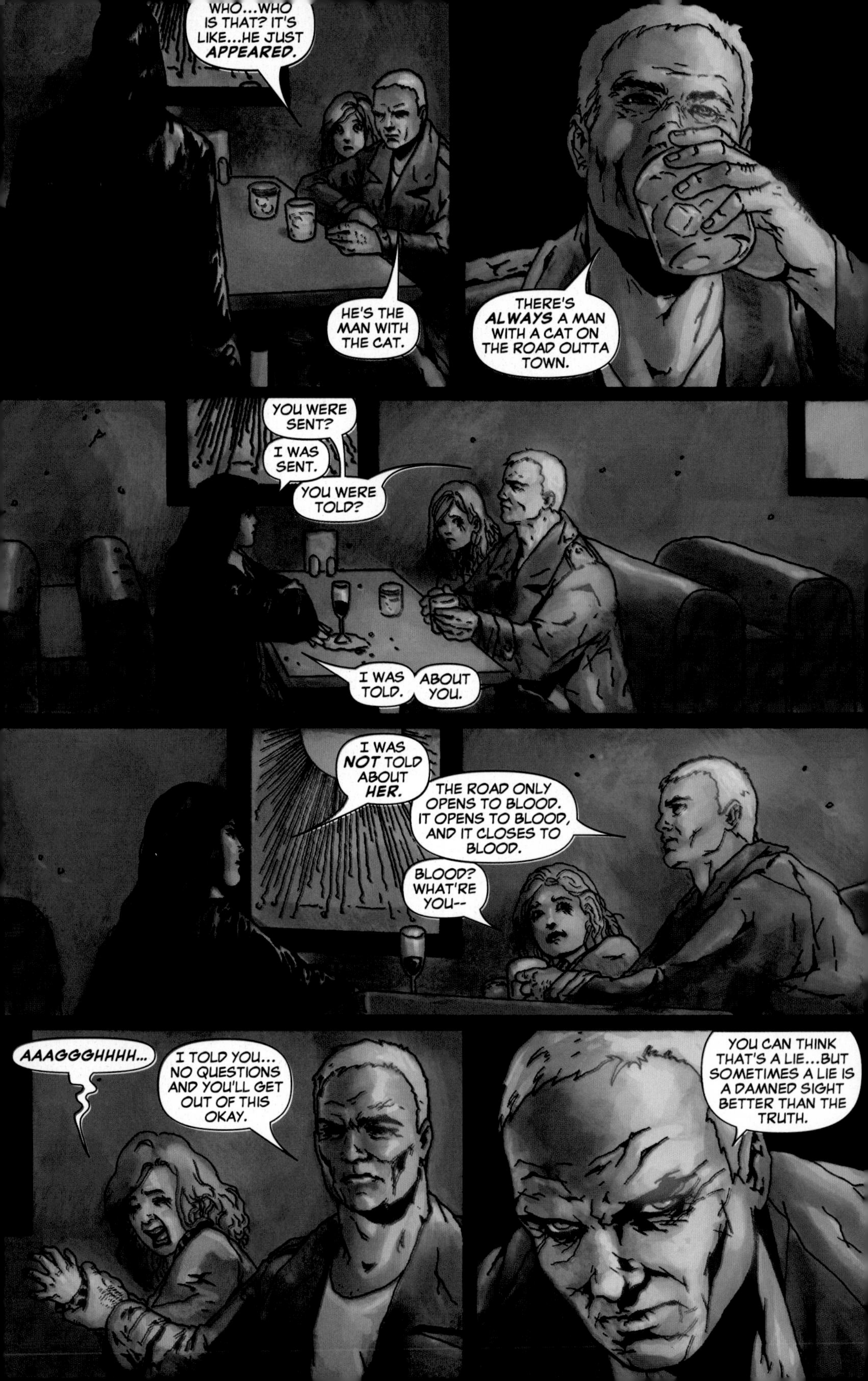
WHO...WHO IS THAT? IT'S LIKE...HE JUST APPEARED.
HE'S THE MAN WITH THE CAT.
THERE'S ALWAYS A MAN WITH A CAT ON THE ROAD OUTTA TOWN.
YOU WERE SENT?
I WAS SENT.
YOU WERE TOLD?
I WAS TOLD.
ABOUT YOU.
I WAS NOT TOLD ABOUT HER.
THE ROAD ONLY OPENS TO BLOOD. IT OPENS TO BLOOD, AND IT CLOSES TO BLOOD.
BLOOD? WHAT'RE YOU--
AAAGGGHHHH...
I TOLD YOU... NO QUESTIONS AND YOU'LL GET OUT OF THIS OKAY.
YOU CAN THINK THAT'S A LIE...BUT SOMETIMES A LIE IS A DAMNED SIGHT BETTER THAN THE TRUTH.

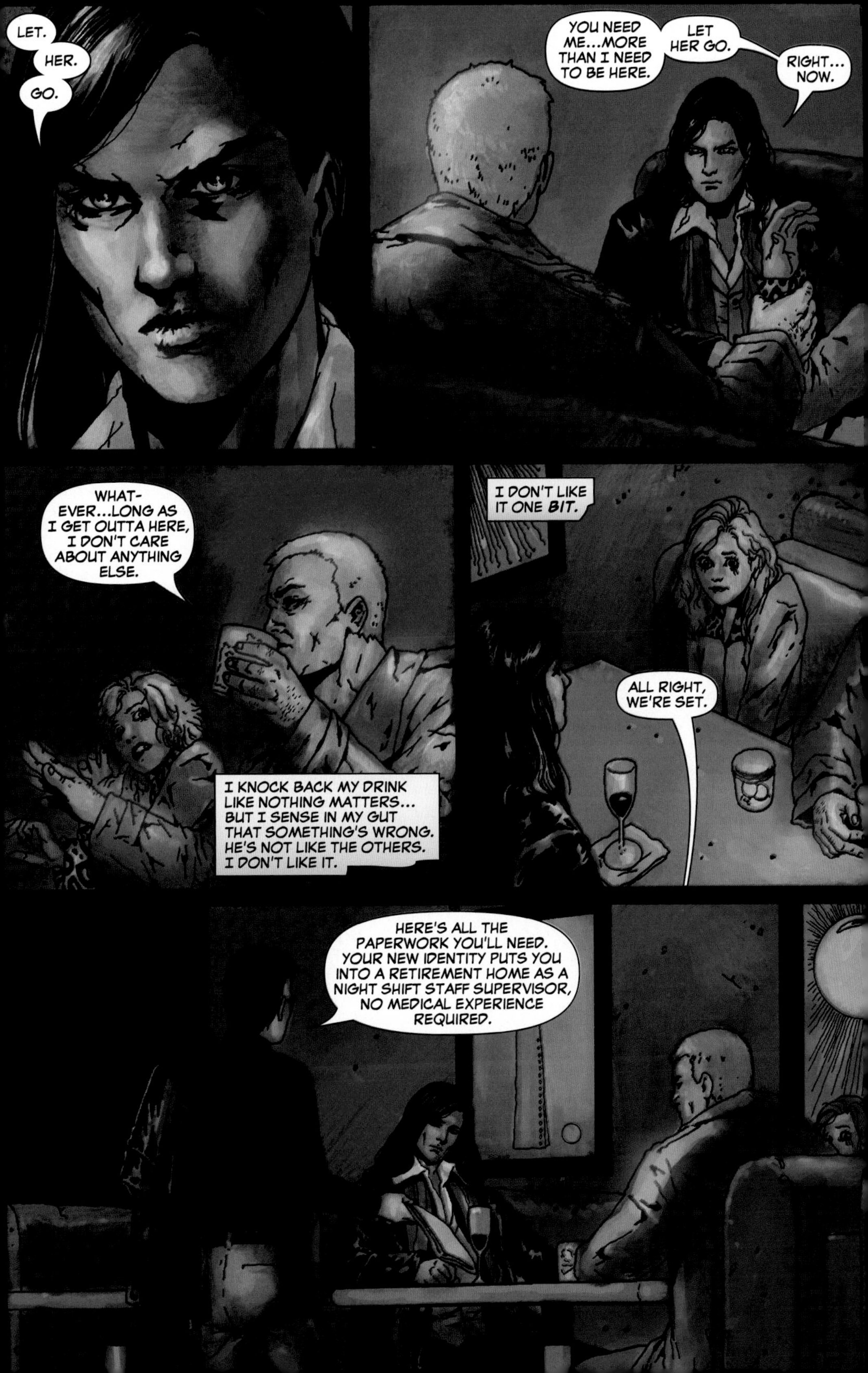
LET.
HER.
GO.
YOU NEED ME...MORE THAN I NEED TO BE HERE.
LET HER GO.
RIGHT... NOW.
WHAT-EVER...LONG AS I GET OUTTA HERE, I DON'T CARE ABOUT ANYTHING ELSE.
I KNOCK BACK MY DRINK LIKE NOTHING MATTERS... BUT I SENSE IN MY GUT THAT SOMETHING'S WRONG. HE'S NOT LIKE THE OTHERS. I DON'T LIKE IT.
I DON'T LIKE IT ONE *BIT*.
ALL RIGHT, WE'RE SET.
HERE'S ALL THE PAPERWORK YOU'LL NEED. YOUR NEW IDENTITY PUTS YOU INTO A RETIREMENT HOME AS A NIGHT SHIFT STAFF SUPERVISOR, NO MEDICAL EXPERIENCE REQUIRED.

"IT'S THE BEST I COULD DO ON SUCH SHORT NOTICE. STILL, IT'LL LET YOU FOLLOW YOUR HEART'S DESIRE WHILE WE FIND SOMETHING A BIT MORE...DIGNIFIED."

NOW, IF YOU'LL COME THIS WAY... WE DON'T HAVE ALL NIGHT, AFTER ALL.

WELL, *YOU* DON'T, ANYWAY.

HE LEADS US TOWARD A DOOR I SWEAR WASN'T THERE A MINUTE EARLIER.

BUT THEN, I *NEVER* SEE THE DOOR HE OPENS BEFORE HE OPENS IT.

GO ON, QUICKLY NOW.

THIS IS THE PART THAT ALWAYS CREEPS ME OUT. NOT THE BIT WITH THE EYES, NOT THE STITCHES, NOT EVEN THE DOOR APPEARING LIKE THAT.

IT'S WHAT'S WAITING ON THE OTHER SIDE

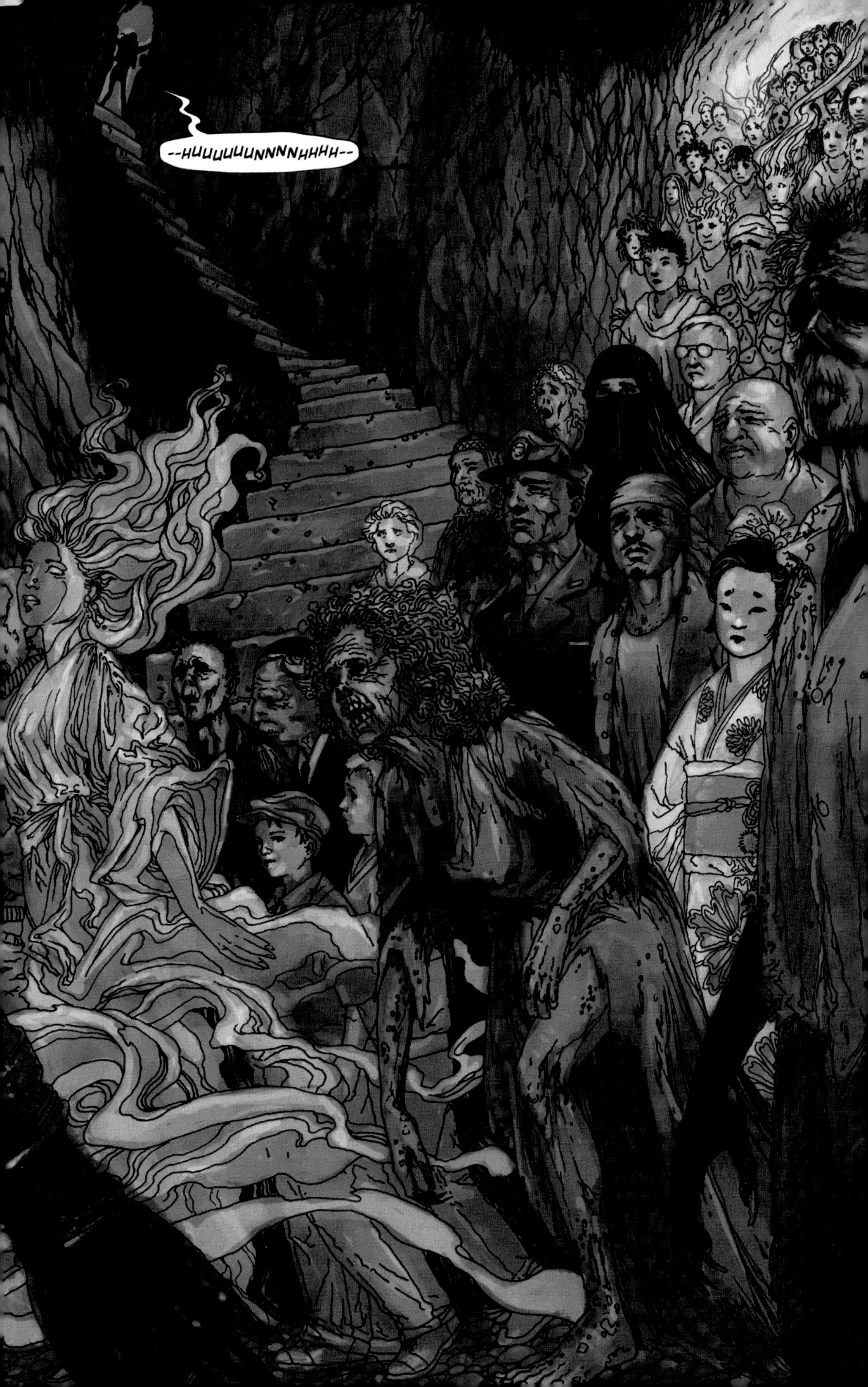
--HUUUUUUNNNHHHH--

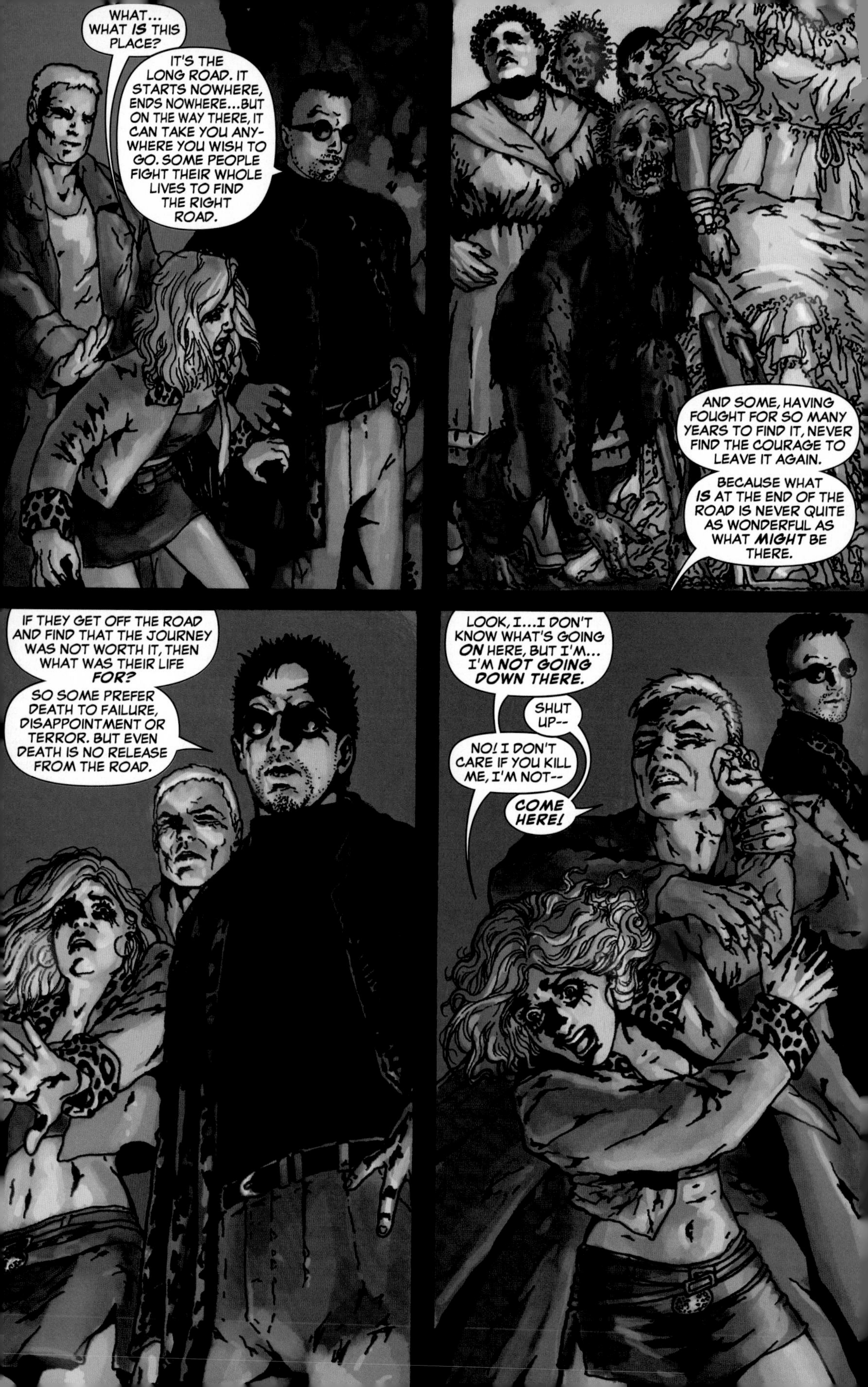
WHAT... WHAT IS THIS PLACE?
IT'S THE LONG ROAD. IT STARTS NOWHERE, ENDS NOWHERE...BUT ON THE WAY THERE, IT CAN TAKE YOU ANYWHERE YOU WISH TO GO. SOME PEOPLE FIGHT THEIR WHOLE LIVES TO FIND THE RIGHT ROAD.
AND SOME, HAVING FOUGHT FOR SO MANY YEARS TO FIND IT, NEVER FIND THE COURAGE TO LEAVE IT AGAIN.
BECAUSE WHAT IS AT THE END OF THE ROAD IS NEVER QUITE AS WONDERFUL AS WHAT MIGHT BE THERE.
IF THEY GET OFF THE ROAD AND FIND THAT THE JOURNEY WAS NOT WORTH IT, THEN WHAT WAS THEIR LIFE FOR?
SO SOME PREFER DEATH TO FAILURE, DISAPPOINTMENT OR TERROR. BUT EVEN DEATH IS NO RELEASE FROM THE ROAD.
LOOK, I...I DON'T KNOW WHAT'S GOING ON HERE, BUT I'M... I'M NOT GOING DOWN THERE.
SHUT UP--
NO! I DON'T CARE IF YOU KILL ME, I'M NOT--
COME HERE!

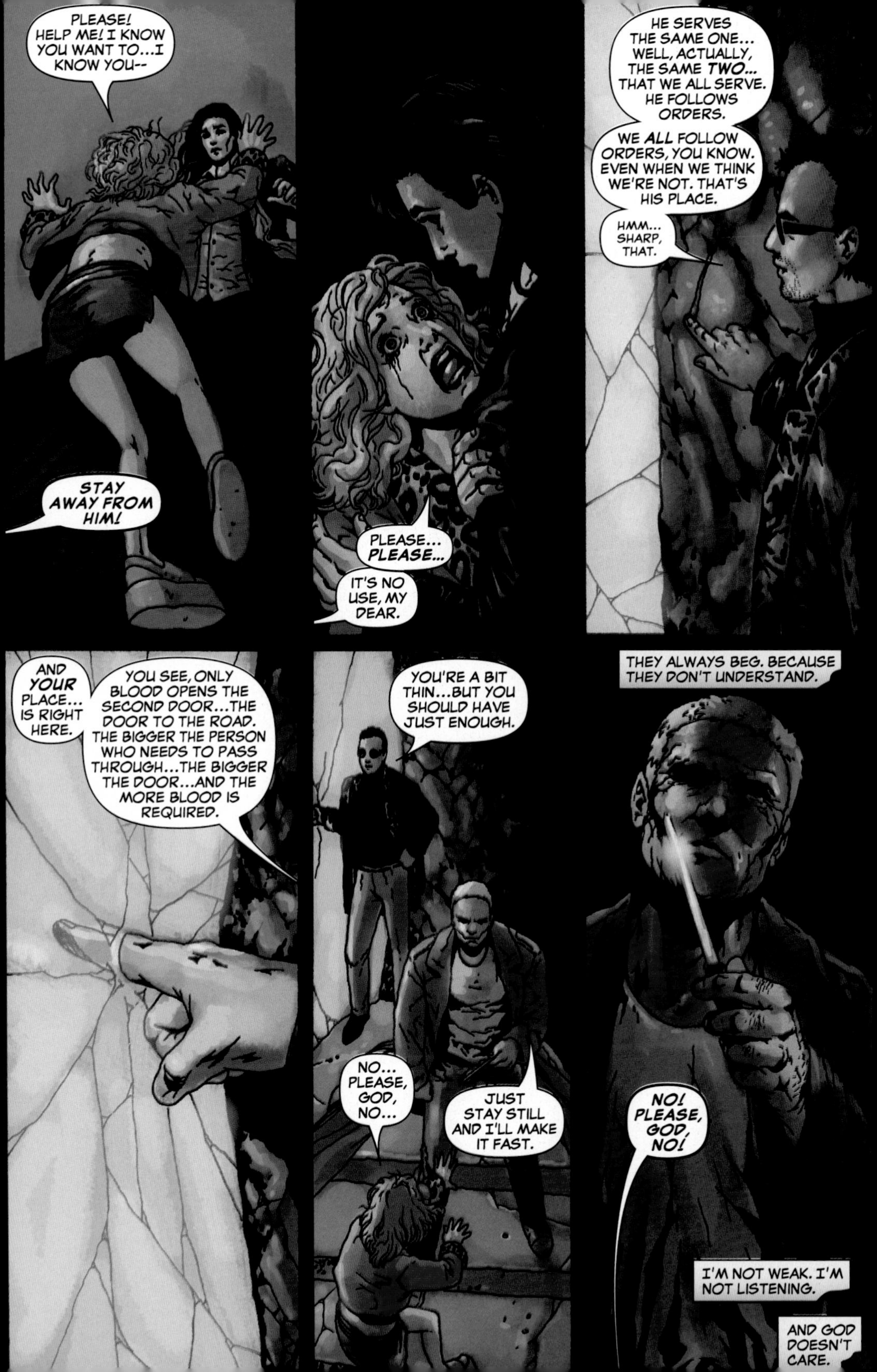
PLEASE! HELP ME! I KNOW YOU WANT TO...I KNOW YOU--
STAY AWAY FROM HIM!
PLEASE... PLEASE...
IT'S NO USE, MY DEAR.
HE SERVES THE SAME ONE... WELL, ACTUALLY, THE SAME TWO... THAT WE ALL SERVE. HE FOLLOWS ORDERS.
WE ALL FOLLOW ORDERS, YOU KNOW. EVEN WHEN WE THINK WE'RE NOT. THAT'S HIS PLACE.
HMM... SHARP, THAT.
AND YOUR PLACE... IS RIGHT HERE.
YOU SEE, ONLY BLOOD OPENS THE SECOND DOOR...THE DOOR TO THE ROAD. THE BIGGER THE PERSON WHO NEEDS TO PASS THROUGH...THE BIGGER THE DOOR...AND THE MORE BLOOD IS REQUIRED.
YOU'RE A BIT THIN...BUT YOU SHOULD HAVE JUST ENOUGH.
NO... PLEASE, GOD, NO...
JUST STAY STILL AND I'LL MAKE IT FAST.
THEY ALWAYS BEG. BECAUSE THEY DON'T UNDERSTAND.
NO! PLEASE, GOD, NO!
I'M NOT WEAK. I'M NOT LISTENING.
AND GOD DOESN'T CARE.

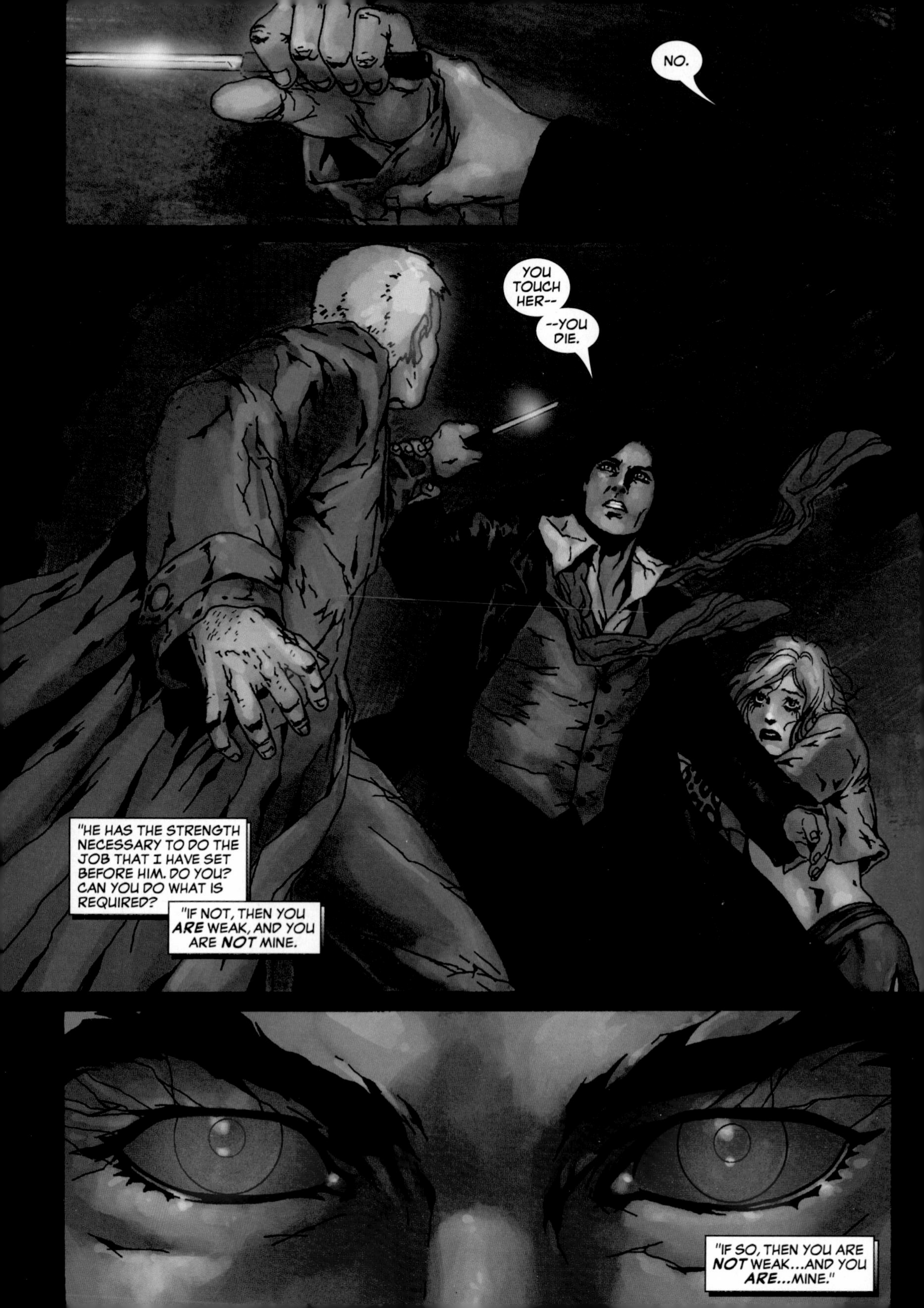
NO.
YOU TOUCH HER--
--YOU DIE.
"HE HAS THE STRENGTH NECESSARY TO DO THE JOB THAT I HAVE SET BEFORE HIM. DO YOU? CAN YOU DO WHAT IS REQUIRED?
"IF NOT, THEN YOU ARE WEAK, AND YOU ARE NOT MINE.
"IF SO, THEN YOU ARE NOT WEAK...AND YOU ARE...MINE."

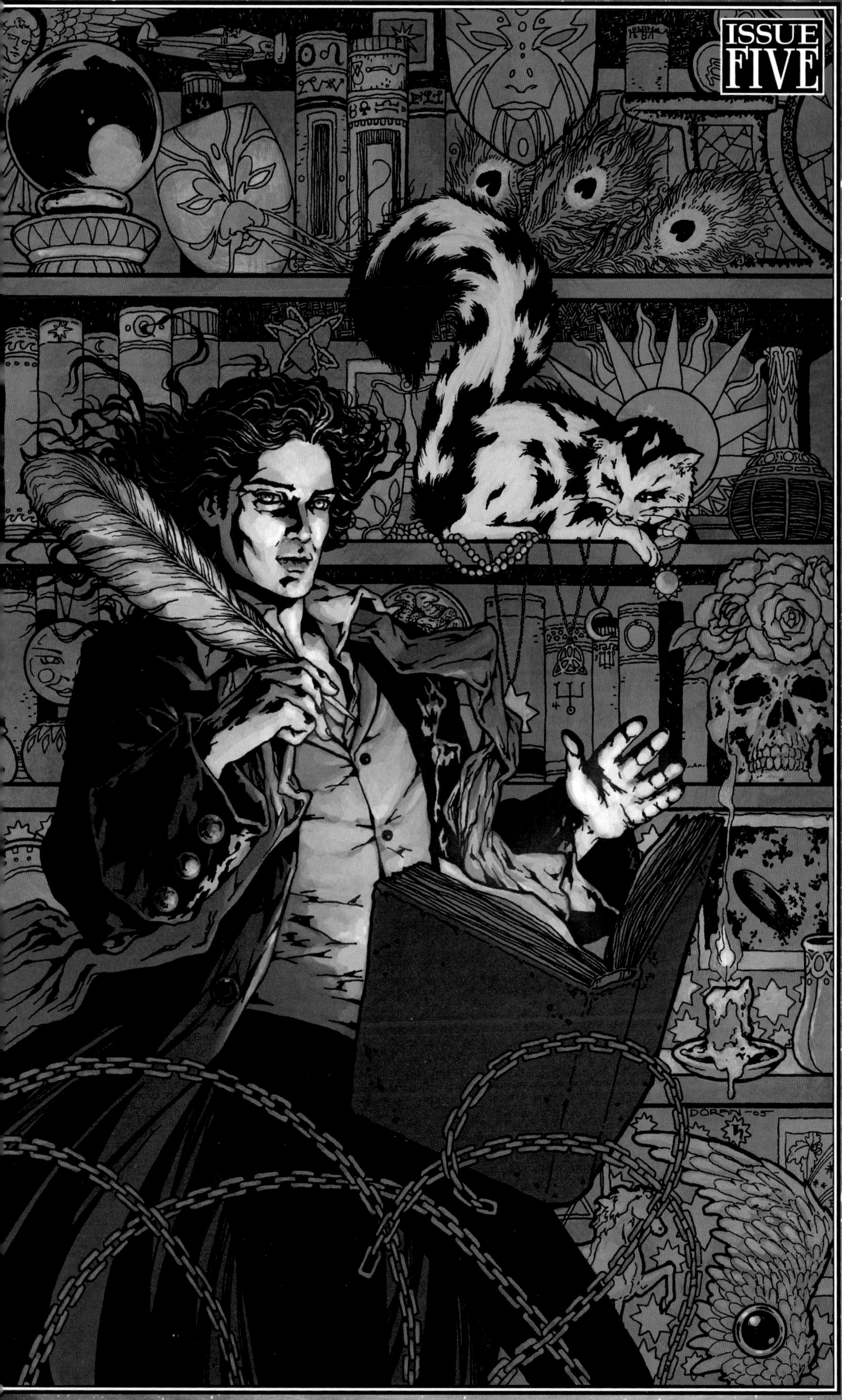
ISSUE FIVE
DORAN '05

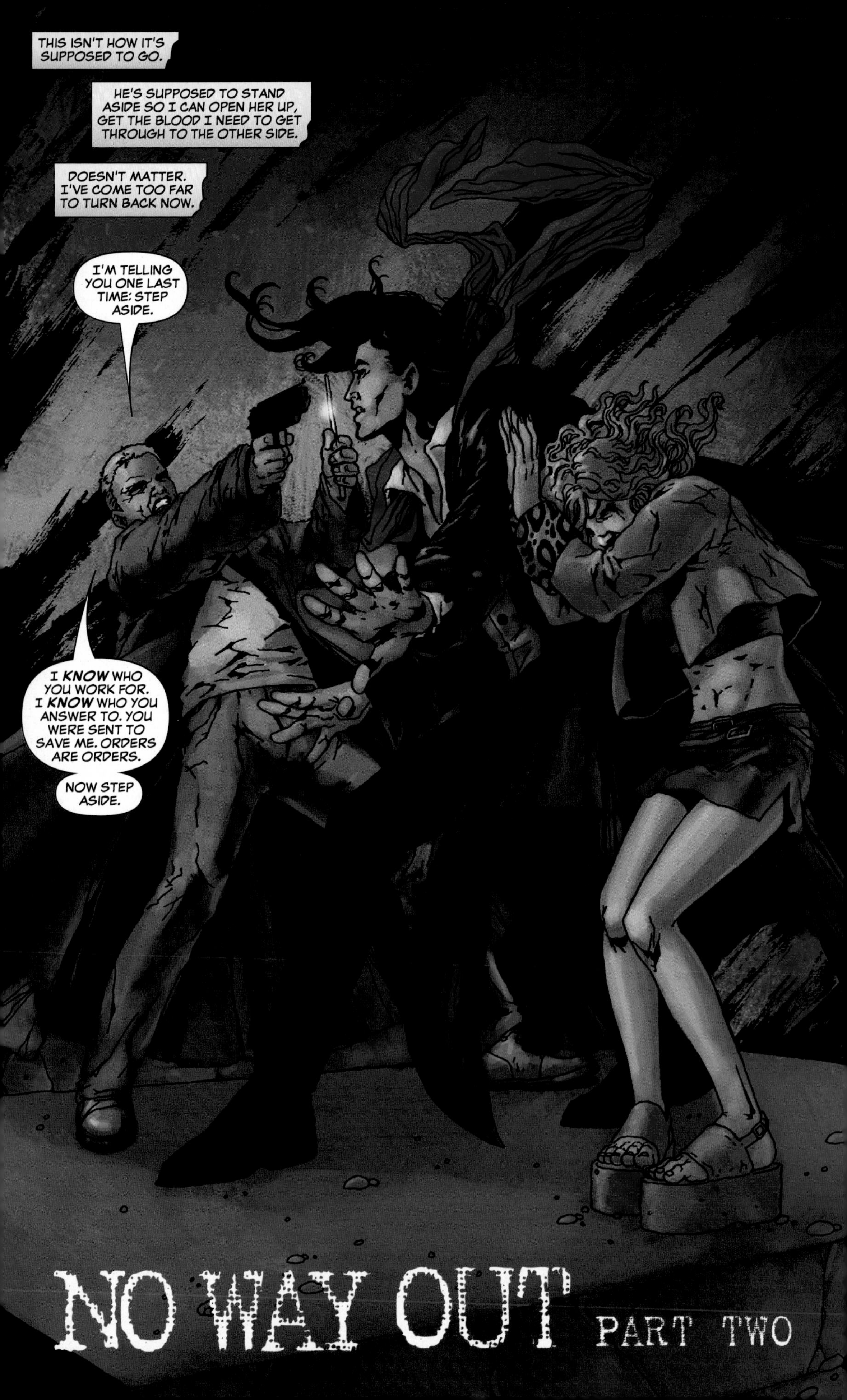
THIS ISN'T HOW IT'S SUPPOSED TO GO.
HE'S SUPPOSED TO STAND ASIDE SO I CAN OPEN HER UP, GET THE BLOOD I NEED TO GET THROUGH TO THE OTHER SIDE.
DOESN'T MATTER. I'VE COME TOO FAR TO TURN BACK NOW.
I'M TELLING YOU ONE LAST TIME: STEP ASIDE.
I KNOW WHO YOU WORK FOR. I KNOW WHO YOU ANSWER TO. YOU WERE SENT TO SAVE ME. ORDERS ARE ORDERS.
NOW STEP ASIDE.
NO WAY OUT PART TWO

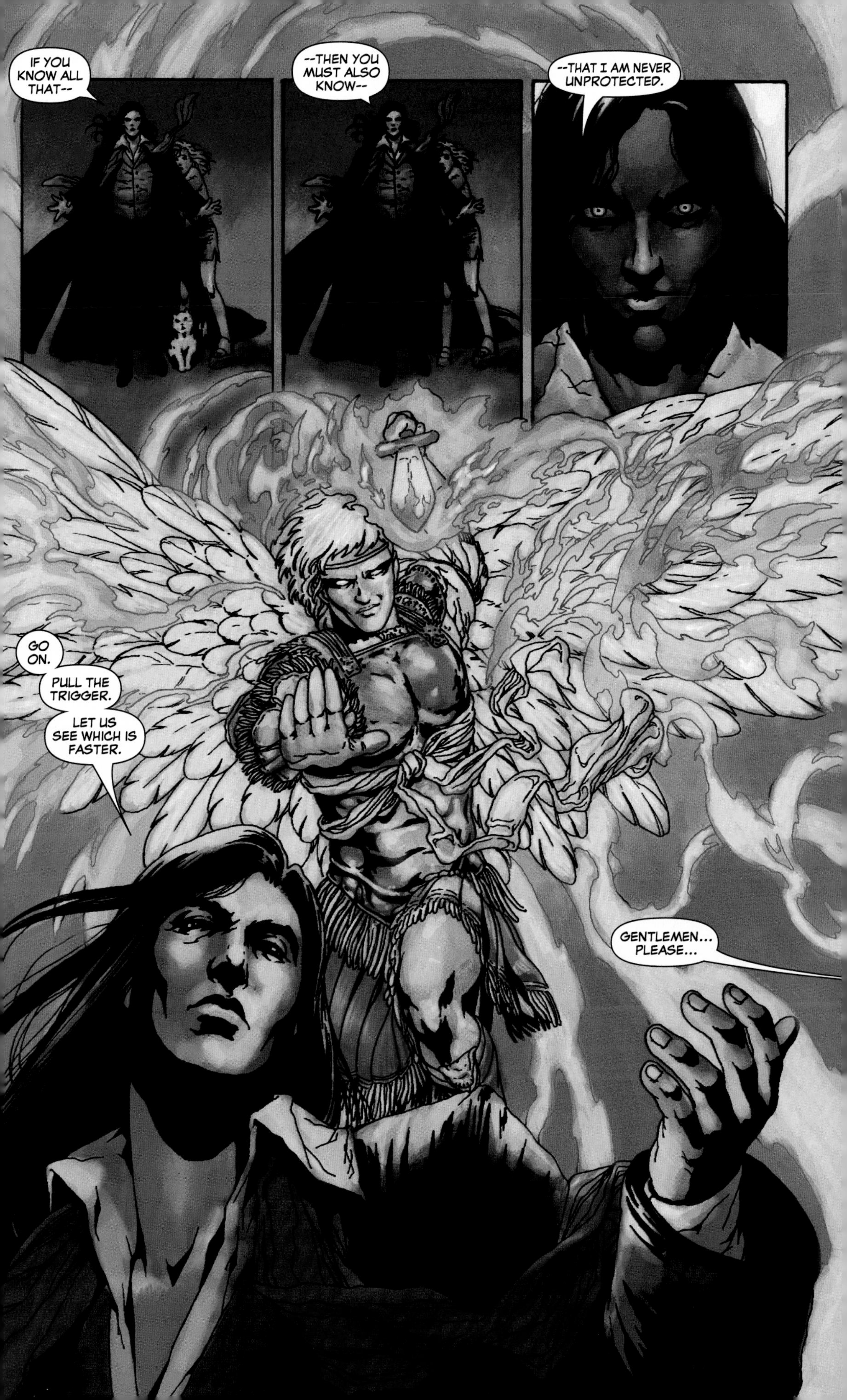
IF YOU KNOW ALL THAT--
--THEN YOU MUST ALSO KNOW--
--THAT I AM NEVER UNPROTECTED.
GO ON.
PULL THE TRIGGER.
LET US SEE WHICH IS FASTER.
GENTLEMEN... PLEASE...

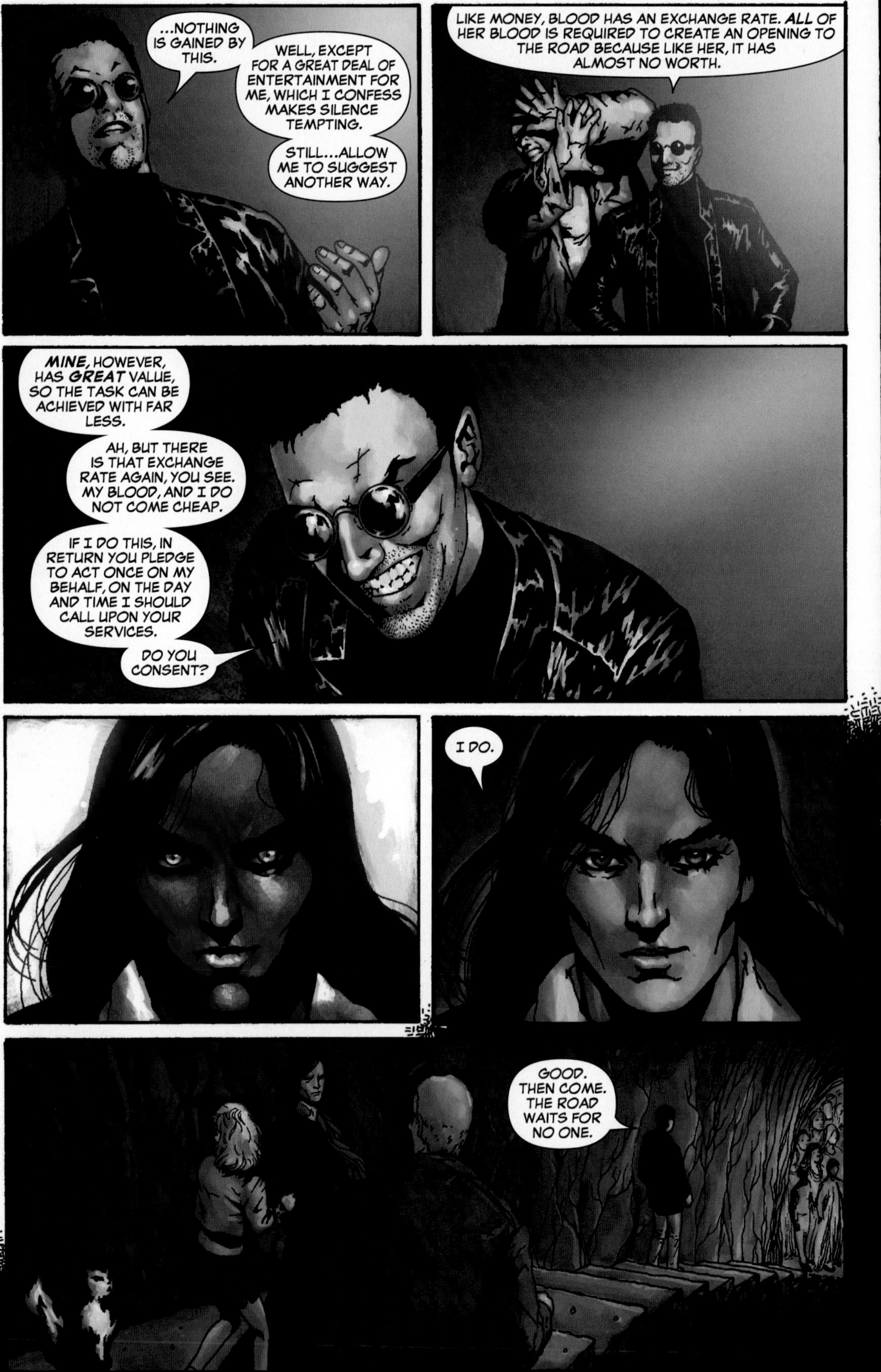

...NOTHING IS GAINED BY THIS.
WELL, EXCEPT FOR A GREAT DEAL OF ENTERTAINMENT FOR ME, WHICH I CONFESS MAKES SILENCE TEMPTING.
STILL...ALLOW ME TO SUGGEST ANOTHER WAY.
LIKE MONEY, BLOOD HAS AN EXCHANGE RATE. ALL OF HER BLOOD IS REQUIRED TO CREATE AN OPENING TO THE ROAD BECAUSE LIKE HER, IT HAS ALMOST NO WORTH.
MINE, HOWEVER, HAS GREAT VALUE, SO THE TASK CAN BE ACHIEVED WITH FAR LESS.
AH, BUT THERE IS THAT EXCHANGE RATE AGAIN, YOU SEE. MY BLOOD, AND I DO NOT COME CHEAP.
IF I DO THIS, IN RETURN YOU PLEDGE TO ACT ONCE ON MY BEHALF, ON THE DAY AND TIME I SHOULD CALL UPON YOUR SERVICES.
DO YOU CONSENT?
I DO.
GOOD. THEN COME. THE ROAD WAITS FOR NO ONE.

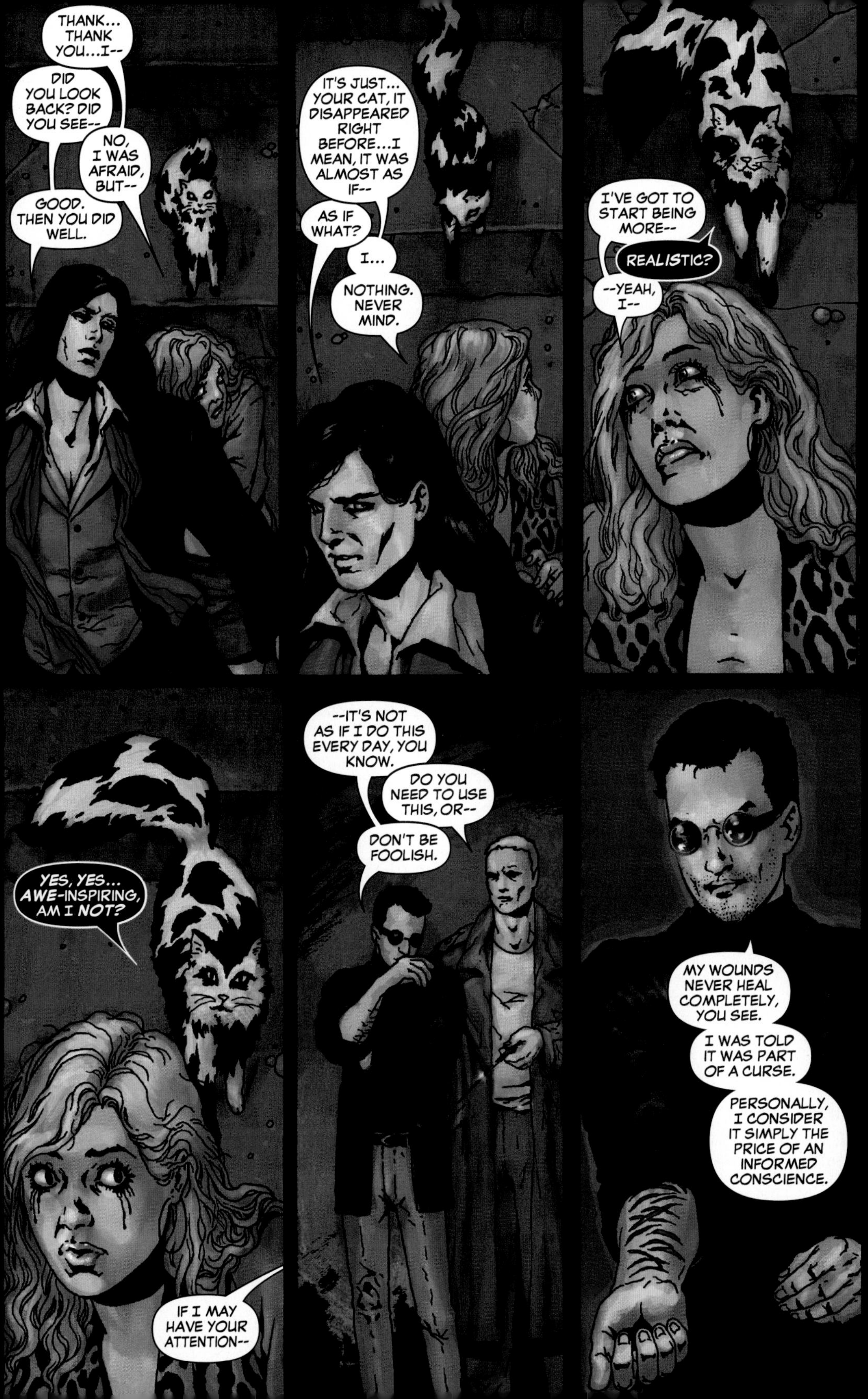
THANK... THANK YOU...I--
DID YOU LOOK BACK? DID YOU SEE--
NO, I WAS AFRAID, BUT--
GOOD. THEN YOU DID WELL.
IT'S JUST... YOUR CAT, IT DISAPPEARED RIGHT BEFORE...I MEAN, IT WAS ALMOST AS IF--
AS IF WHAT?
I...
NOTHING. NEVER MIND.
I'VE GOT TO START BEING MORE--
REALISTIC?
--YEAH, I--
YES, YES... AWE-INSPIRING, AM I NOT?
IF I MAY HAVE YOUR ATTENTION--
--IT'S NOT AS IF I DO THIS EVERY DAY, YOU KNOW.
DO YOU NEED TO USE THIS, OR--
DON'T BE FOOLISH.
MY WOUNDS NEVER HEAL COMPLETELY, YOU SEE.
I WAS TOLD IT WAS PART OF A CURSE.
PERSONALLY, I CONSIDER IT SIMPLY THE PRICE OF AN INFORMED CONSCIENCE.

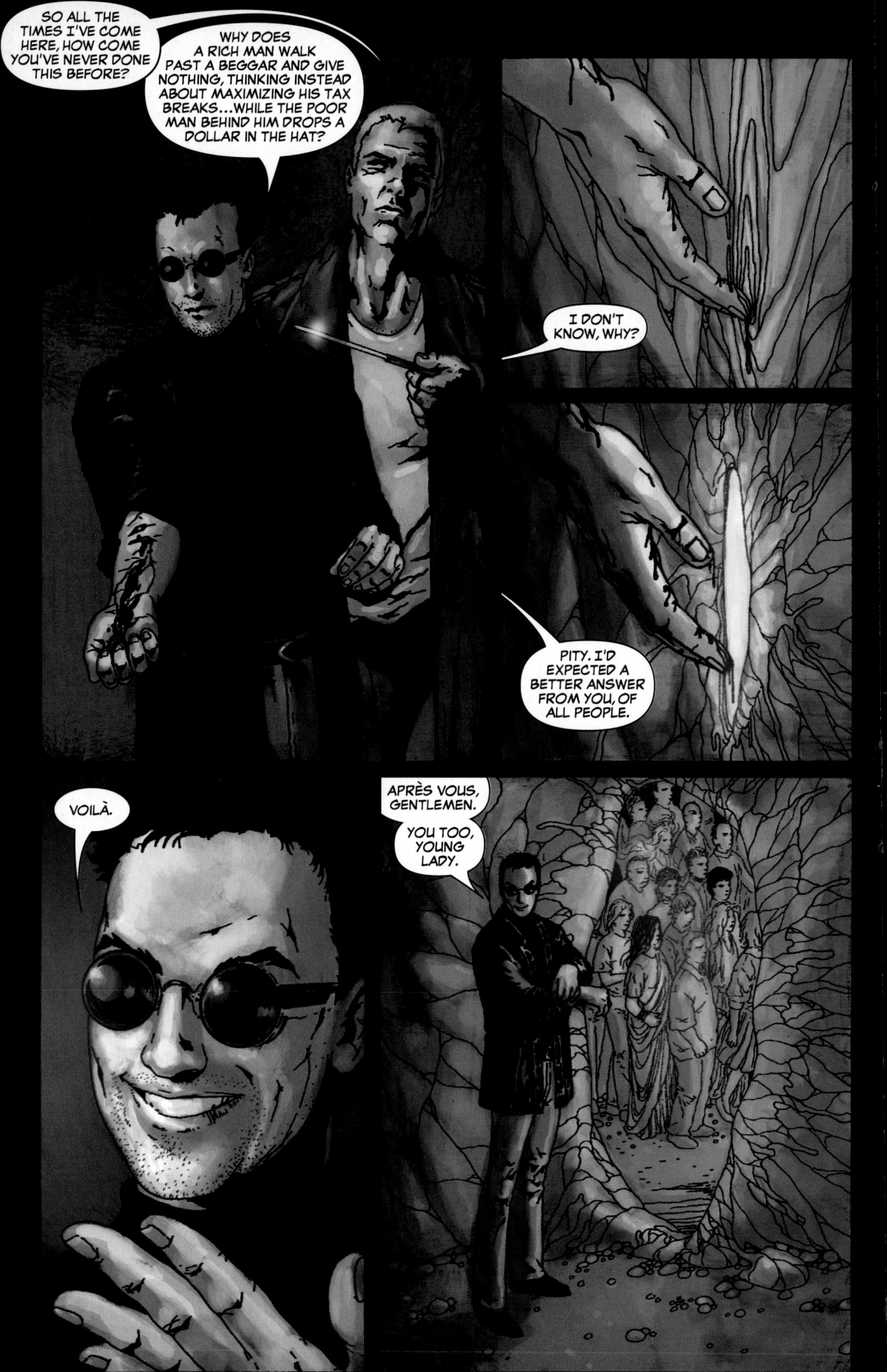
SO ALL THE TIMES I'VE COME HERE, HOW COME YOU'VE NEVER DONE THIS BEFORE?
WHY DOES A RICH MAN WALK PAST A BEGGAR AND GIVE NOTHING, THINKING INSTEAD ABOUT MAXIMIZING HIS TAX BREAKS...WHILE THE POOR MAN BEHIND HIM DROPS A DOLLAR IN THE HAT?
I DON'T KNOW, WHY?
PITY. I'D EXPECTED A BETTER ANSWER FROM YOU, OF ALL PEOPLE.
VOILÀ.
APRÈS VOUS, GENTLEMEN.
YOU TOO, YOUNG LADY.

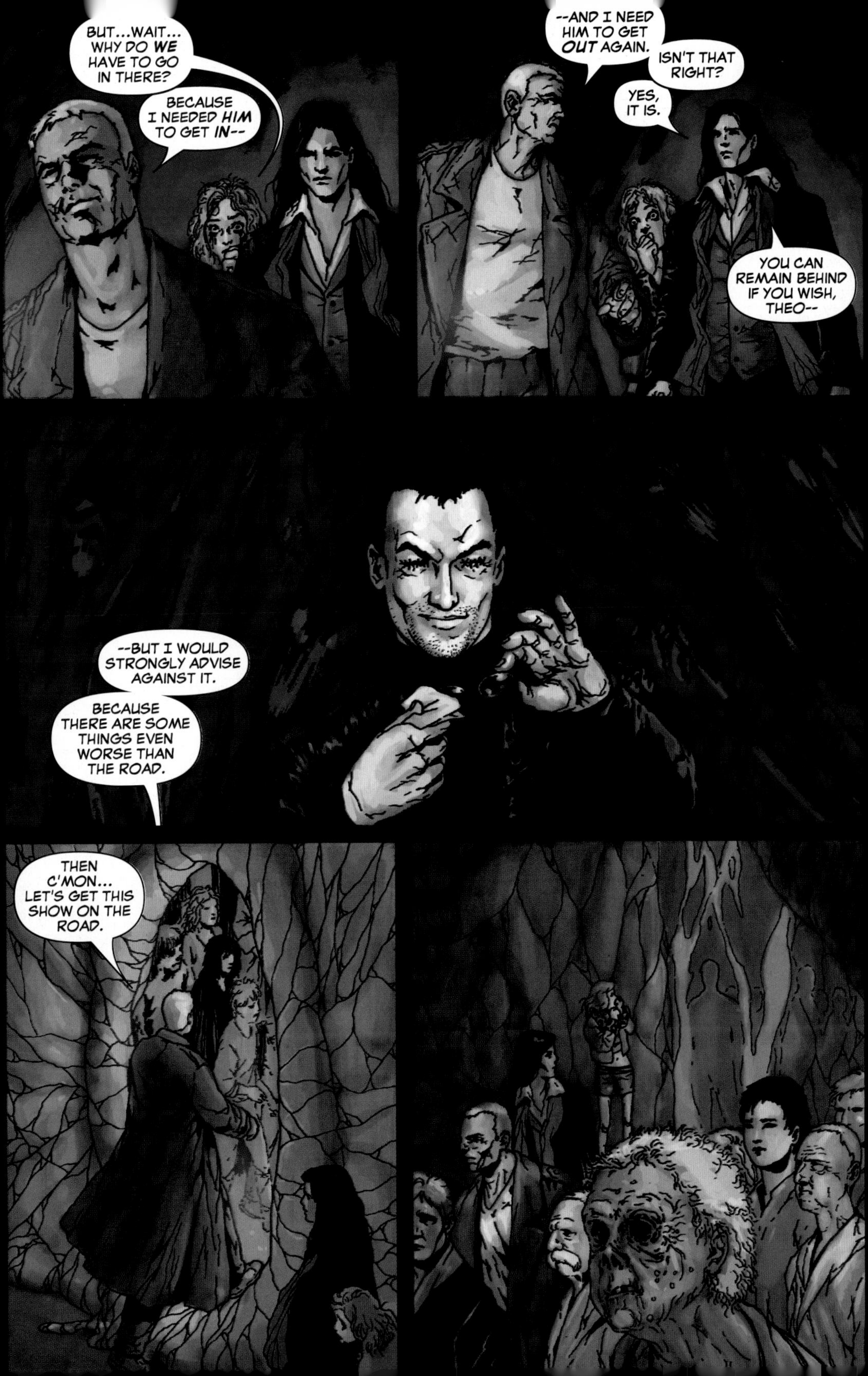

BUT...WAIT... WHY DO WE HAVE TO GO IN THERE?
BECAUSE I NEEDED HIM TO GET IN--
--AND I NEED HIM TO GET OUT AGAIN.
ISN'T THAT RIGHT?
YES, IT IS.
YOU CAN REMAIN BEHIND IF YOU WISH, THEO--
--BUT I WOULD STRONGLY ADVISE AGAINST IT.
BECAUSE THERE ARE SOME THINGS EVEN WORSE THAN THE ROAD.
THEN C'MON... LET'S GET THIS SHOW ON THE ROAD.

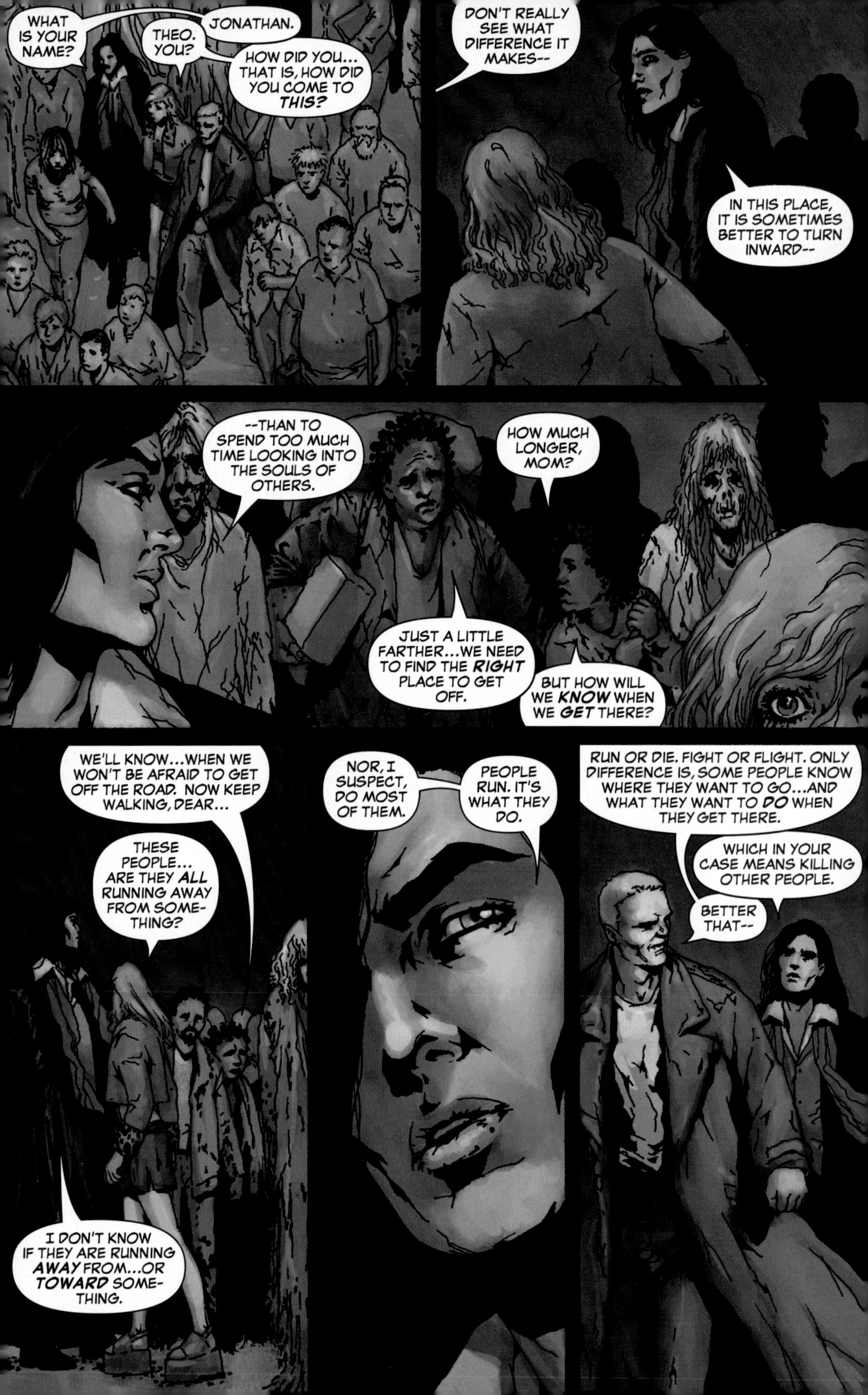
WHAT IS YOUR NAME?
JONATHAN.
THEO. YOU?
HOW DID YOU... THAT IS, HOW DID YOU COME TO THIS?
DON'T REALLY SEE WHAT DIFFERENCE IT MAKES--
IN THIS PLACE, IT IS SOMETIMES BETTER TO TURN INWARD--
--THAN TO SPEND TOO MUCH TIME LOOKING INTO THE SOULS OF OTHERS.
HOW MUCH LONGER, MOM?
JUST A LITTLE FARTHER...WE NEED TO FIND THE RIGHT PLACE TO GET OFF.
BUT HOW WILL WE KNOW WHEN WE GET THERE?
WE'LL KNOW...WHEN WE WON'T BE AFRAID TO GET OFF THE ROAD. NOW KEEP WALKING, DEAR...
THESE PEOPLE... ARE THEY ALL RUNNING AWAY FROM SOME-THING?
I DON'T KNOW IF THEY ARE RUNNING AWAY FROM...OR TOWARD SOME-THING.
PEOPLE RUN. IT'S WHAT THEY DO.
NOR, I SUSPECT, DO MOST OF THEM.
RUN OR DIE. FIGHT OR FLIGHT. ONLY DIFFERENCE IS, SOME PEOPLE KNOW WHERE THEY WANT TO GO...AND WHAT THEY WANT TO DO WHEN THEY GET THERE.
WHICH IN YOUR CASE MEANS KILLING OTHER PEOPLE.
BETTER THAT--

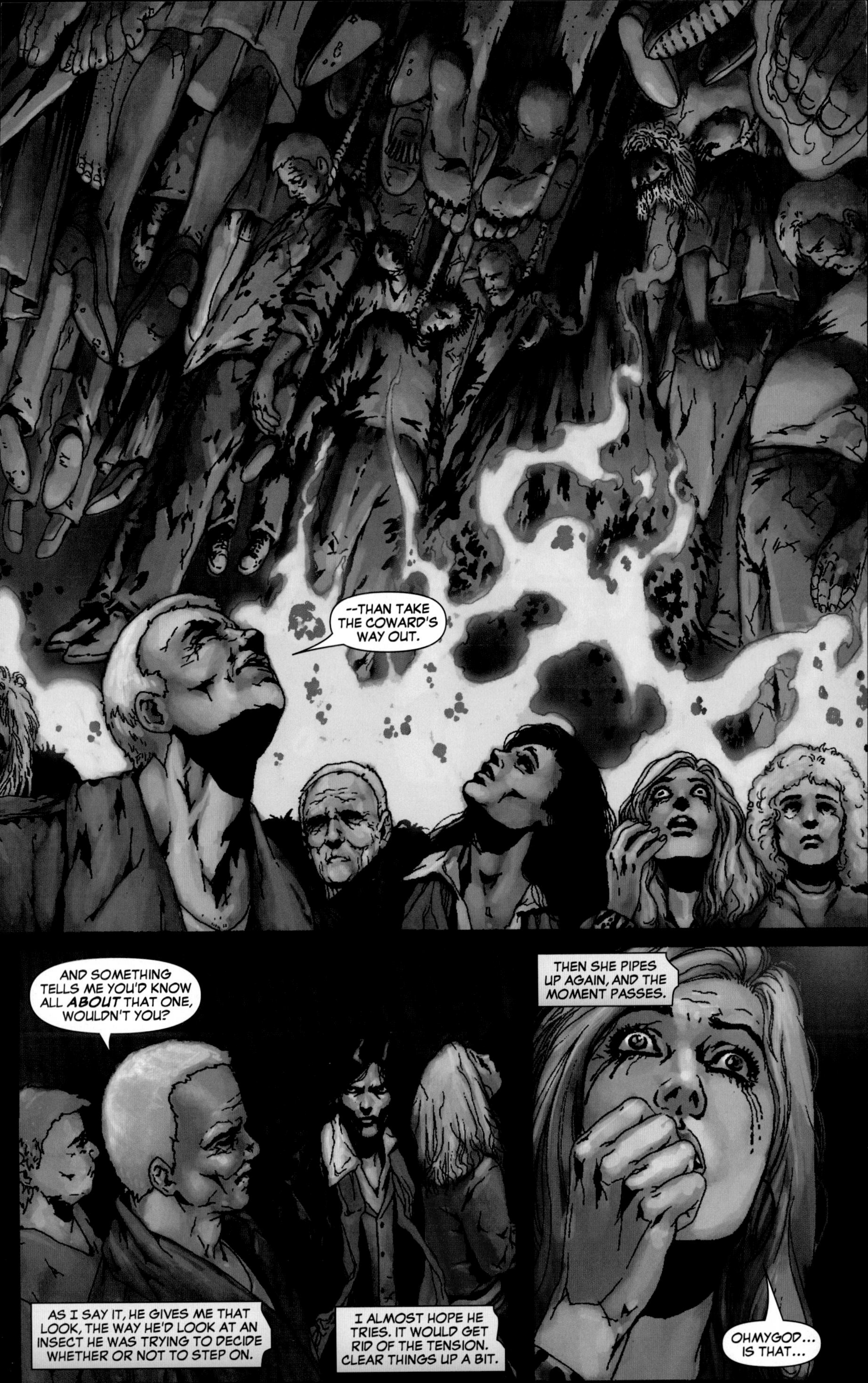
--THAN TAKE THE COWARD'S WAY OUT.
AND SOMETHING TELLS ME YOU'D KNOW ALL *ABOUT* THAT ONE, WOULDN'T YOU?
AS I SAY IT, HE GIVES ME THAT LOOK, THE WAY HE'D LOOK AT AN INSECT HE WAS TRYING TO DECIDE WHETHER OR NOT TO STEP ON.
I ALMOST HOPE HE TRIES. IT WOULD GET RID OF THE TENSION. CLEAR THINGS UP A BIT.
THEN SHE PIPES UP AGAIN, AND THE MOMENT PASSES.
OHMYGOD... IS THAT...

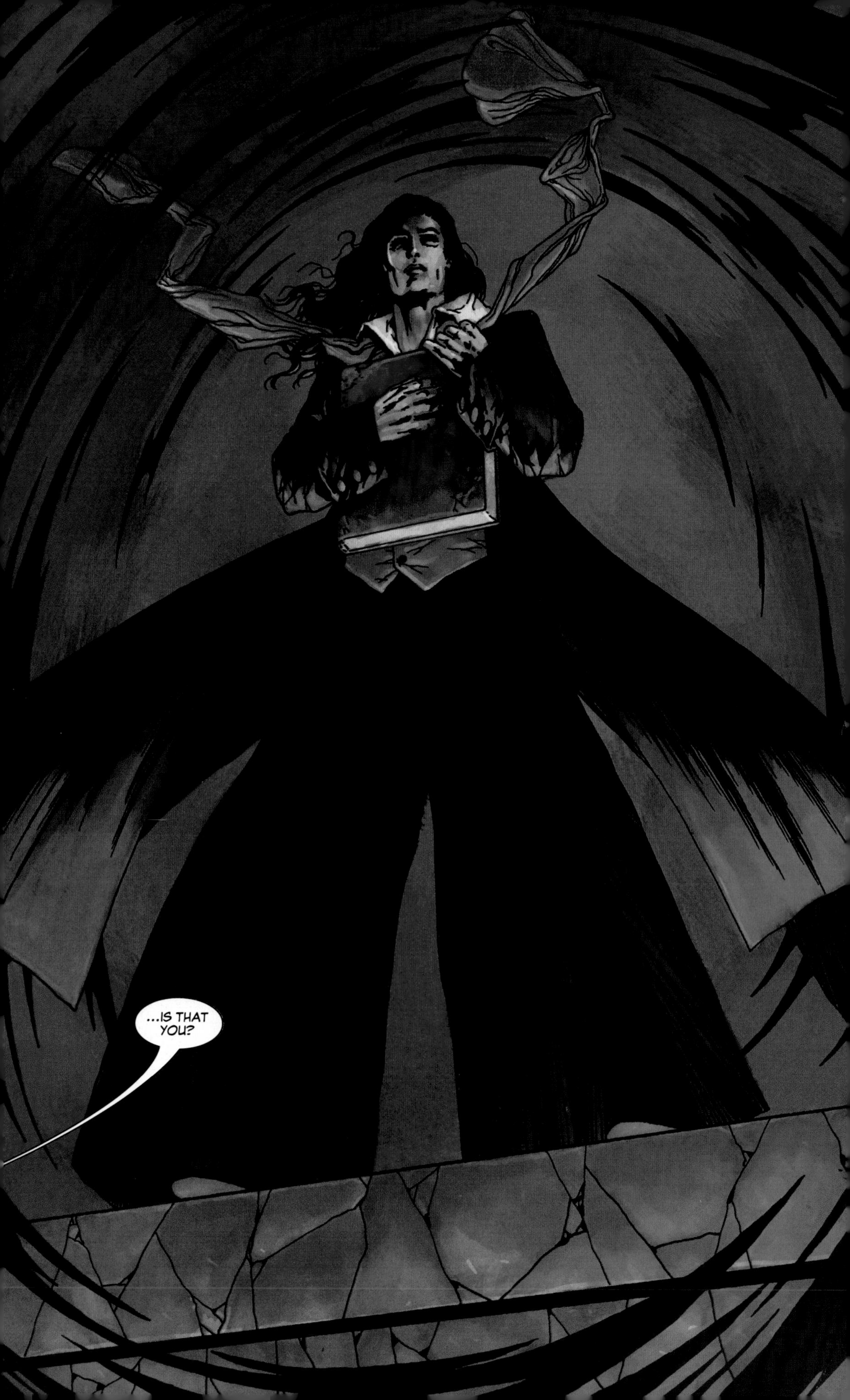
...IS THAT YOU?

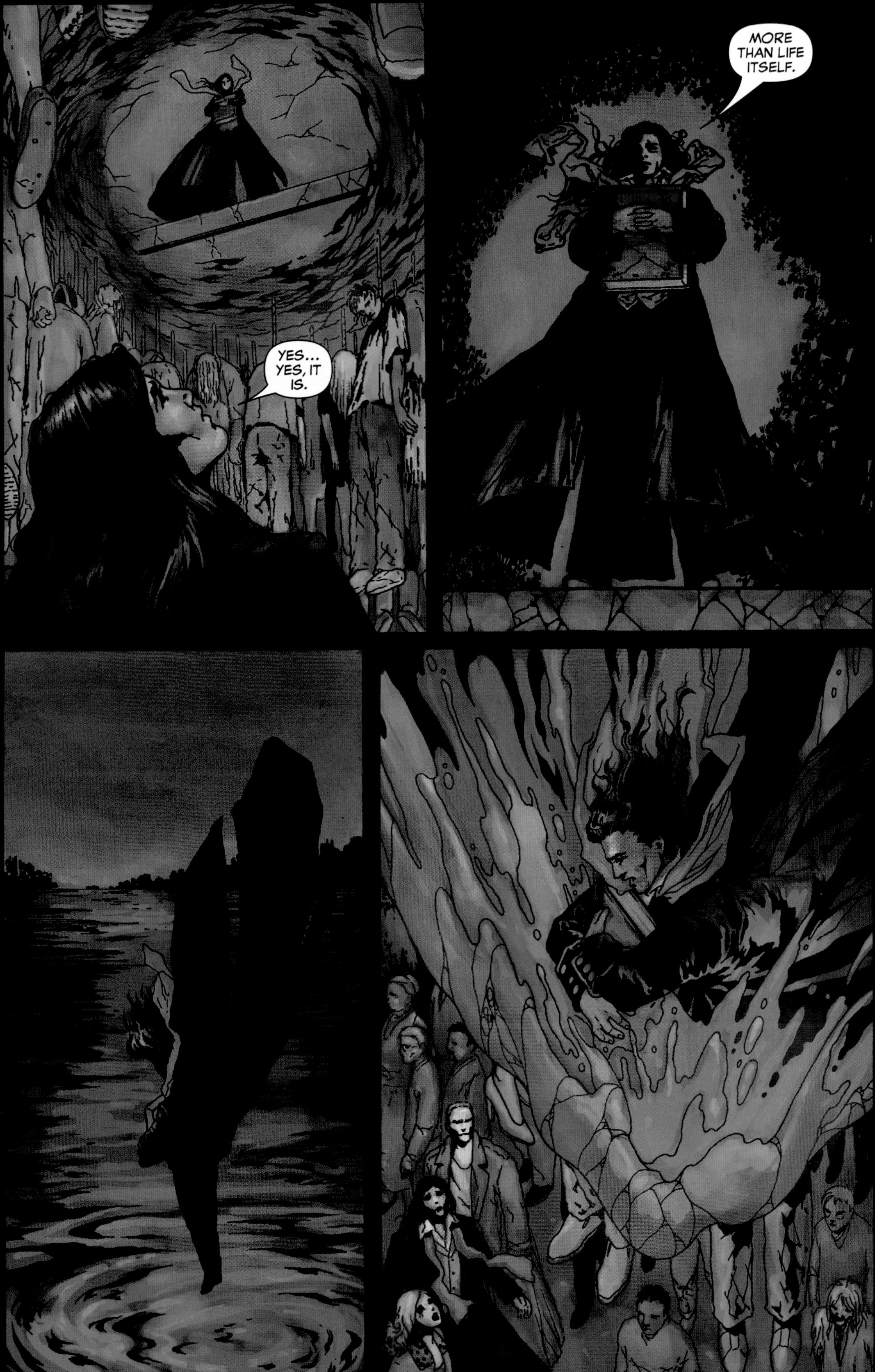
YES... YES, IT IS.
MORE THAN LIFE ITSELF.

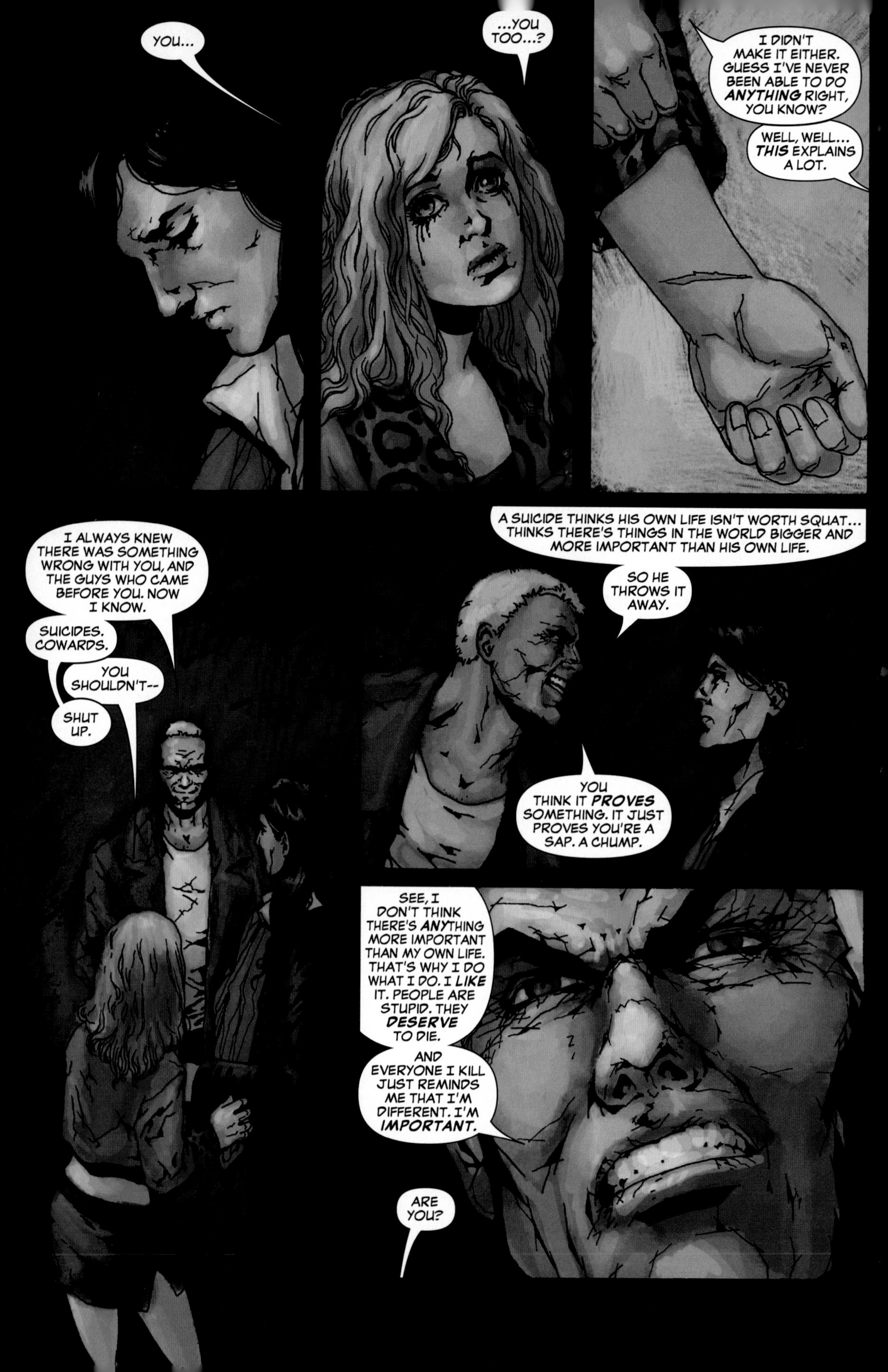
YOU...
...YOU TOO...?
I DIDN'T MAKE IT EITHER. GUESS I'VE NEVER BEEN ABLE TO DO ANYTHING RIGHT, YOU KNOW?
WELL, WELL... THIS EXPLAINS A LOT.
I ALWAYS KNEW THERE WAS SOMETHING WRONG WITH YOU, AND THE GUYS WHO CAME BEFORE YOU. NOW I KNOW.
SUICIDES. COWARDS.
YOU SHOULDN'T--
SHUT UP.
A SUICIDE THINKS HIS OWN LIFE ISN'T WORTH SQUAT... THINKS THERE'S THINGS IN THE WORLD BIGGER AND MORE IMPORTANT THAN HIS OWN LIFE.
SO HE THROWS IT AWAY.
YOU THINK IT PROVES SOMETHING. IT JUST PROVES YOU'RE A SAP. A CHUMP.
SEE, I DON'T THINK THERE'S ANYTHING MORE IMPORTANT THAN MY OWN LIFE. THAT'S WHY I DO WHAT I DO. I LIKE IT. PEOPLE ARE STUPID. THEY DESERVE TO DIE.
AND EVERYONE I KILL JUST REMINDS ME THAT I'M DIFFERENT. I'M IMPORTANT.
ARE YOU?

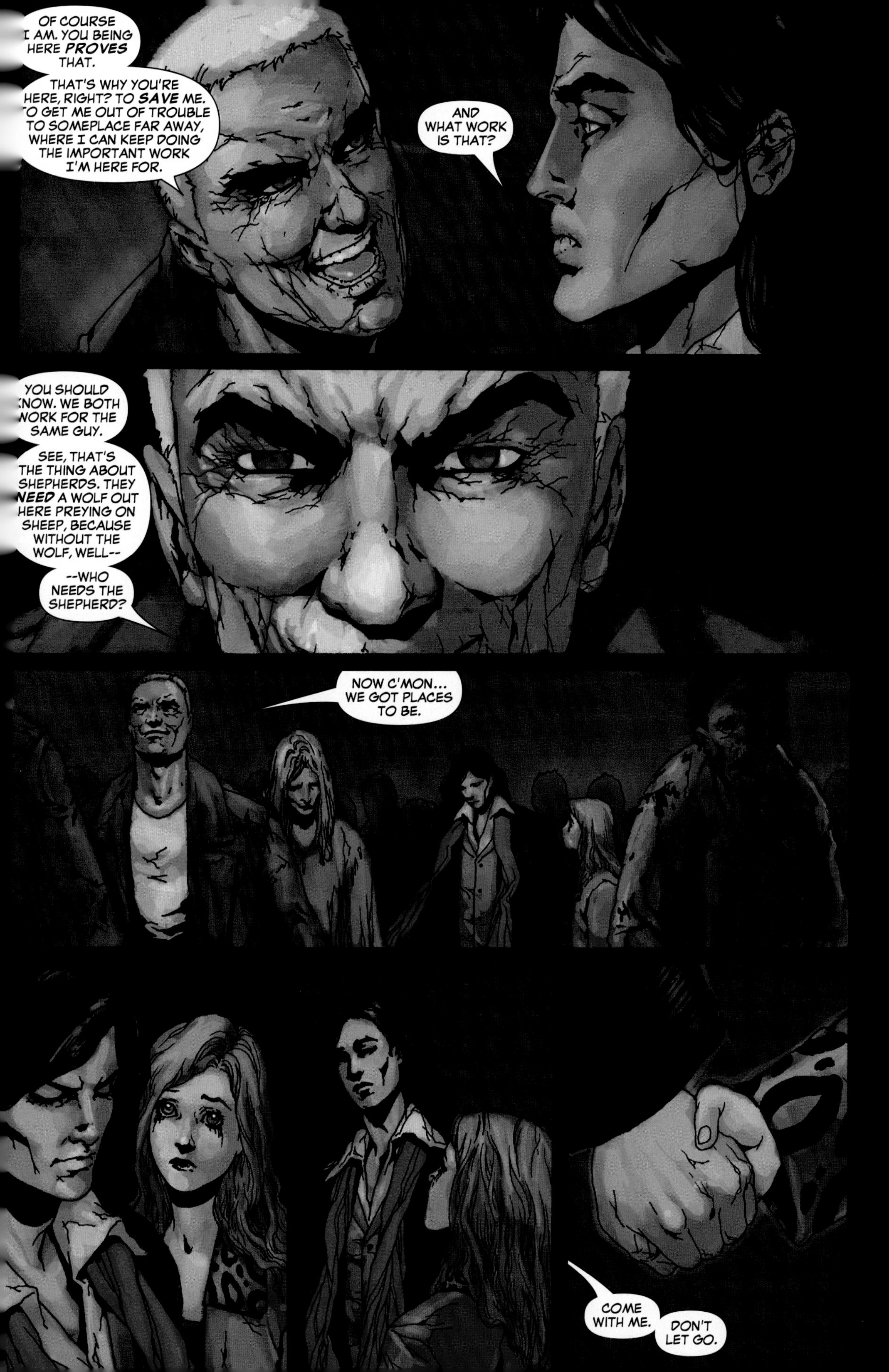
OF COURSE I AM. YOU BEING HERE PROVES THAT.
THAT'S WHY YOU'RE HERE, RIGHT? TO SAVE ME. TO GET ME OUT OF TROUBLE TO SOMEPLACE FAR AWAY, WHERE I CAN KEEP DOING THE IMPORTANT WORK I'M HERE FOR.
AND WHAT WORK IS THAT?
YOU SHOULD KNOW. WE BOTH WORK FOR THE SAME GUY.
SEE, THAT'S THE THING ABOUT SHEPHERDS. THEY NEED A WOLF OUT HERE PREYING ON SHEEP, BECAUSE WITHOUT THE WOLF, WELL--
--WHO NEEDS THE SHEPHERD?
NOW C'MON... WE GOT PLACES TO BE.
COME WITH ME.
DON'T LET GO.

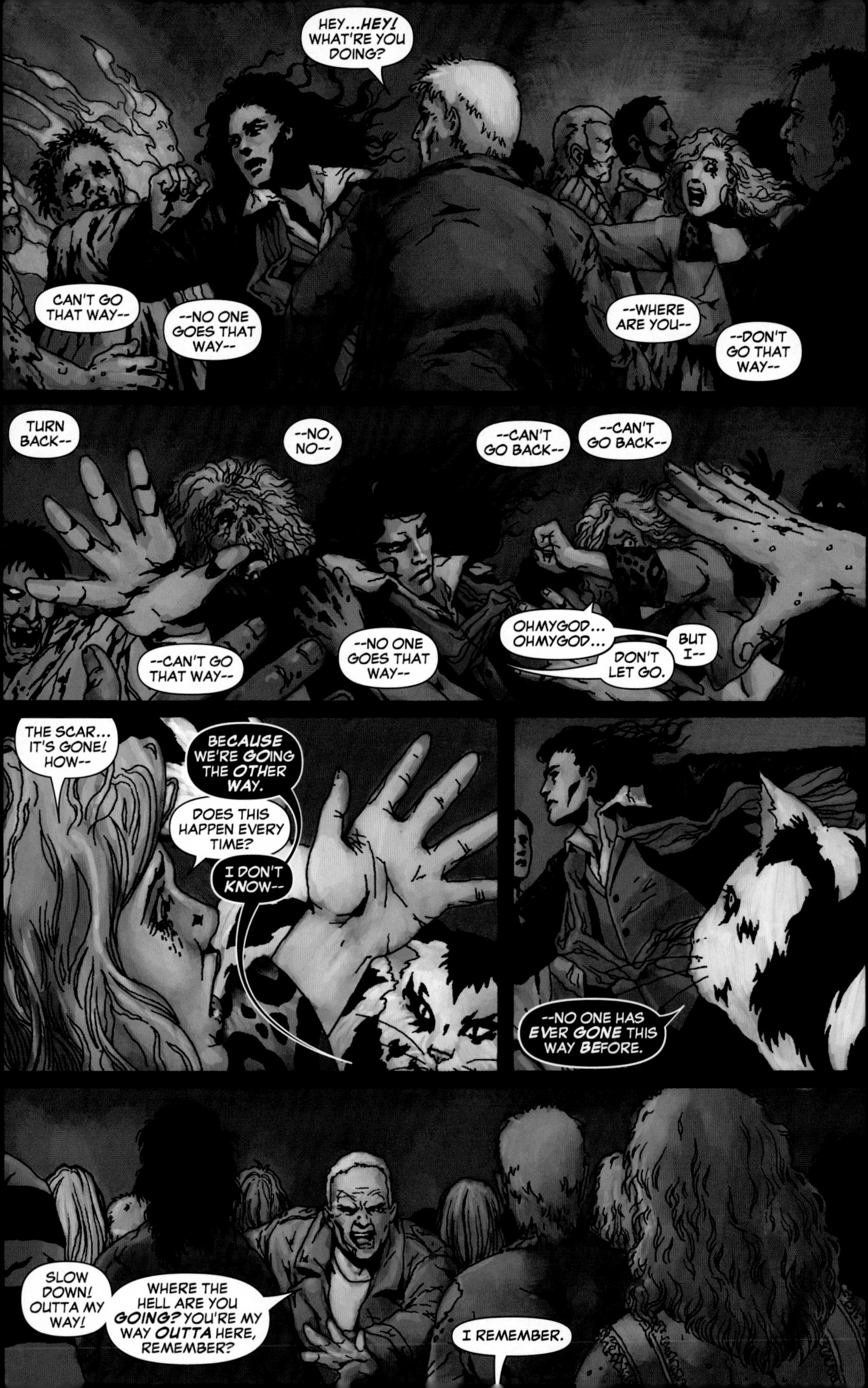
HEY...HEY! WHAT'RE YOU DOING?
CAN'T GO THAT WAY--
--NO ONE GOES THAT WAY--
--WHERE ARE YOU--
--DON'T GO THAT WAY--
TURN BACK--
--NO, NO--
--CAN'T GO BACK--
--CAN'T GO BACK--
--CAN'T GO THAT WAY--
--NO ONE GOES THAT WAY--
OHMYGOD... OHMYGOD...
BUT I--
DON'T LET GO.
THE SCAR... IT'S GONE! HOW--
BECAUSE WE'RE GOING THE OTHER WAY.
DOES THIS HAPPEN EVERY TIME?
I DON'T KNOW--
--NO ONE HAS EVER GONE THIS WAY BEFORE.
SLOW DOWN! OUTTA MY WAY!
WHERE THE HELL ARE YOU GOING? YOU'RE MY WAY OUTTA HERE, REMEMBER?
I REMEMBER.

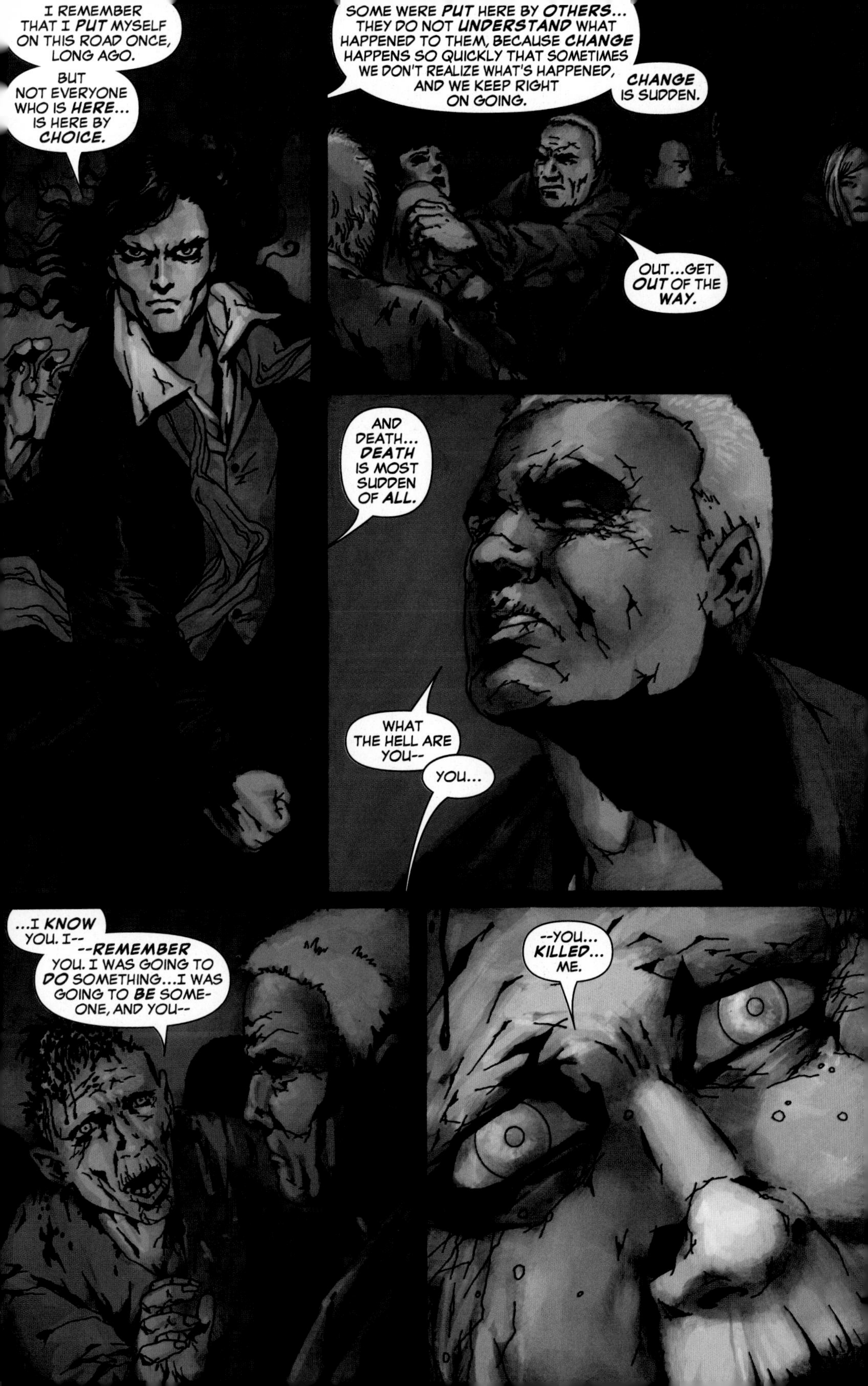
I REMEMBER THAT I PUT MYSELF ON THIS ROAD ONCE, LONG AGO.
BUT NOT EVERYONE WHO IS HERE... IS HERE BY CHOICE.
SOME WERE PUT HERE BY OTHERS... THEY DO NOT UNDERSTAND WHAT HAPPENED TO THEM, BECAUSE CHANGE HAPPENS SO QUICKLY THAT SOMETIMES WE DON'T REALIZE WHAT'S HAPPENED, AND WE KEEP RIGHT ON GOING.
CHANGE IS SUDDEN.
OUT...GET OUT OF THE WAY.
AND DEATH... DEATH IS MOST SUDDEN OF ALL.
WHAT THE HELL ARE YOU--
YOU...
...I KNOW YOU. I--
--REMEMBER YOU. I WAS GOING TO DO SOMETHING...I WAS GOING TO BE SOME-ONE, AND YOU--
--YOU... KILLED... ME.

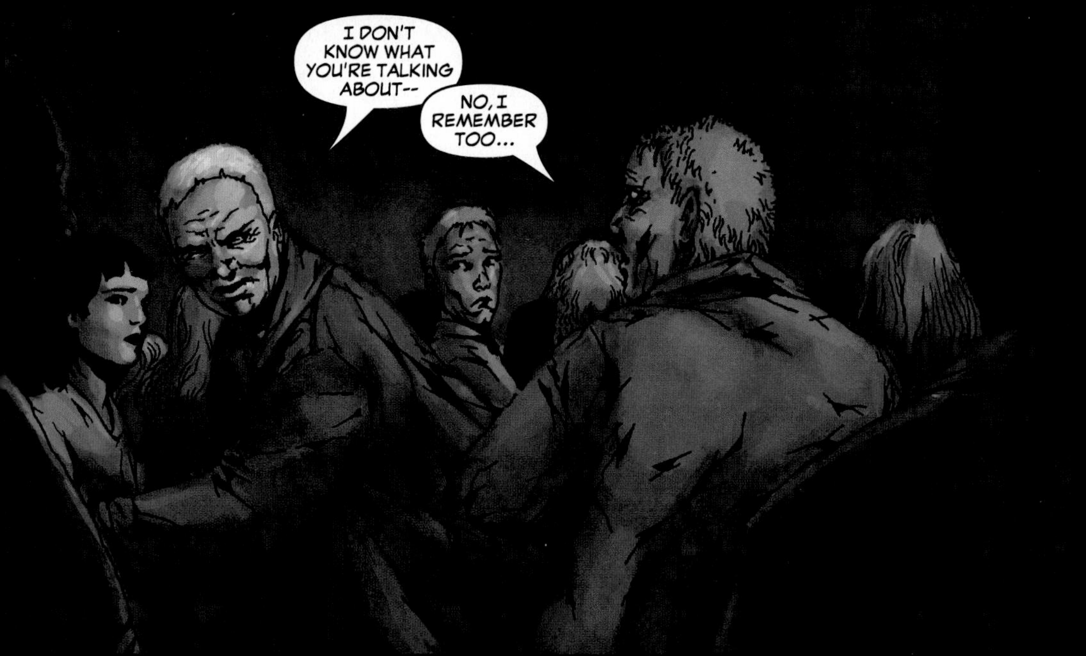
I DON'T KNOW WHAT YOU'RE TALKING ABOUT--
NO, I REMEMBER TOO...

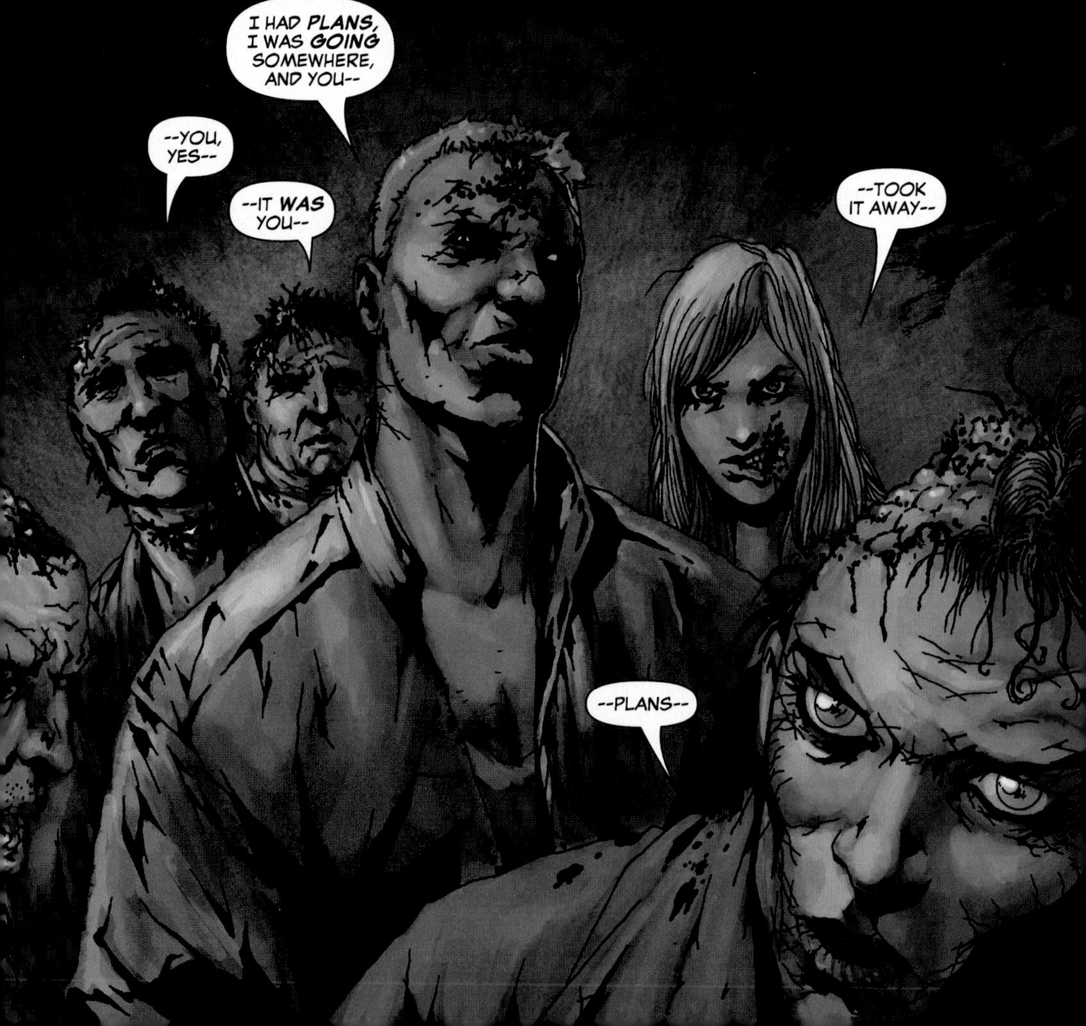
I HAD PLANS, I WAS GOING SOMEWHERE, AND YOU--
--YOU, YES--
--IT WAS YOU--
--TOOK IT AWAY--
--PLANS--

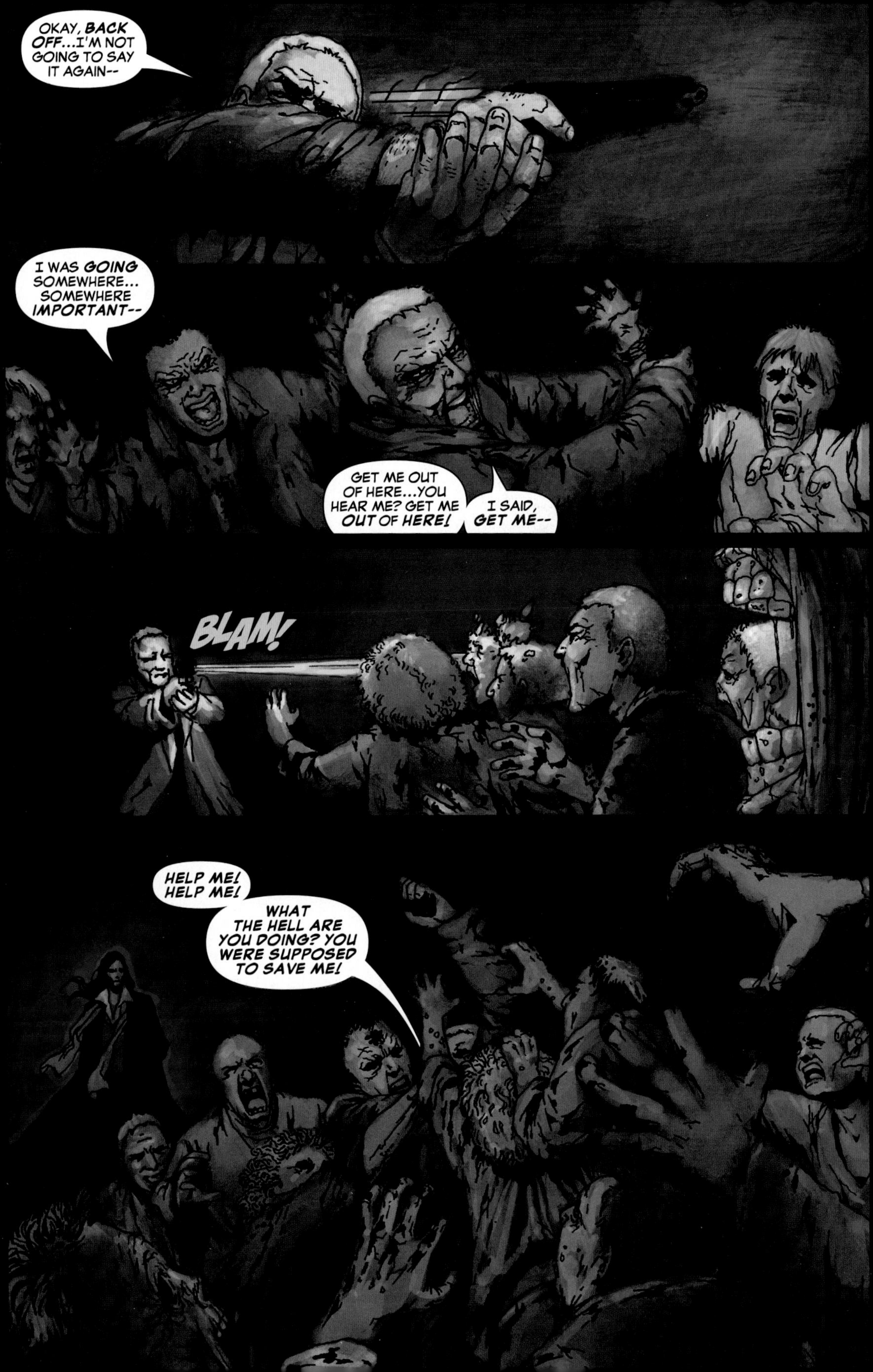
OKAY, BACK OFF...I'M NOT GOING TO SAY IT AGAIN--
I WAS GOING SOMEWHERE... SOMEWHERE IMPORTANT--
GET ME OUT OF HERE...YOU HEAR ME? GET ME OUT OF HERE!
I SAID, GET ME--
BLAM!
HELP ME! HELP ME!
WHAT THE HELL ARE YOU DOING? YOU WERE SUPPOSED TO SAVE ME!

I SAVE--

I WANT HIM SAVED.

--I SAVE--

AH, WELL--

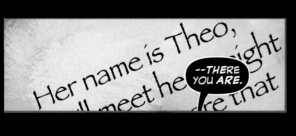

Her name is Theo,
'll meet he ight
re that

--THERE YOU ARE.

--WHAT I CHOOSE TO SAVE.

I SAVE... WHAT CAN BE SAVED.

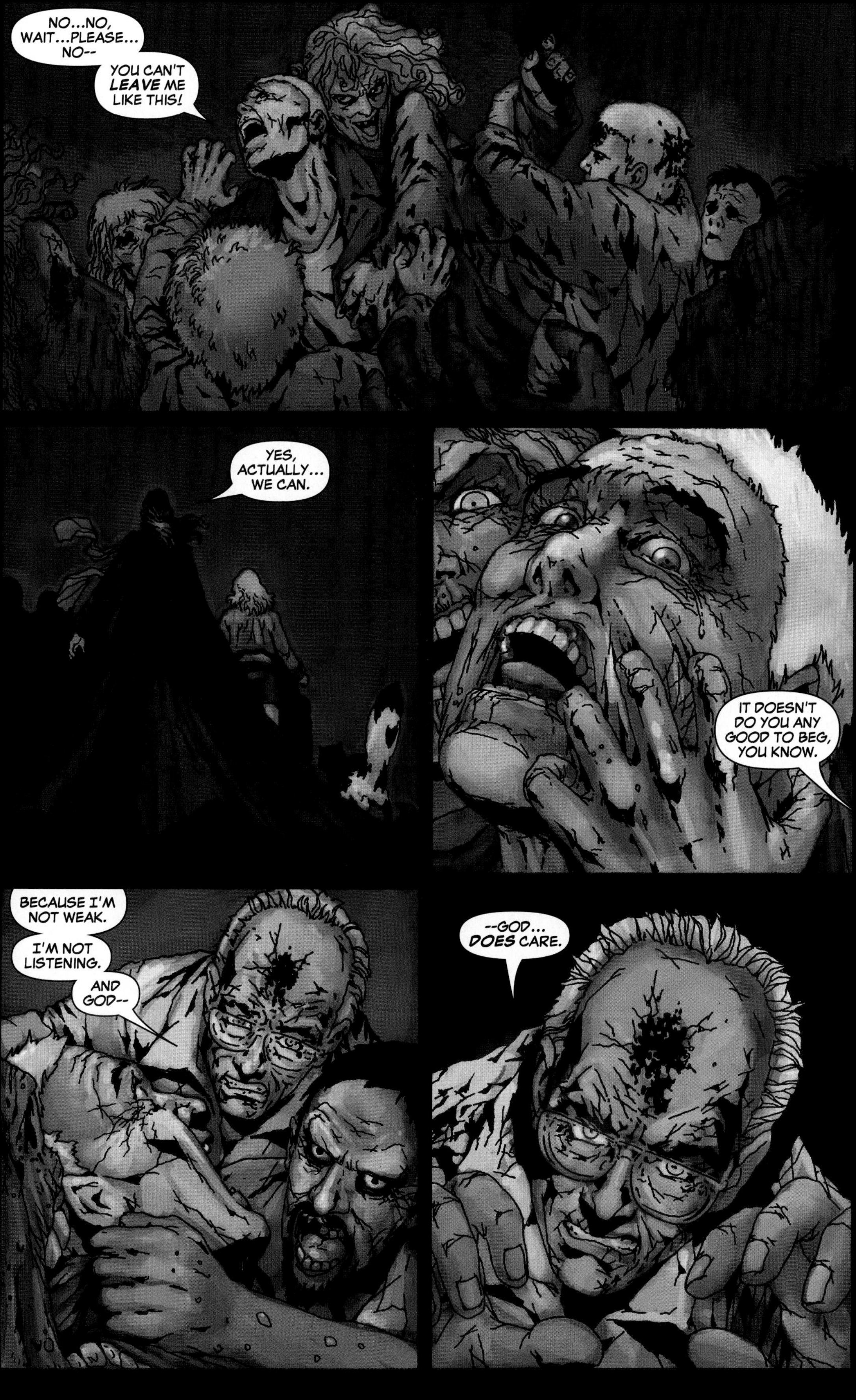
NO...NO, WAIT...PLEASE... NO--
YOU CAN'T *LEAVE* ME LIKE THIS!
YES, ACTUALLY... WE CAN.
IT DOESN'T DO YOU ANY GOOD TO BEG, YOU KNOW.
BECAUSE I'M NOT WEAK.
I'M NOT LISTENING.
AND GOD--
--GOD... *DOES* CARE.

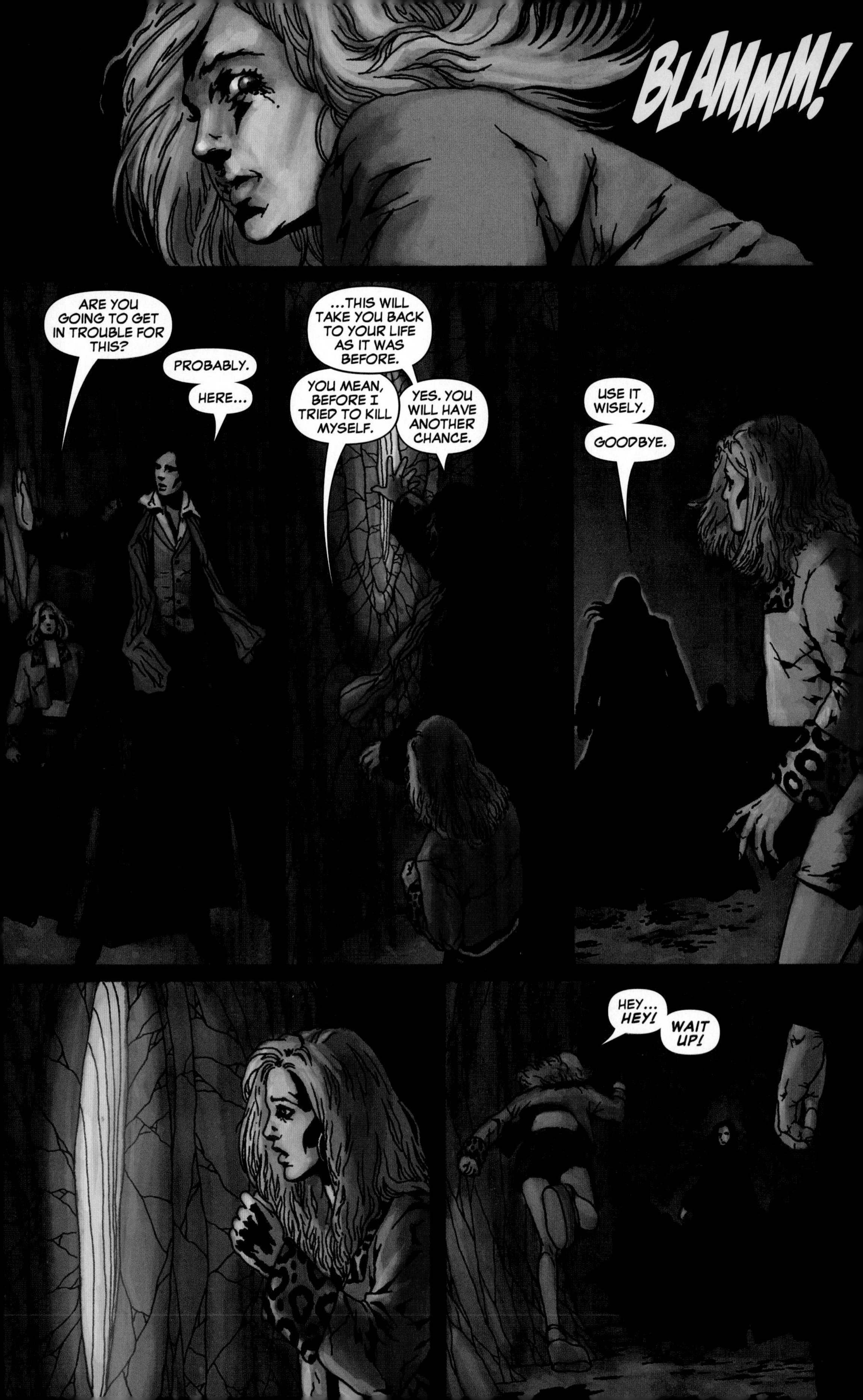
BLAMMM!
ARE YOU GOING TO GET IN TROUBLE FOR THIS?
PROBABLY.
HERE...
...THIS WILL TAKE YOU BACK TO YOUR LIFE AS IT WAS BEFORE.
YOU MEAN, BEFORE I TRIED TO KILL MYSELF.
YES. YOU WILL HAVE ANOTHER CHANCE.
USE IT WISELY.
GOODBYE.
HEY... HEY!
WAIT UP!

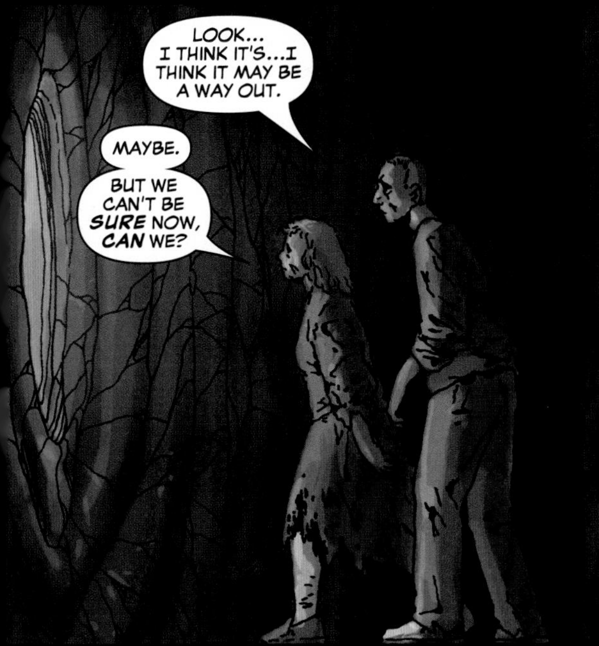
LOOK... I THINK IT'S...I THINK IT MAY BE A WAY OUT.
MAYBE.
BUT WE CAN'T BE **SURE** NOW, **CAN** WE?

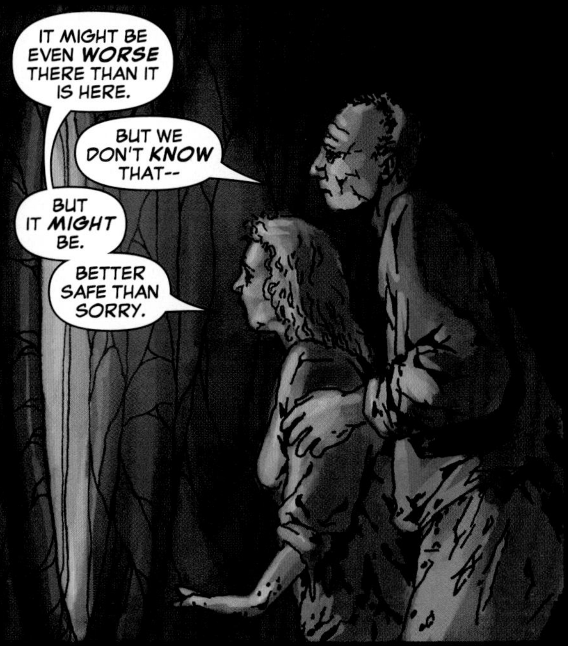
IT MIGHT BE EVEN **WORSE** THERE THAN IT IS HERE.
BUT WE DON'T **KNOW** THAT--
BUT IT **MIGHT** BE.
BETTER SAFE THAN SORRY.

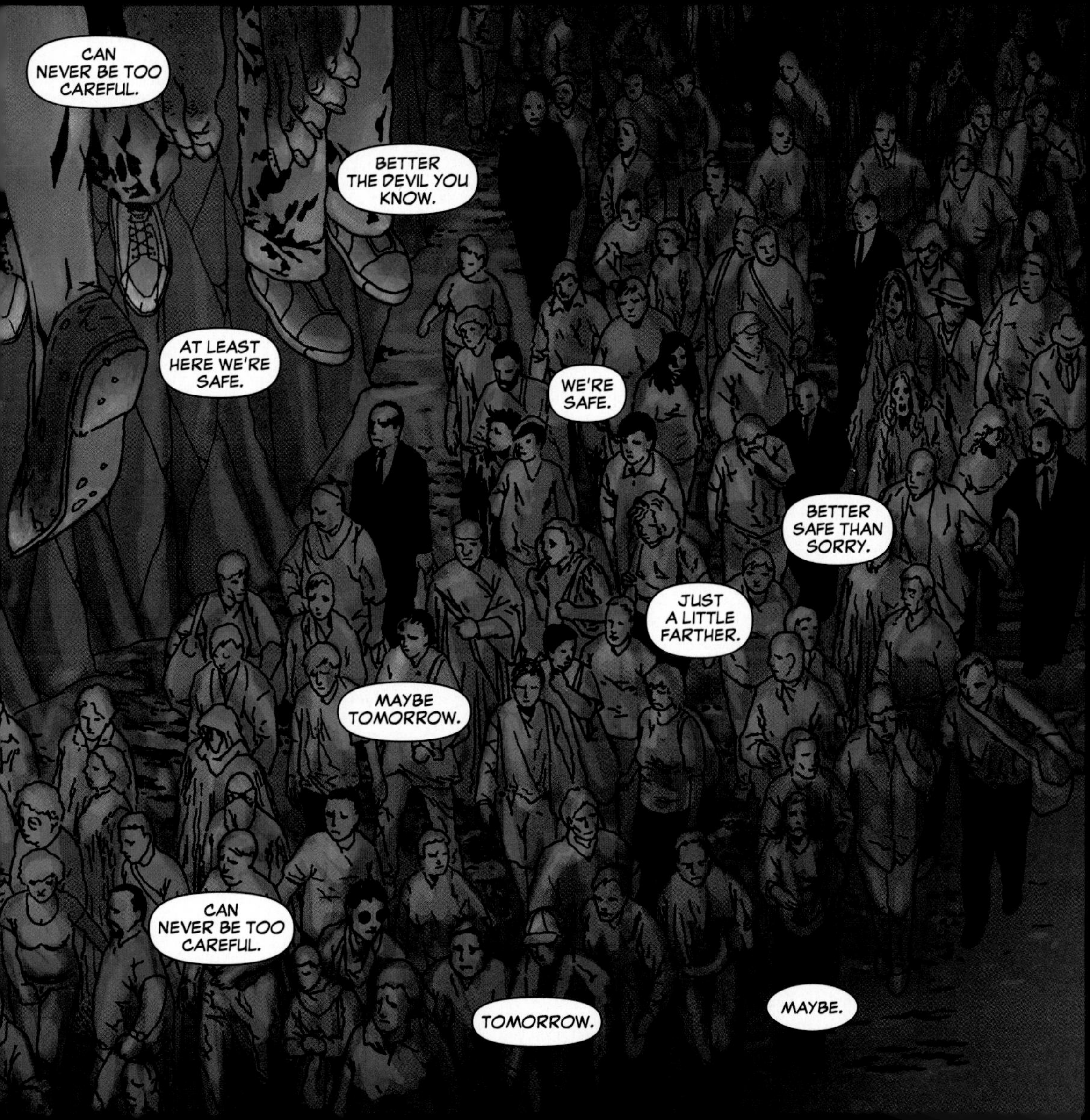
CAN NEVER BE TOO CAREFUL.
BETTER THE DEVIL YOU KNOW.
AT LEAST HERE WE'RE SAFE.
WE'RE SAFE.
BETTER SAFE THAN SORRY.
JUST A LITTLE FARTHER.
MAYBE TOMORROW.
CAN NEVER BE TOO CAREFUL.
TOMORROW.
MAYBE.

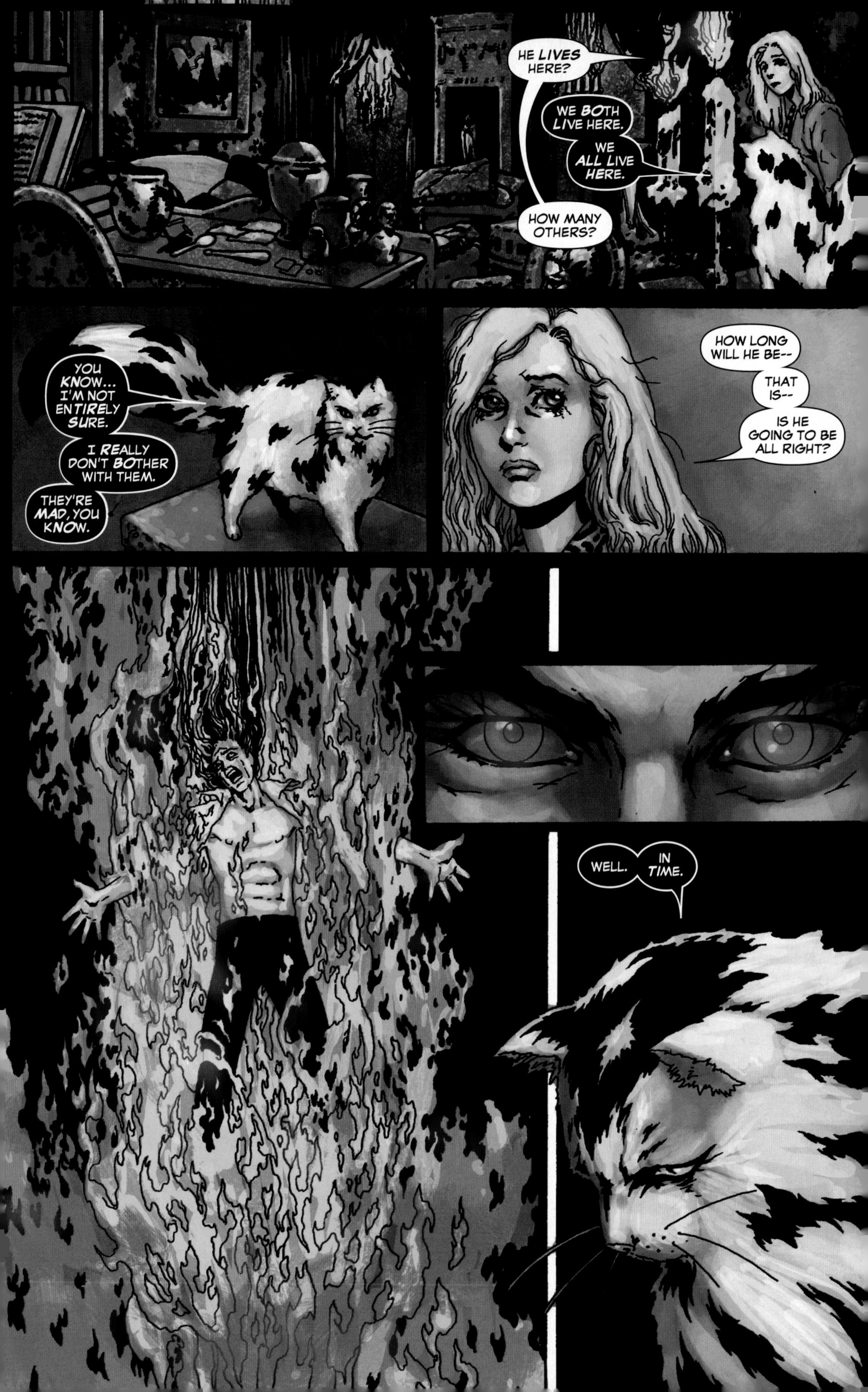
HE LIVES HERE?
WE BOTH LIVE HERE.
WE ALL LIVE HERE.
HOW MANY OTHERS?
YOU KNOW... I'M NOT ENTIRELY SURE.
I REALLY DON'T BOTHER WITH THEM.
THEY'RE MAD, YOU KNOW.
HOW LONG WILL HE BE--
THAT IS--
IS HE GOING TO BE ALL RIGHT?
WELL.
IN TIME.

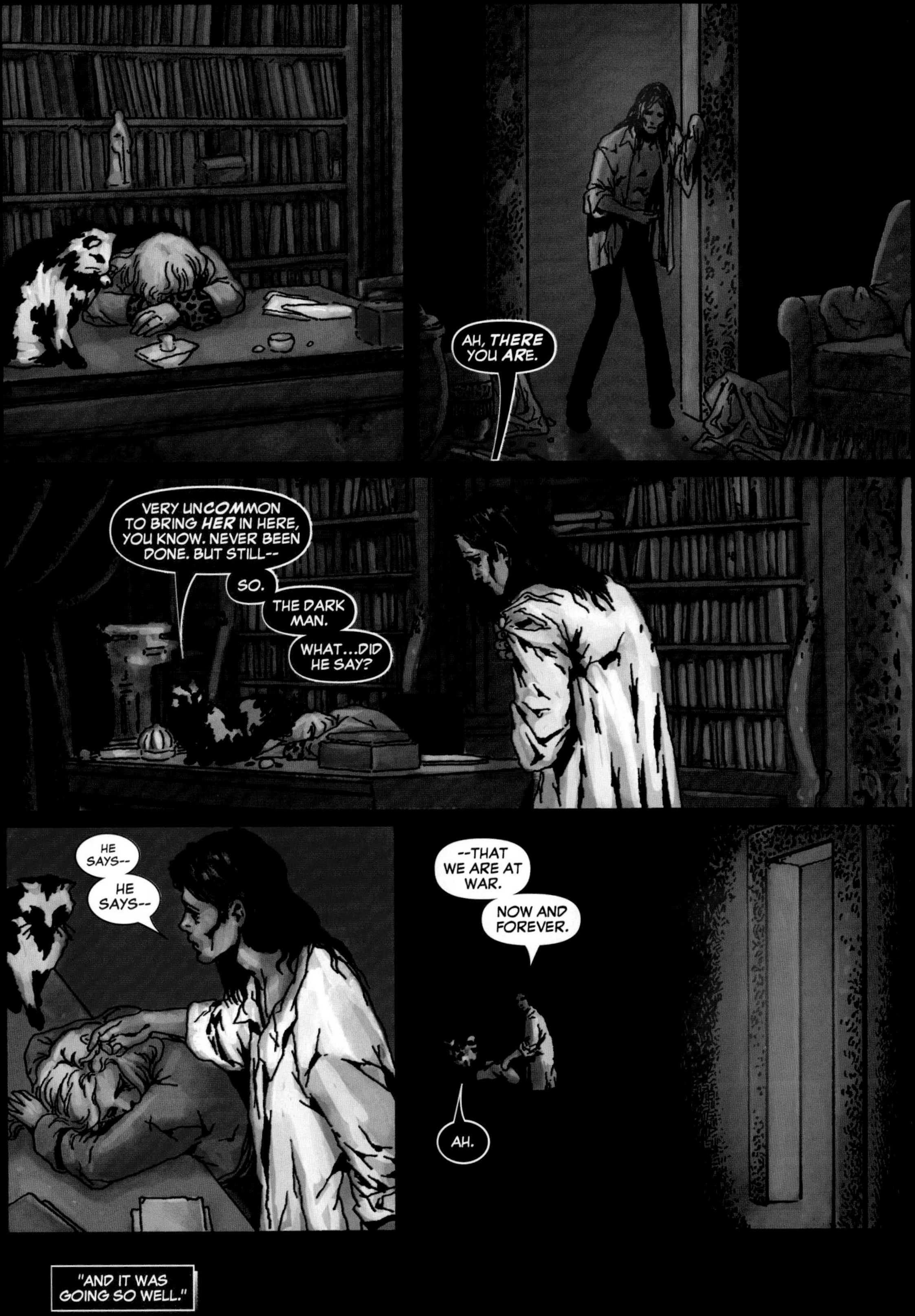
AH, THERE YOU ARE.
VERY UNCOMMON TO BRING HER IN HERE, YOU KNOW. NEVER BEEN DONE. BUT STILL--
SO.
THE DARK MAN.
WHAT...DID HE SAY?
HE SAYS--
HE SAYS--
--THAT WE ARE AT WAR.
NOW AND FOREVER.
AH.
"AND IT WAS GOING SO WELL."

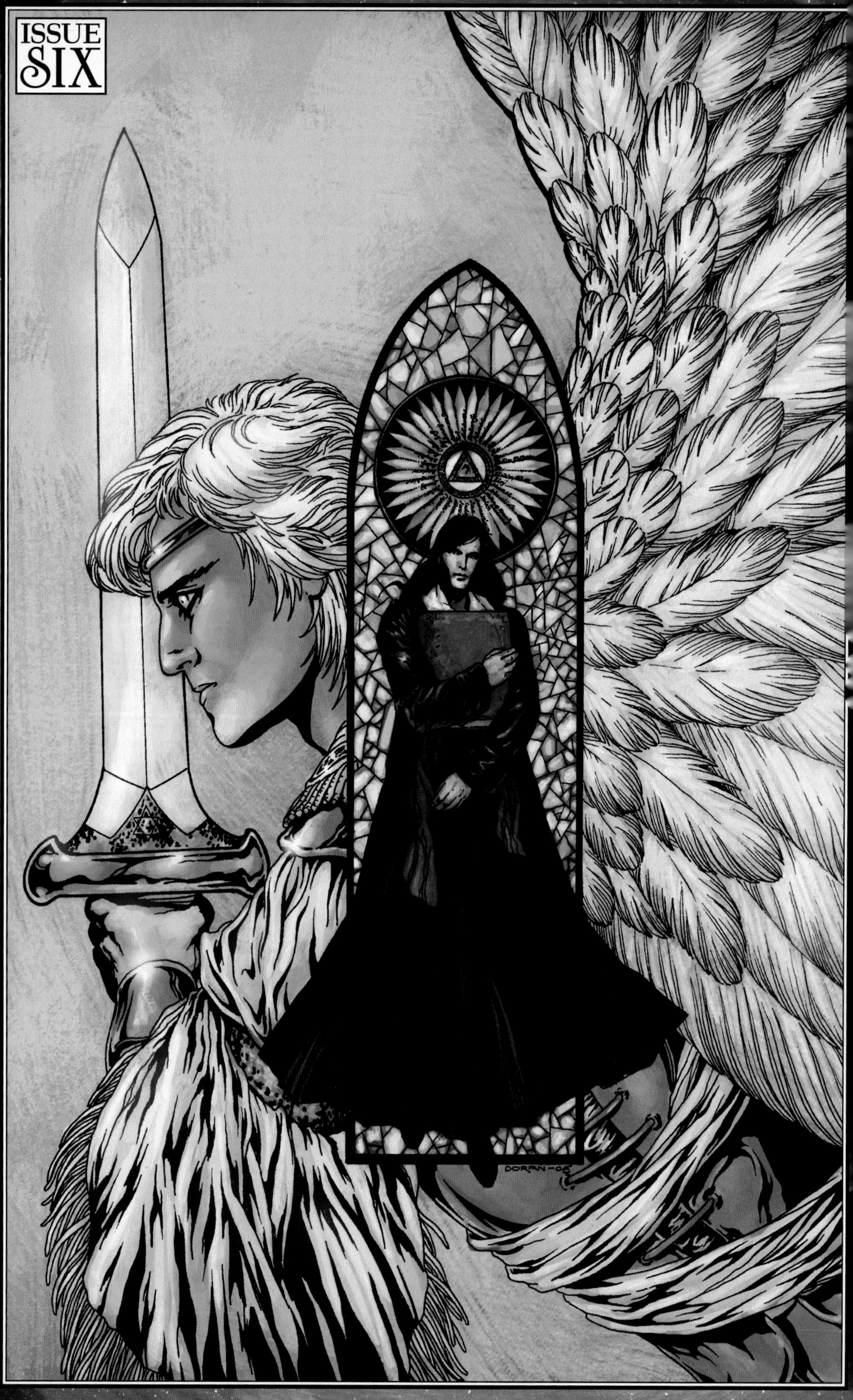
ISSUE SIX
DORAN-05

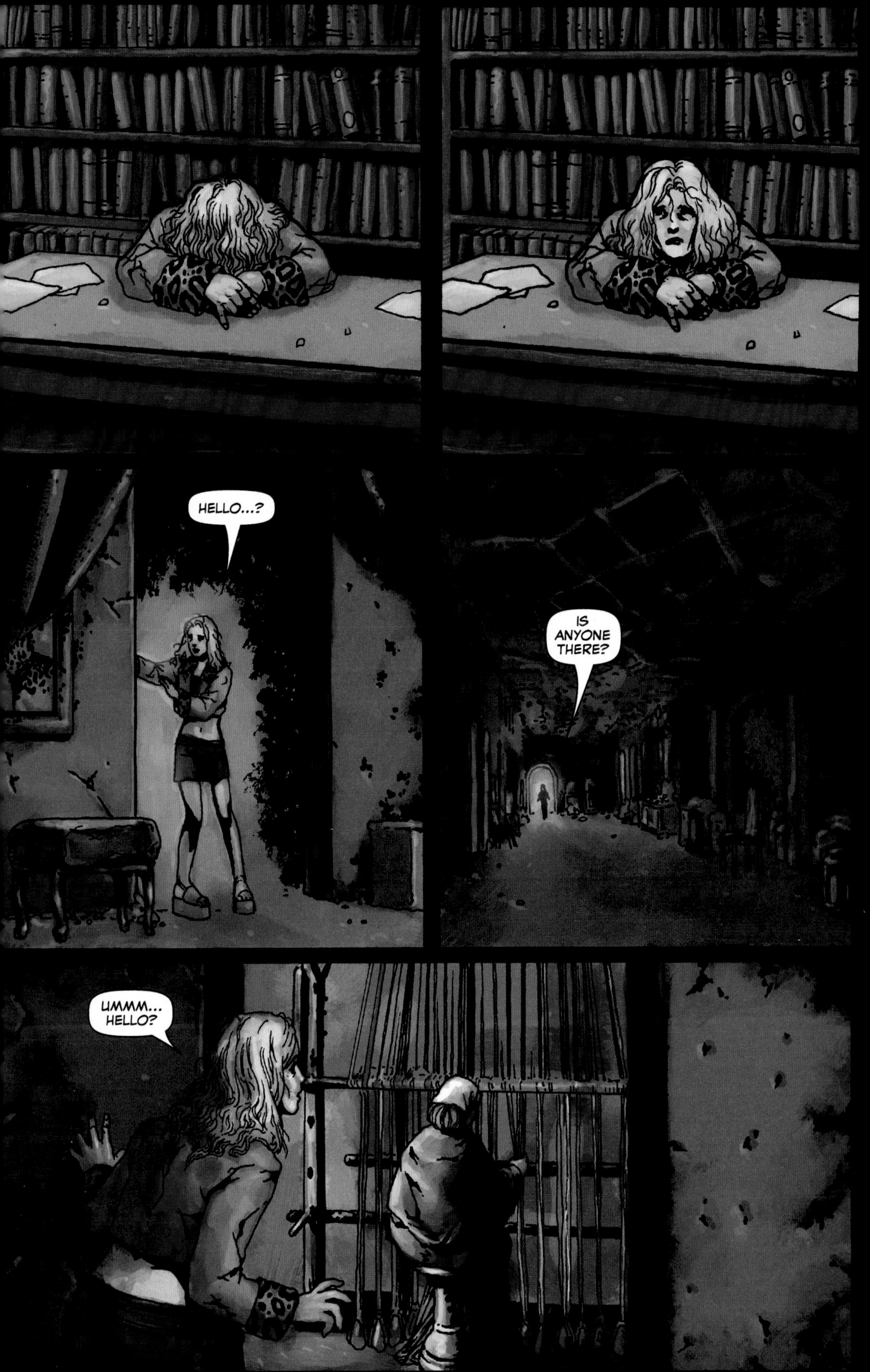
HELLO...?
IS ANYONE THERE?
UMMM... HELLO?

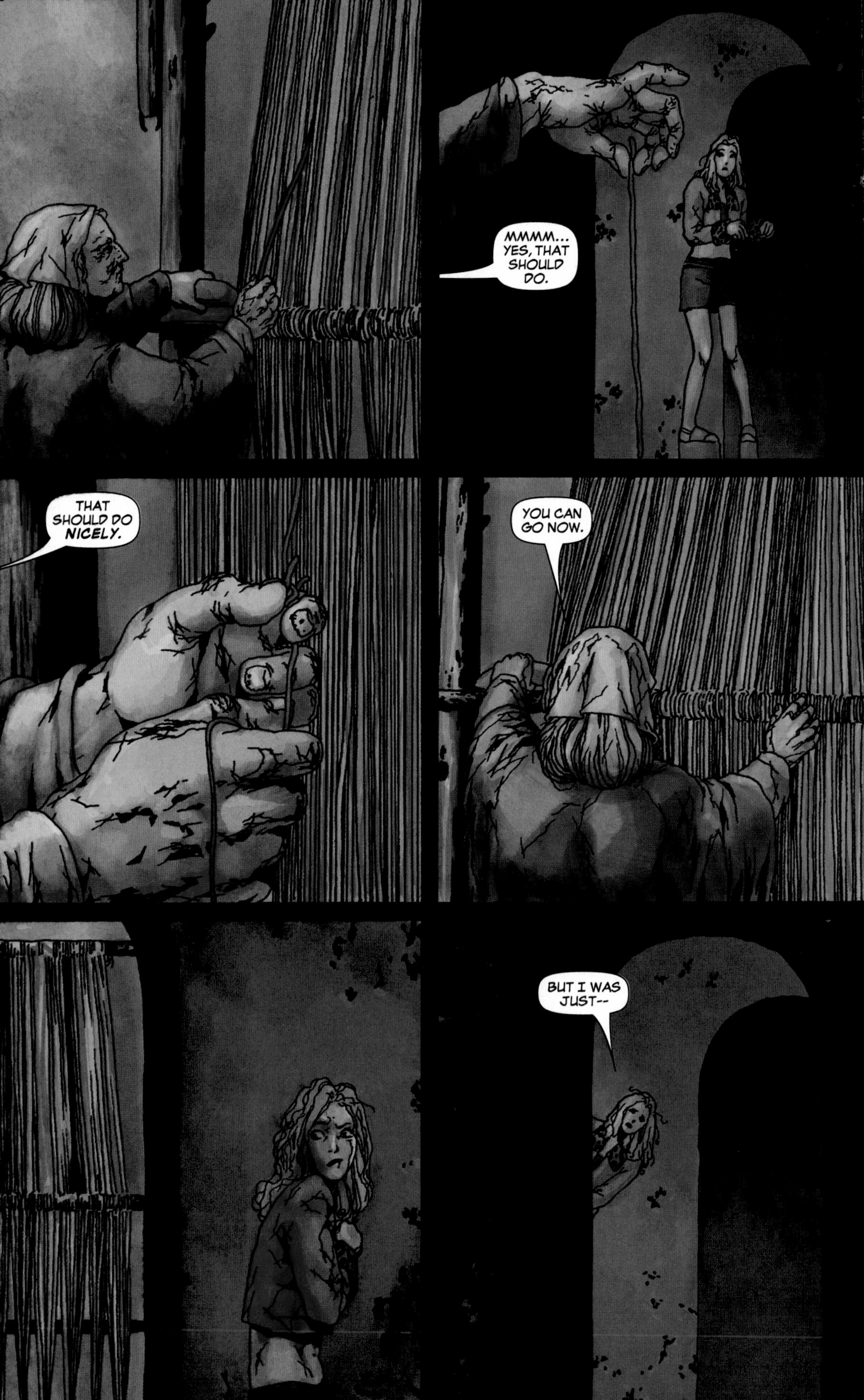
MMMM... YES, THAT SHOULD DO.
THAT SHOULD DO NICELY.
YOU CAN GO NOW.
BUT I WAS JUST--

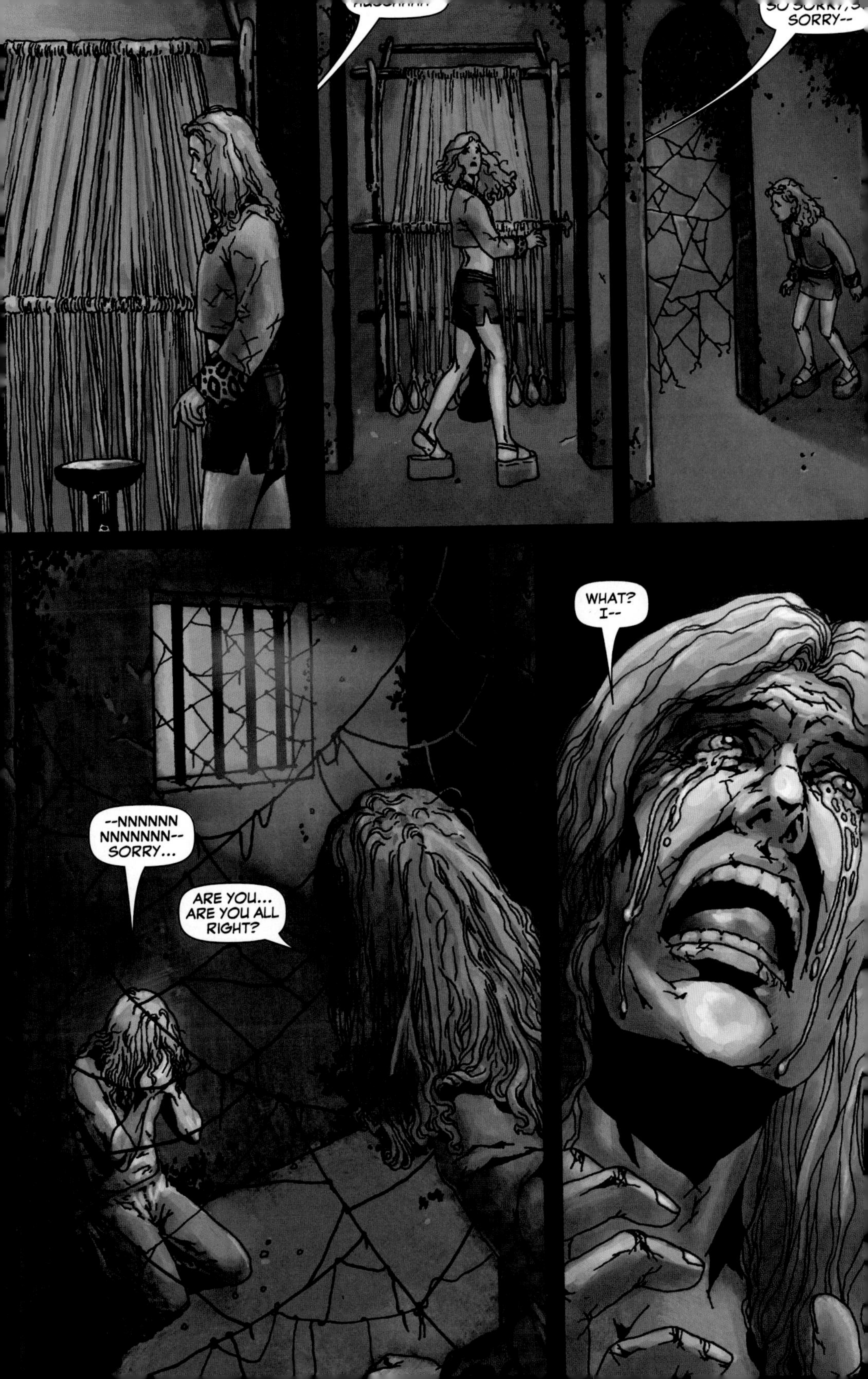
SORRY--
--NNNNNN NNNNNNN-- SORRY...
ARE YOU... ARE YOU ALL RIGHT?
WHAT? I--

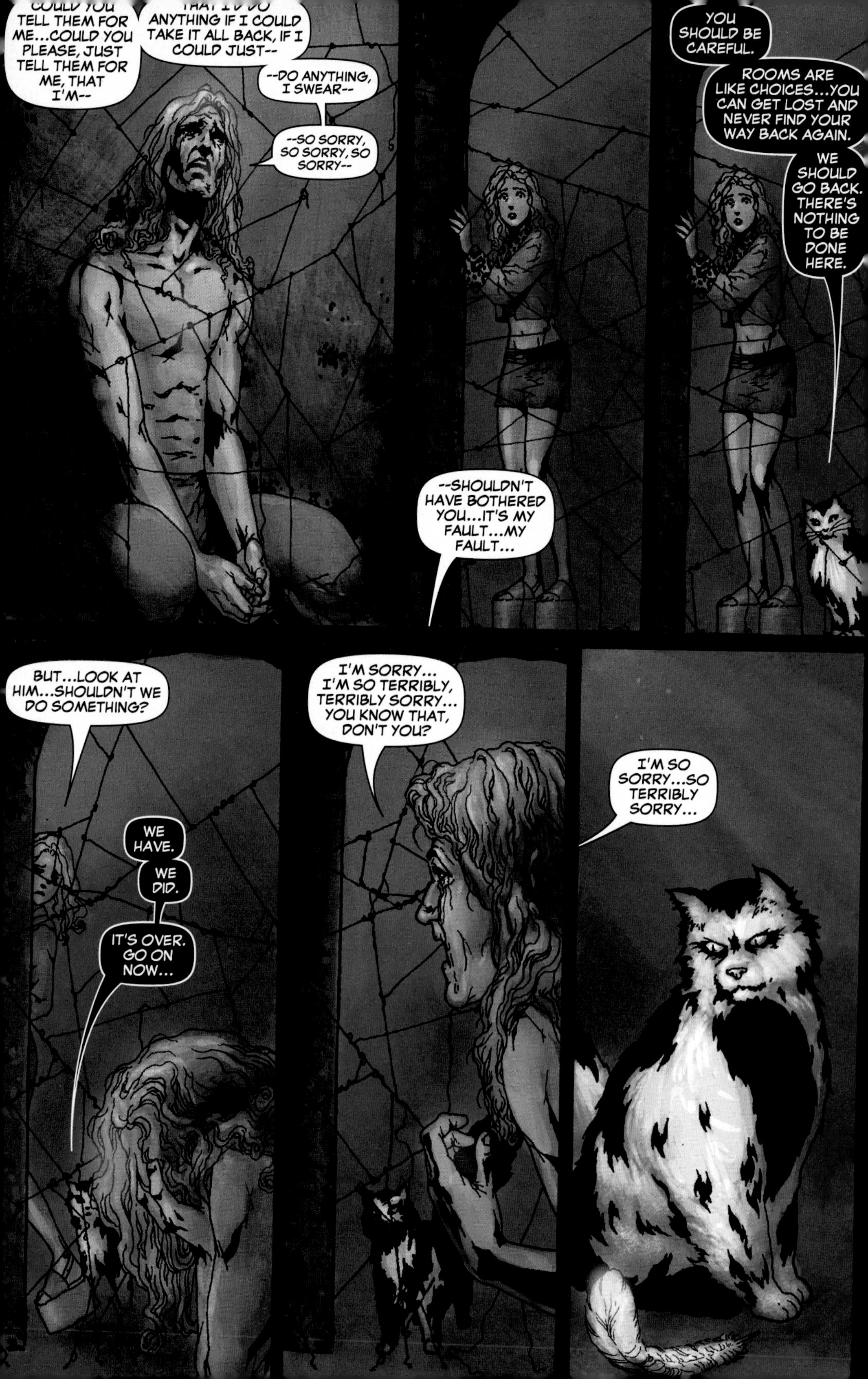
COULD YOU TELL THEM FOR ME...COULD YOU PLEASE, JUST TELL THEM FOR ME, THAT I'M--
THAT I'D DO ANYTHING IF I COULD TAKE IT ALL BACK, IF I COULD JUST--
--DO ANYTHING, I SWEAR--
--SO SORRY, SO SORRY, SO SORRY--
--SHOULDN'T HAVE BOTHERED YOU...IT'S MY FAULT...MY FAULT...
YOU SHOULD BE CAREFUL.
ROOMS ARE LIKE CHOICES...YOU CAN GET LOST AND NEVER FIND YOUR WAY BACK AGAIN.
WE SHOULD GO BACK. THERE'S NOTHING TO BE DONE HERE.
BUT...LOOK AT HIM...SHOULDN'T WE DO SOMETHING?
WE HAVE.
WE DID.
IT'S OVER. GO ON NOW...
I'M SORRY... I'M SO TERRIBLY, TERRIBLY SORRY... YOU KNOW THAT, DON'T YOU?
I'M SO SORRY...SO TERRIBLY SORRY...

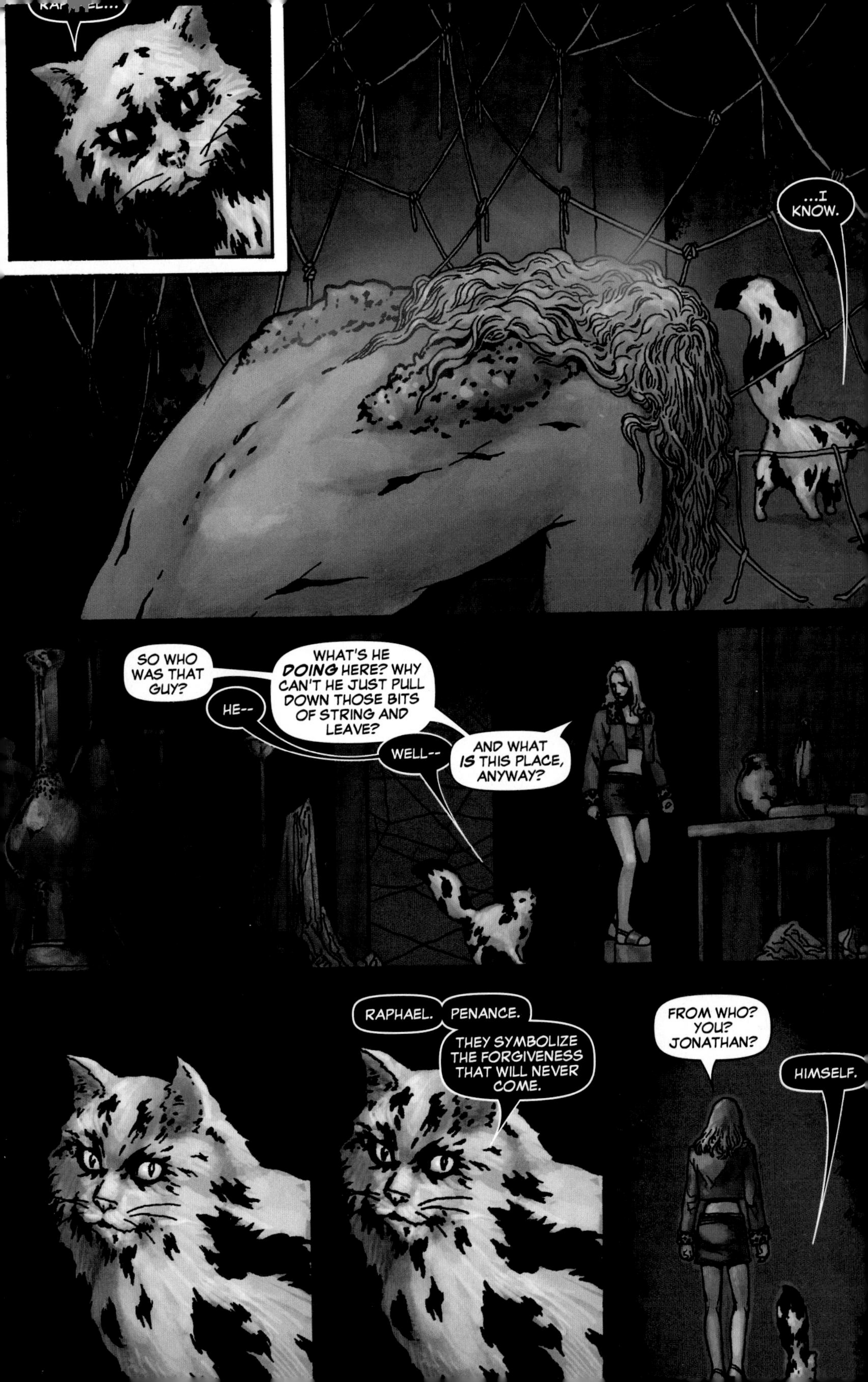
...I KNOW.
SO WHO WAS THAT GUY?
WHAT'S HE DOING HERE? WHY CAN'T HE JUST PULL DOWN THOSE BITS OF STRING AND LEAVE?
HE--
WELL--
AND WHAT IS THIS PLACE, ANYWAY?
RAPHAEL.
PENANCE.
THEY SYMBOLIZE THE FORGIVENESS THAT WILL NEVER COME.
FROM WHO? YOU? JONATHAN?
HIMSELF.

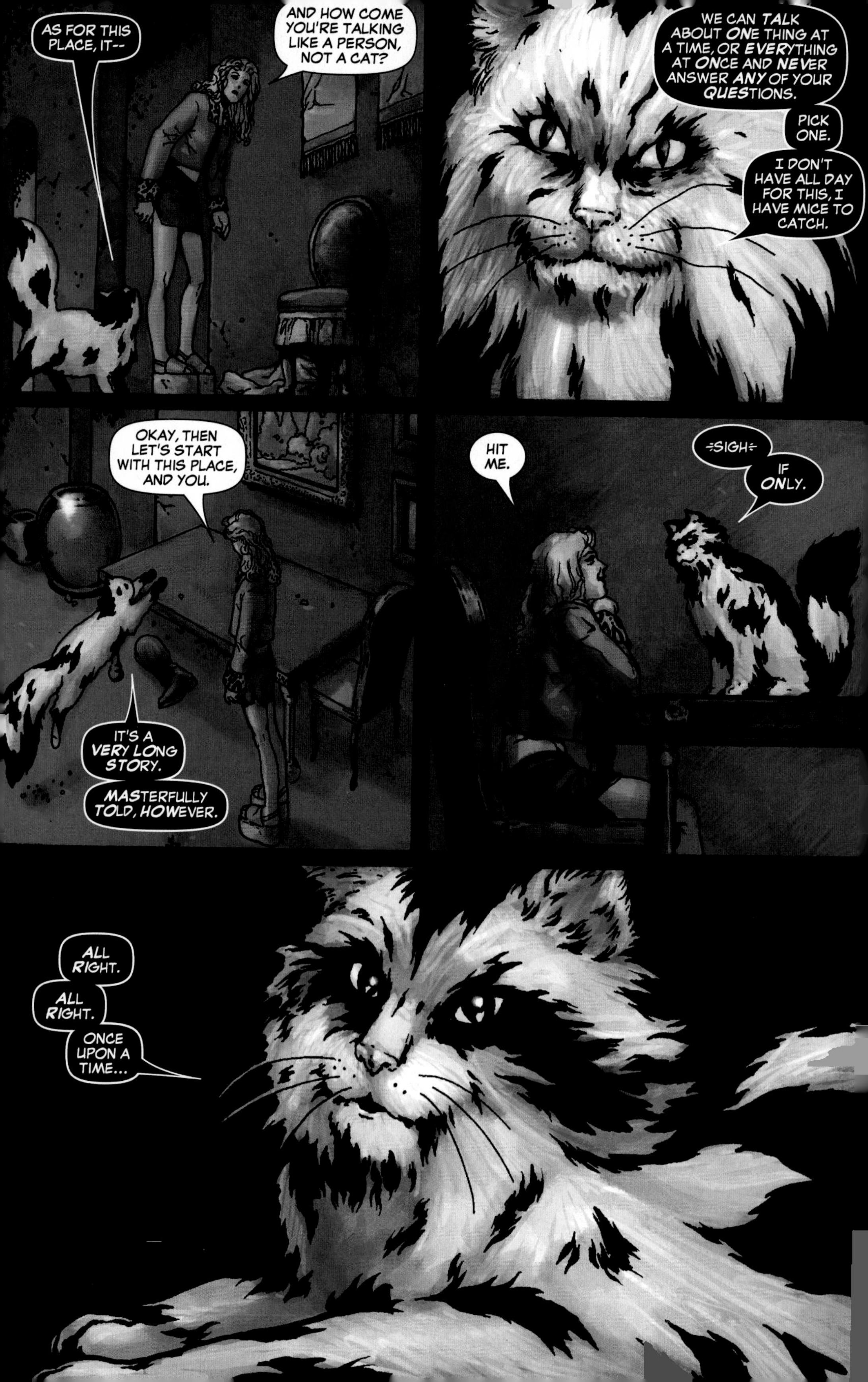
AS FOR THIS PLACE, IT--
AND HOW COME YOU'RE TALKING LIKE A PERSON, NOT A CAT?
WE CAN TALK ABOUT ONE THING AT A TIME, OR EVERYTHING AT ONCE AND NEVER ANSWER ANY OF YOUR QUESTIONS.
PICK ONE.
I DON'T HAVE ALL DAY FOR THIS, I HAVE MICE TO CATCH.
OKAY, THEN LET'S START WITH THIS PLACE, AND YOU.
IT'S A VERY LONG STORY.
MASTERFULLY TOLD, HOWEVER.
HIT ME.
=SIGH=
IF ONLY.
ALL RIGHT.
ALL RIGHT.
ONCE UPON A TIME...

"...THERE WAS THE VOID...

"...AND THE TWO...

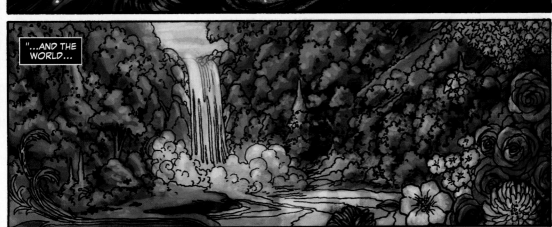

"...AND THE WORLD...

...AND THE TWO.

"THE *OTHER* TWO.

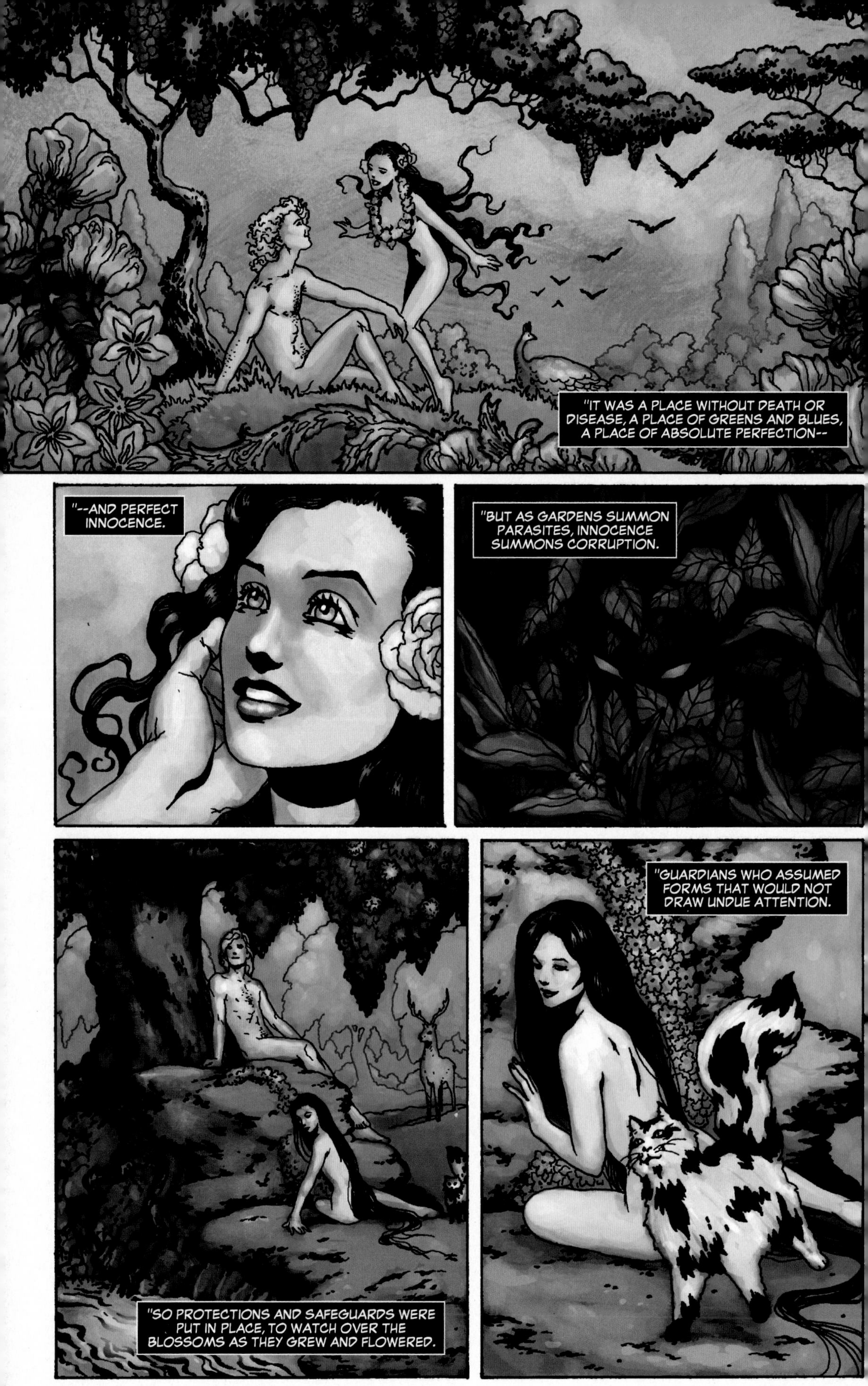
"IT WAS A PLACE WITHOUT DEATH OR DISEASE, A PLACE OF GREENS AND BLUES, A PLACE OF ABSOLUTE PERFECTION--
"--AND PERFECT INNOCENCE.
"BUT AS GARDENS SUMMON PARASITES, INNOCENCE SUMMONS CORRUPTION.
"SO PROTECTIONS AND SAFEGUARDS WERE PUT IN PLACE, TO WATCH OVER THE BLOSSOMS AS THEY GREW AND FLOWERED.
"GUARDIANS WHO ASSUMED FORMS THAT WOULD NOT DRAW UNDUE ATTENTION.

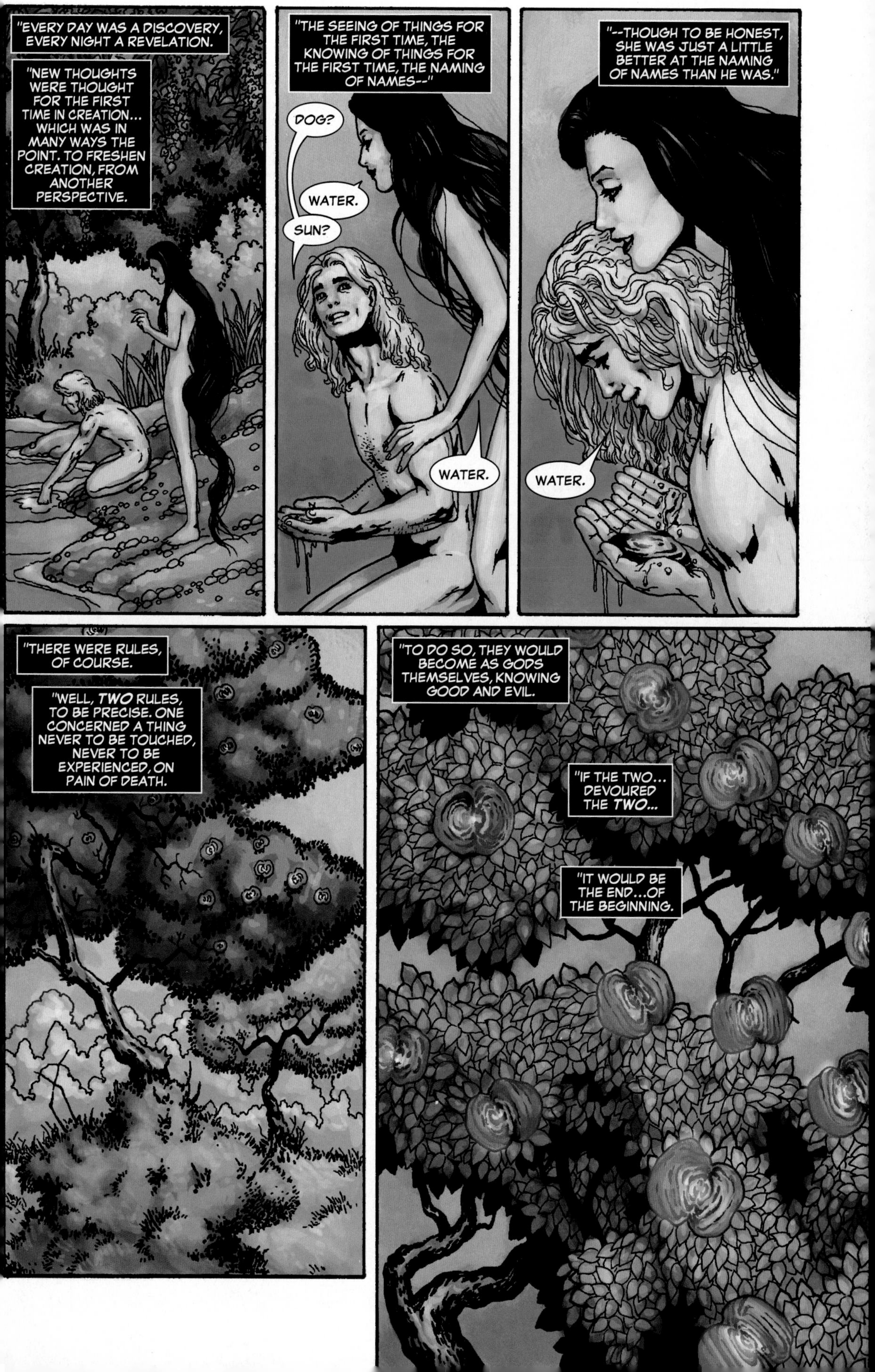
"EVERY DAY WAS A DISCOVERY, EVERY NIGHT A REVELATION.
"NEW THOUGHTS WERE THOUGHT FOR THE FIRST TIME IN CREATION... WHICH WAS IN MANY WAYS THE POINT. TO FRESHEN CREATION, FROM ANOTHER PERSPECTIVE.
"THE SEEING OF THINGS FOR THE FIRST TIME, THE KNOWING OF THINGS FOR THE FIRST TIME, THE NAMING OF NAMES--"
DOG?
WATER.
SUN?
WATER.
"--THOUGH TO BE HONEST, SHE WAS JUST A LITTLE BETTER AT THE NAMING OF NAMES THAN HE WAS."
WATER.
"THERE WERE RULES, OF COURSE.
"WELL, TWO RULES, TO BE PRECISE. ONE CONCERNED A THING NEVER TO BE TOUCHED, NEVER TO BE EXPERIENCED, ON PAIN OF DEATH.
"TO DO SO, THEY WOULD BECOME AS GODS THEMSELVES, KNOWING GOOD AND EVIL.
"IF THE TWO... DEVOURED THE TWO...
"IT WOULD BE THE END...OF THE BEGINNING.

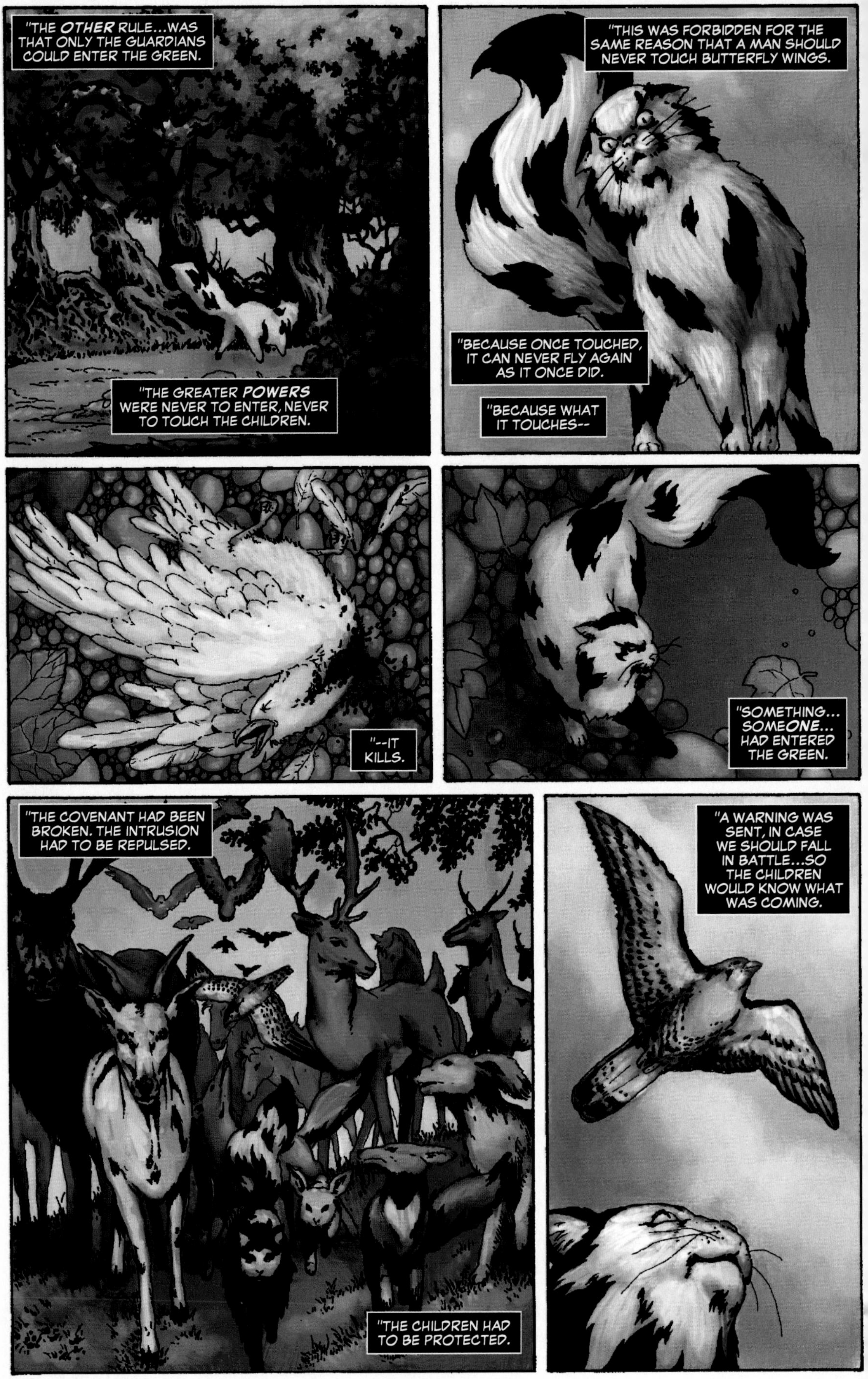
"THE OTHER RULE...WAS THAT ONLY THE GUARDIANS COULD ENTER THE GREEN.
"THE GREATER POWERS WERE NEVER TO ENTER, NEVER TO TOUCH THE CHILDREN.
"THIS WAS FORBIDDEN FOR THE SAME REASON THAT A MAN SHOULD NEVER TOUCH BUTTERFLY WINGS.
"BECAUSE ONCE TOUCHED, IT CAN NEVER FLY AGAIN AS IT ONCE DID.
"BECAUSE WHAT IT TOUCHES--
"--IT KILLS.
"SOMETHING... SOMEONE... HAD ENTERED THE GREEN.
"THE COVENANT HAD BEEN BROKEN. THE INTRUSION HAD TO BE REPULSED.
"THE CHILDREN HAD TO BE PROTECTED.
"A WARNING WAS SENT, IN CASE WE SHOULD FALL IN BATTLE...SO THE CHILDREN WOULD KNOW WHAT WAS COMING.

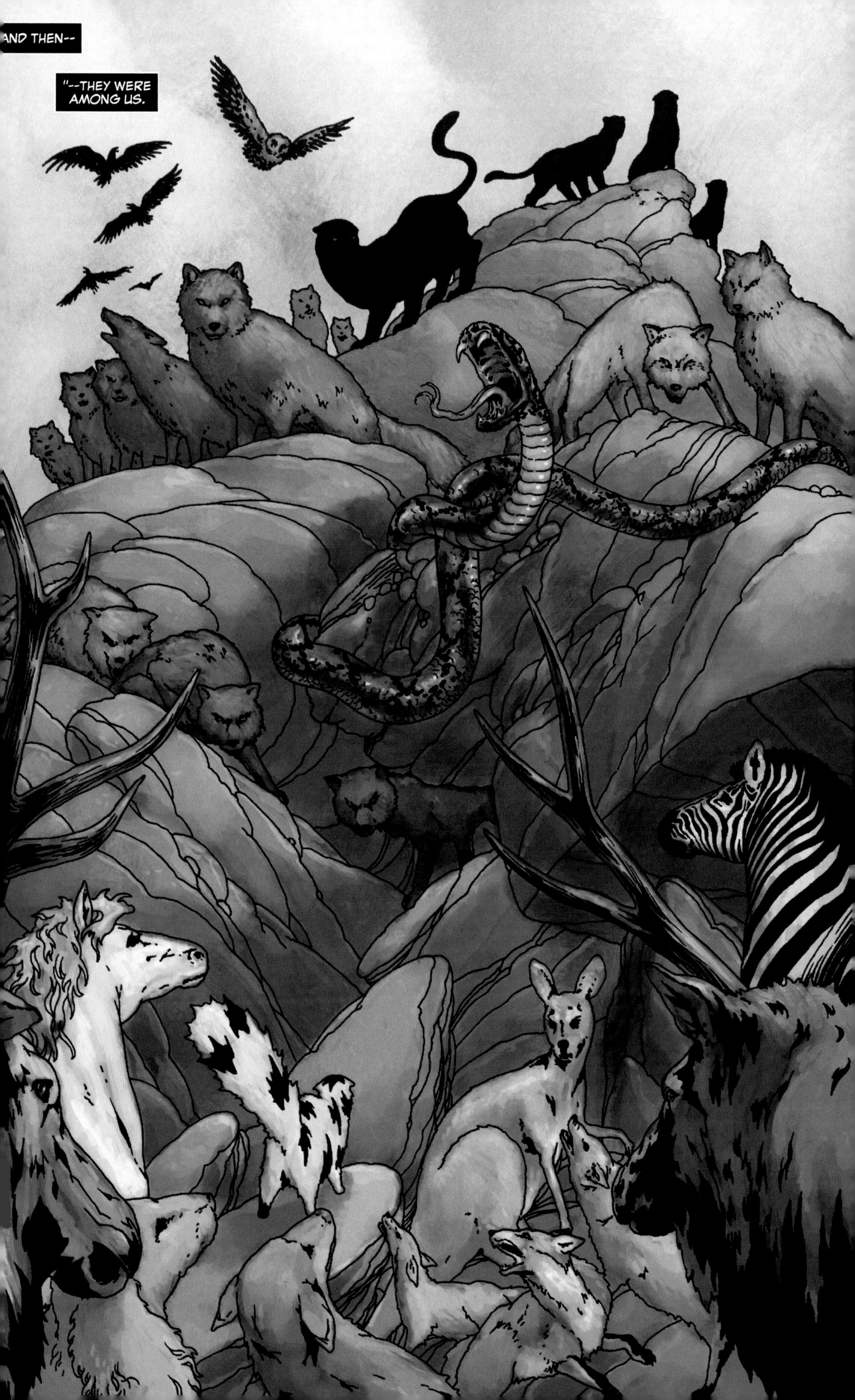
AND THEN--
"--THEY WERE AMONG US.

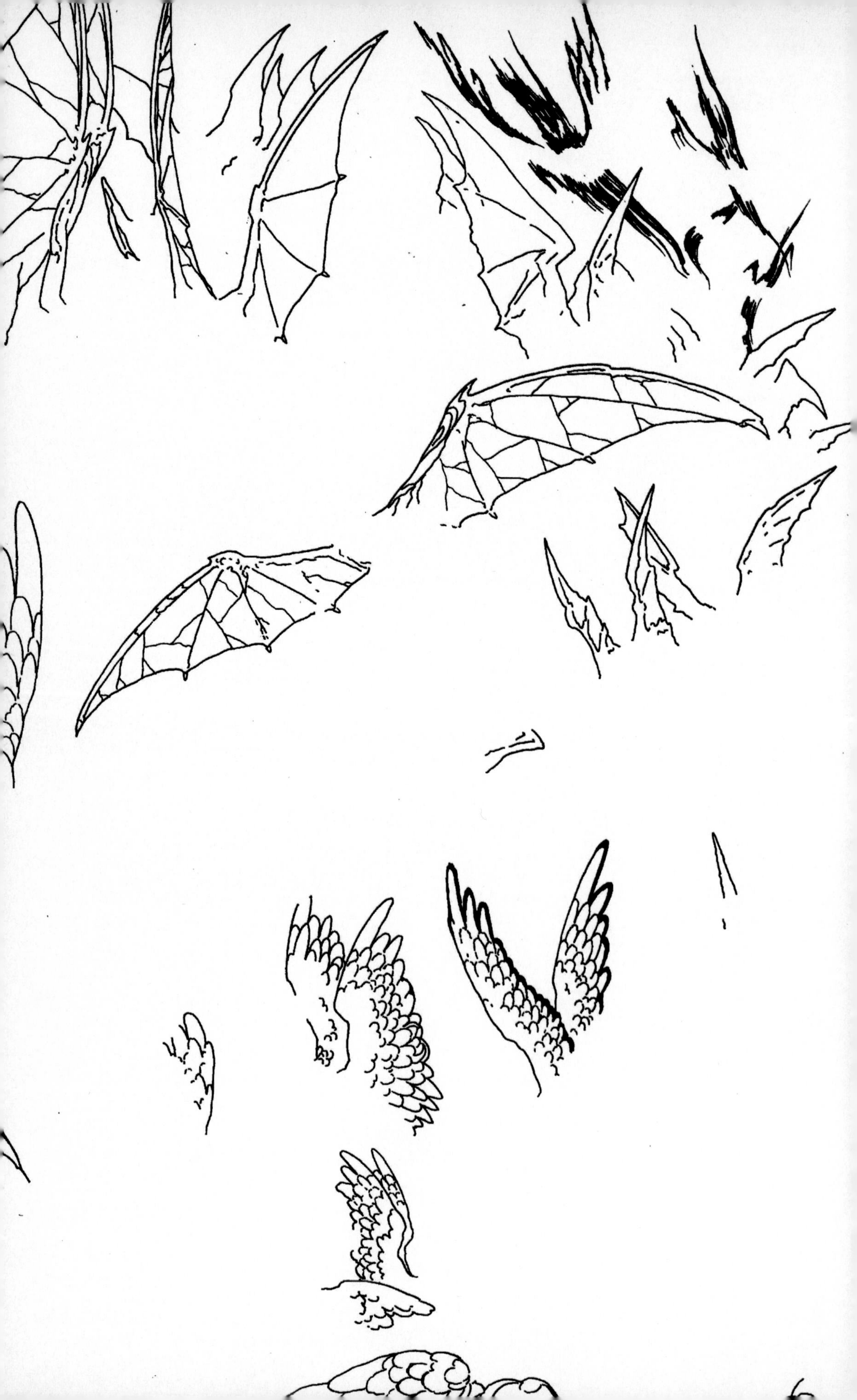

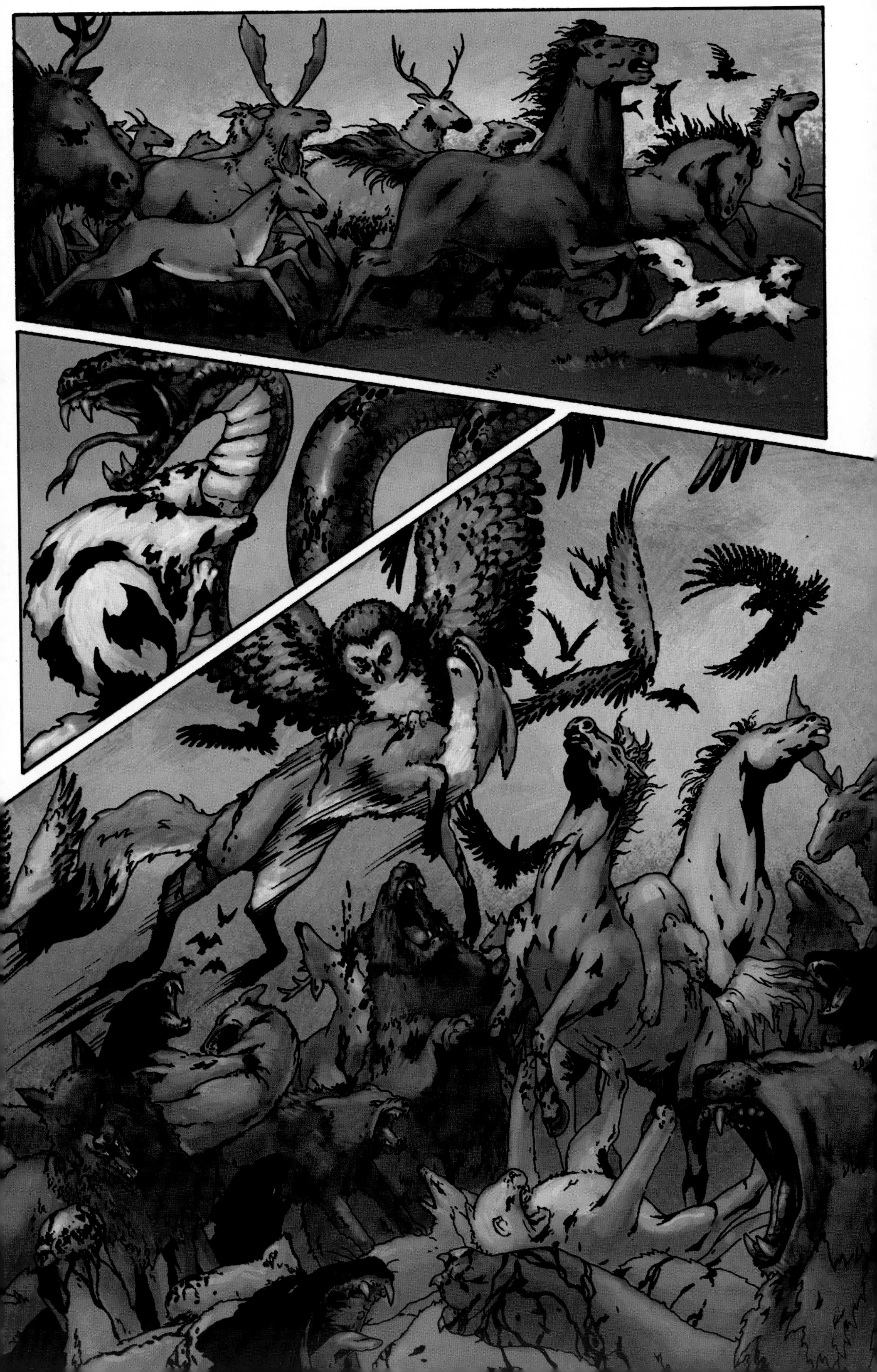

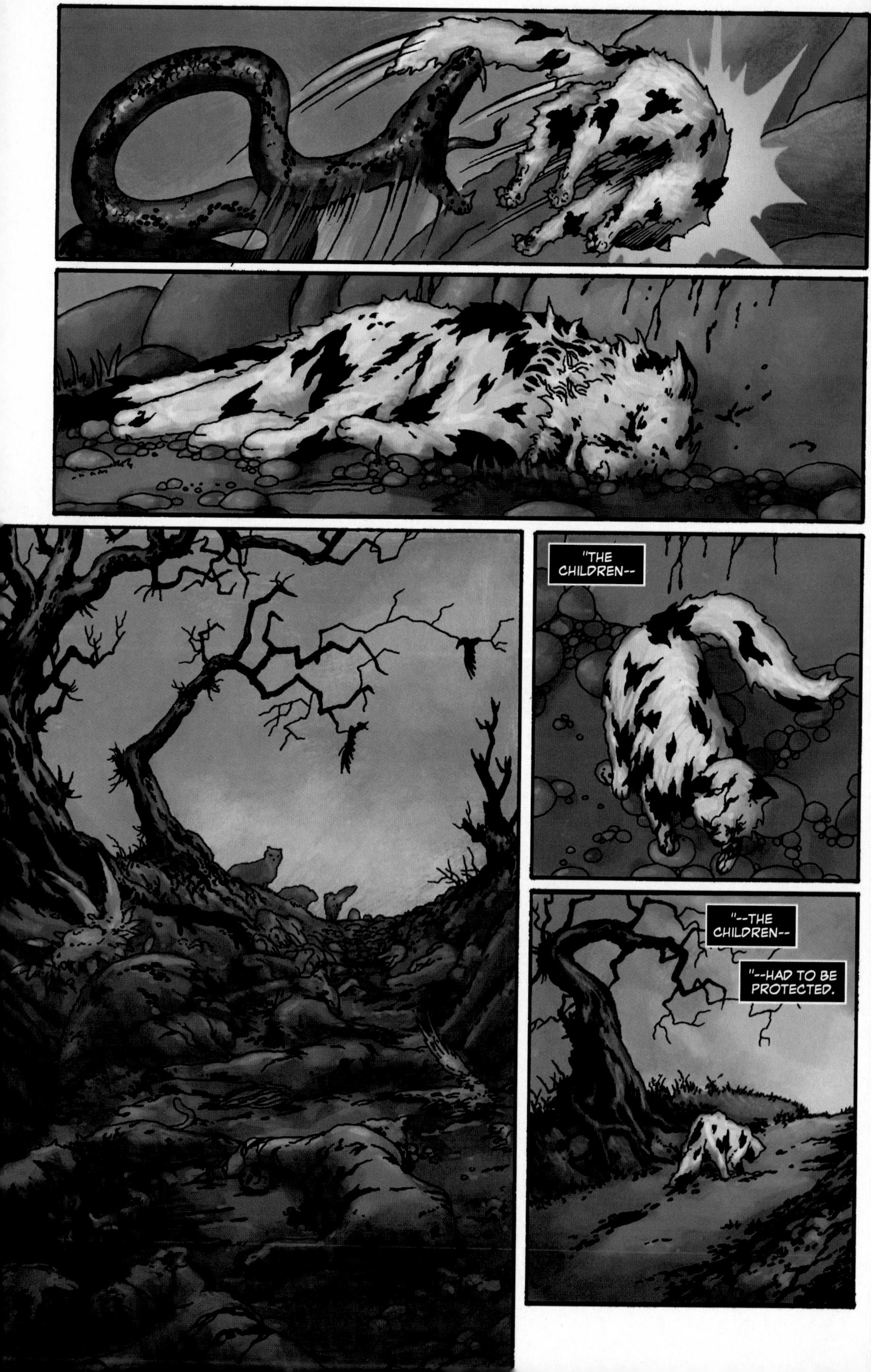
"THE CHILDREN--
"--THE CHILDREN--
"--HAD TO BE PROTECTED.

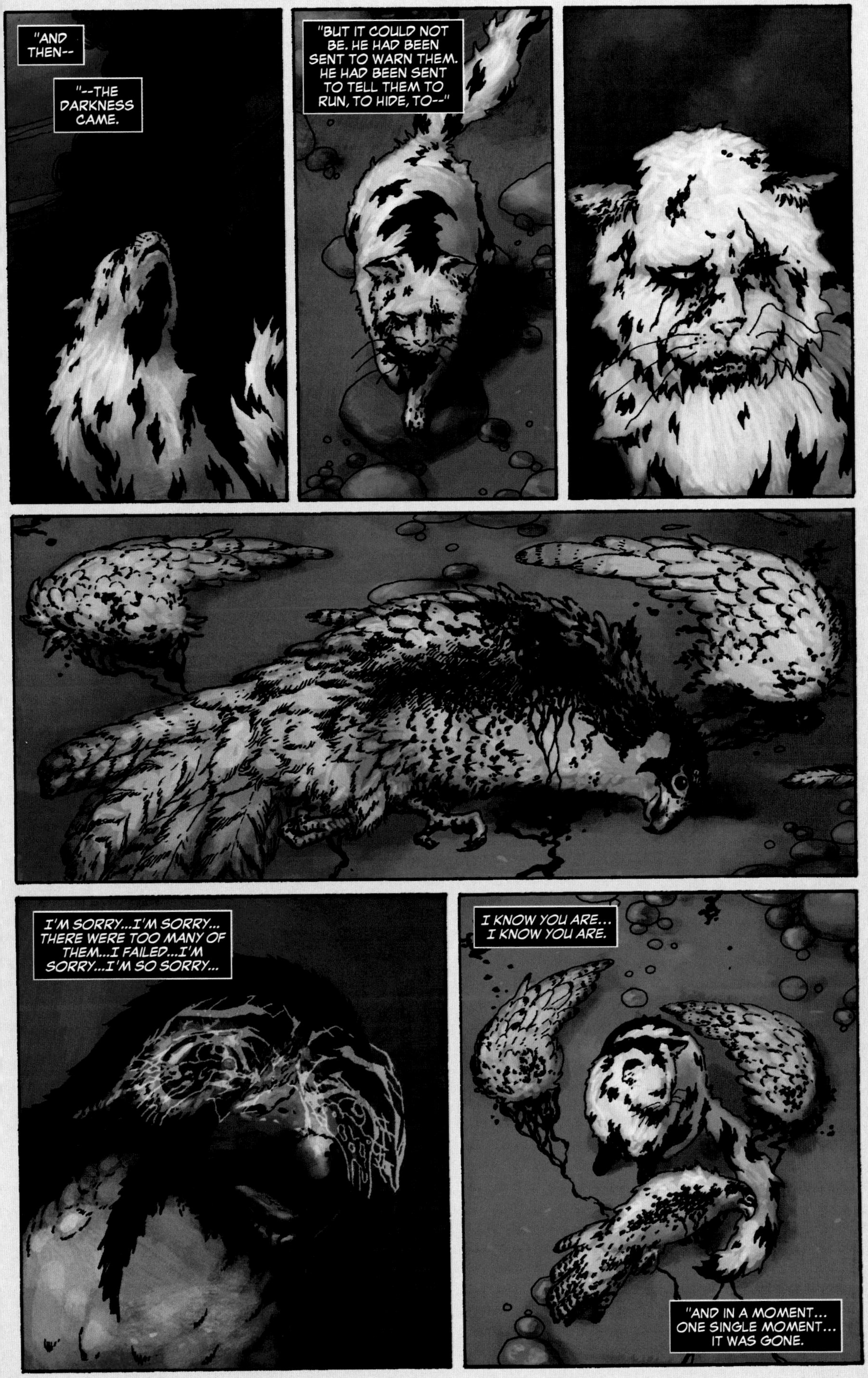
"AND THEN--
"--THE DARKNESS CAME.
"BUT IT COULD NOT BE. HE HAD BEEN SENT TO WARN THEM. HE HAD BEEN SENT TO TELL THEM TO RUN, TO HIDE, TO--"
I'M SORRY...I'M SORRY... THERE WERE TOO MANY OF THEM...I FAILED...I'M SORRY...I'M SO SORRY...
I KNOW YOU ARE... I KNOW YOU ARE.
"AND IN A MOMENT... ONE SINGLE MOMENT... IT WAS GONE.

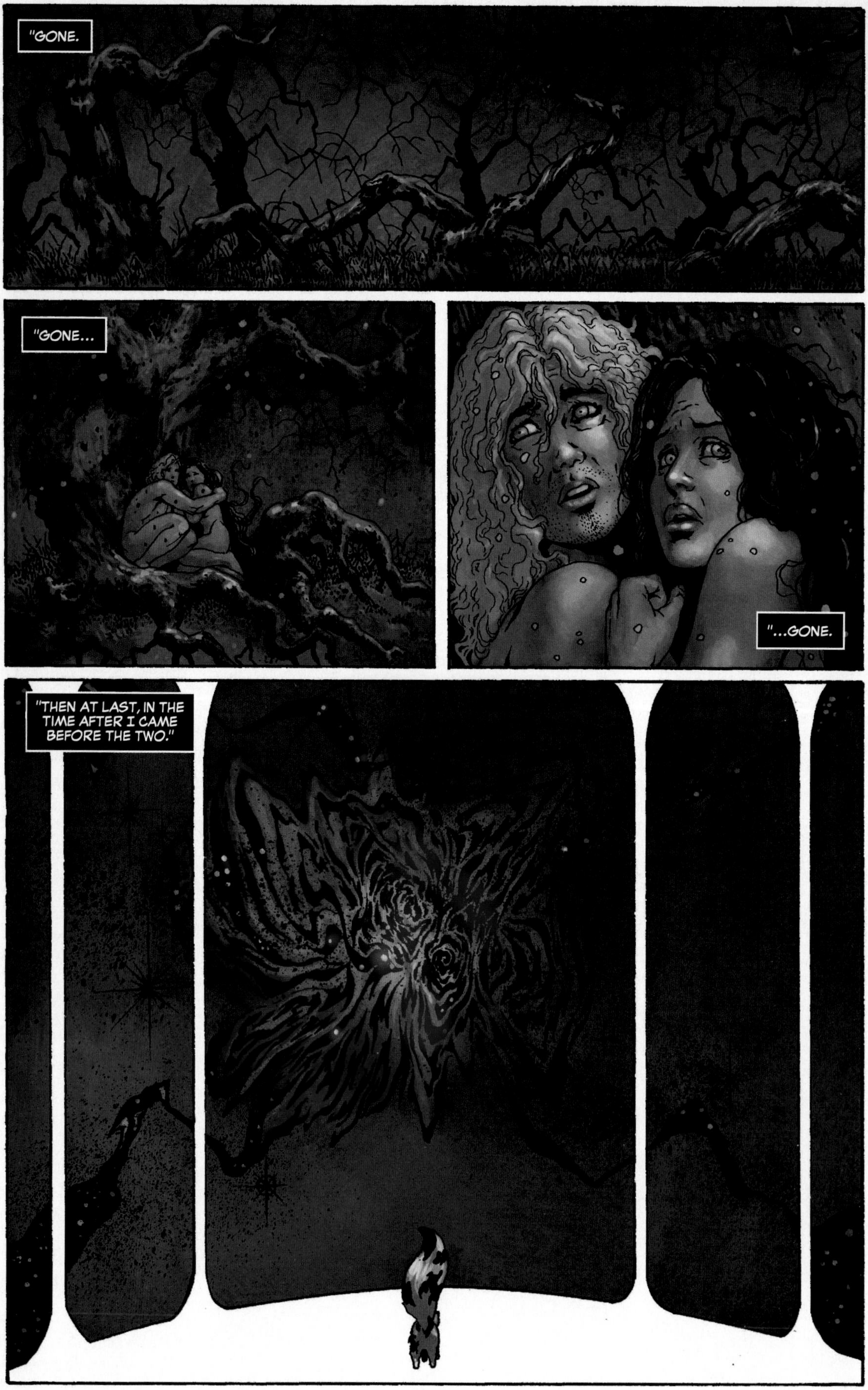
"GONE.
"GONE...
"...GONE.
"THEN AT LAST, IN THE TIME AFTER I CAME BEFORE THE TWO."

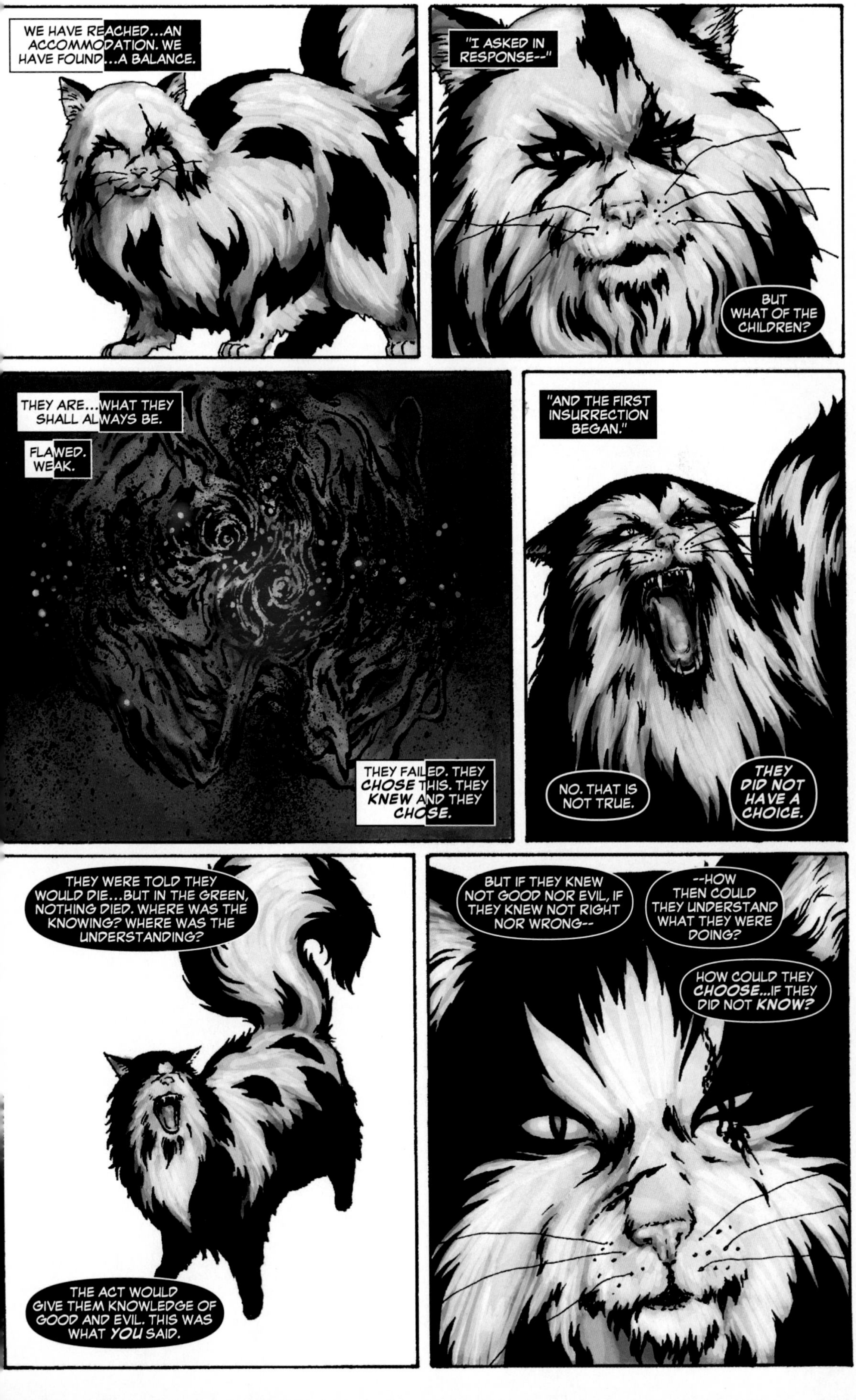
WE HAVE REACHED...AN ACCOMMODATION. WE HAVE FOUND...A BALANCE.
"I ASKED IN RESPONSE--"
BUT WHAT OF THE CHILDREN?
THEY ARE...WHAT THEY SHALL ALWAYS BE.
FLAWED. WEAK.
THEY FAILED. THEY CHOSE THIS. THEY KNEW AND THEY CHOSE.
"AND THE FIRST INSURRECTION BEGAN."
NO. THAT IS NOT TRUE.
THEY DID NOT HAVE A CHOICE.
THEY WERE TOLD THEY WOULD DIE...BUT IN THE GREEN, NOTHING DIED. WHERE WAS THE KNOWING? WHERE WAS THE UNDERSTANDING?
THE ACT WOULD GIVE THEM KNOWLEDGE OF GOOD AND EVIL. THIS WAS WHAT YOU SAID.
BUT IF THEY KNEW NOT GOOD NOR EVIL, IF THEY KNEW NOT RIGHT NOR WRONG--
--HOW THEN COULD THEY UNDERSTAND WHAT THEY WERE DOING?
HOW COULD THEY CHOOSE...IF THEY DID NOT KNOW?

AND THERE IS SOMETHING *ELSE* THEY DID NOT KNOW.

UNTIL THE MOMENT *YOU* CAME... UNTIL THE MOMENT YOU *SPOKE*--

--UNTIL THAT DAY--

--THEY DID NOT KNOW--

--WHAT A *LIE* WAS.

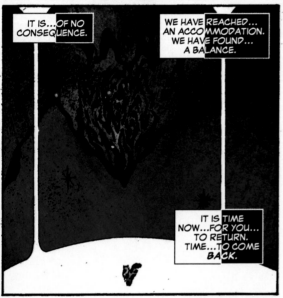

IT IS...OF NO CONSEQUENCE.

WE HAVE REACHED... AN ACCOMMODATION. WE HAVE FOUND... A BALANCE.

IT IS TIME NOW...FOR YOU... TO RETURN. TIME...TO COME *BACK*.

TIME...TO COME *BACK*.

"AND THE SECOND INSURRECTION...BEGAN."

NO.

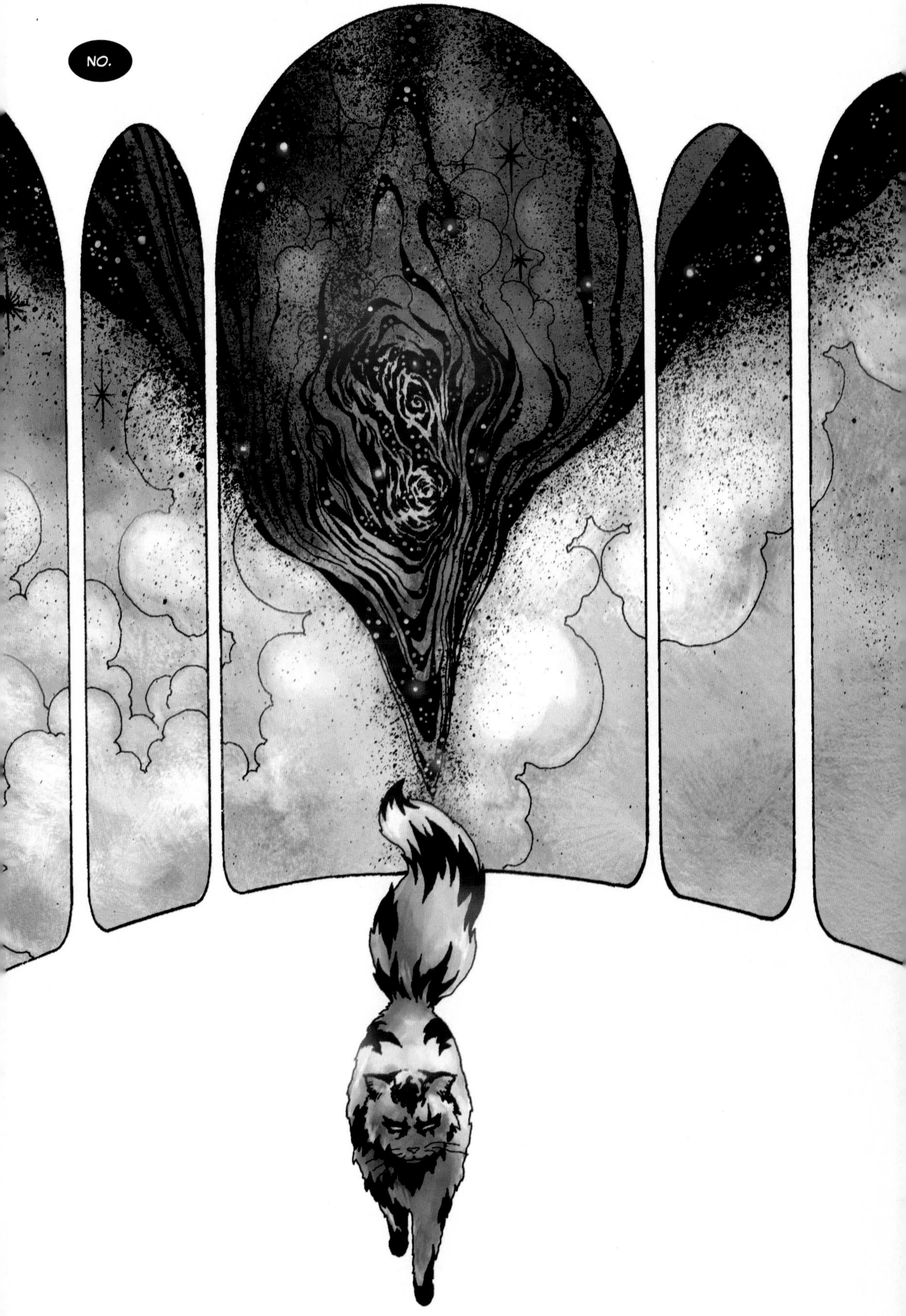
NO.

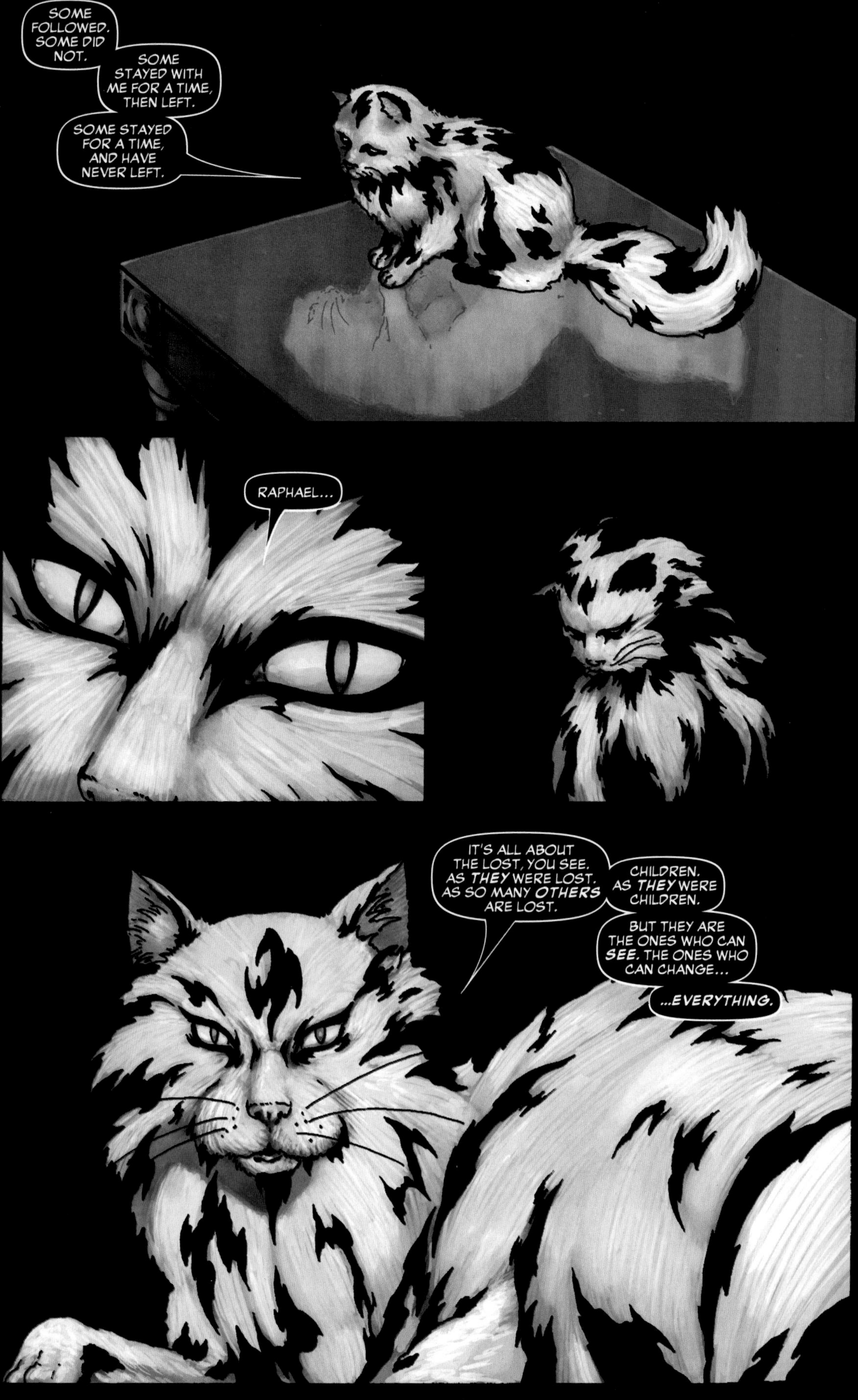
SOME FOLLOWED. SOME DID NOT.
SOME STAYED WITH ME FOR A TIME, THEN LEFT.
SOME STAYED FOR A TIME, AND HAVE NEVER LEFT.
RAPHAEL...
IT'S ALL ABOUT THE LOST, YOU SEE. AS THEY WERE LOST. AS SO MANY OTHERS ARE LOST.
CHILDREN. AS THEY WERE CHILDREN.
BUT THEY ARE THE ONES WHO CAN SEE. THE ONES WHO CAN CHANGE...
...EVERYTHING.

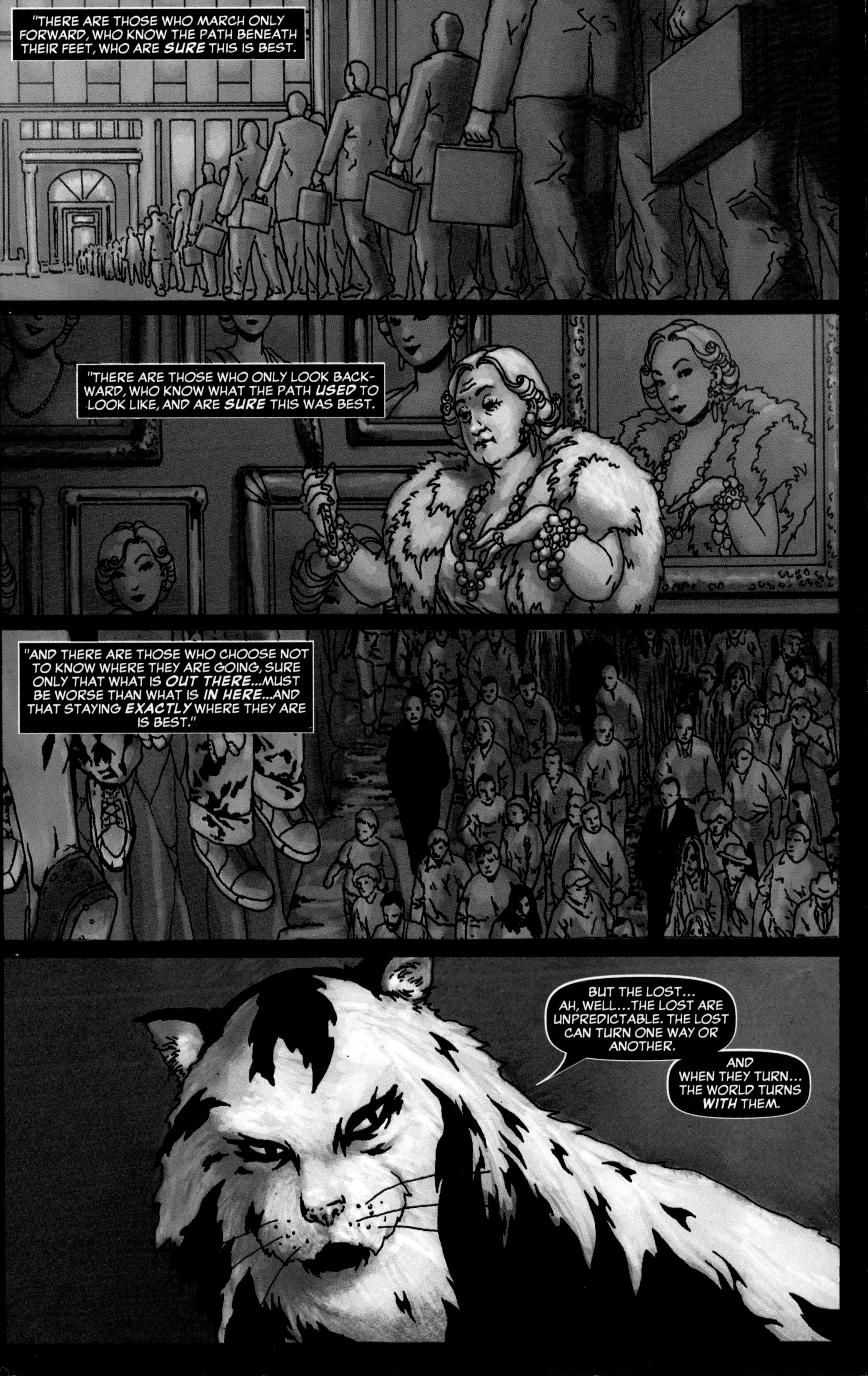
"THERE ARE THOSE WHO MARCH ONLY FORWARD, WHO KNOW THE PATH BENEATH THEIR FEET, WHO ARE SURE THIS IS BEST.
"THERE ARE THOSE WHO ONLY LOOK BACKWARD, WHO KNOW WHAT THE PATH USED TO LOOK LIKE, AND ARE SURE THIS WAS BEST.
"AND THERE ARE THOSE WHO CHOOSE NOT TO KNOW WHERE THEY ARE GOING, SURE ONLY THAT WHAT IS OUT THERE...MUST BE WORSE THAN WHAT IS IN HERE...AND THAT STAYING EXACTLY WHERE THEY ARE IS BEST."
BUT THE LOST... AH, WELL...THE LOST ARE UNPREDICTABLE. THE LOST CAN TURN ONE WAY OR ANOTHER.
AND WHEN THEY TURN... THE WORLD TURNS WITH THEM.

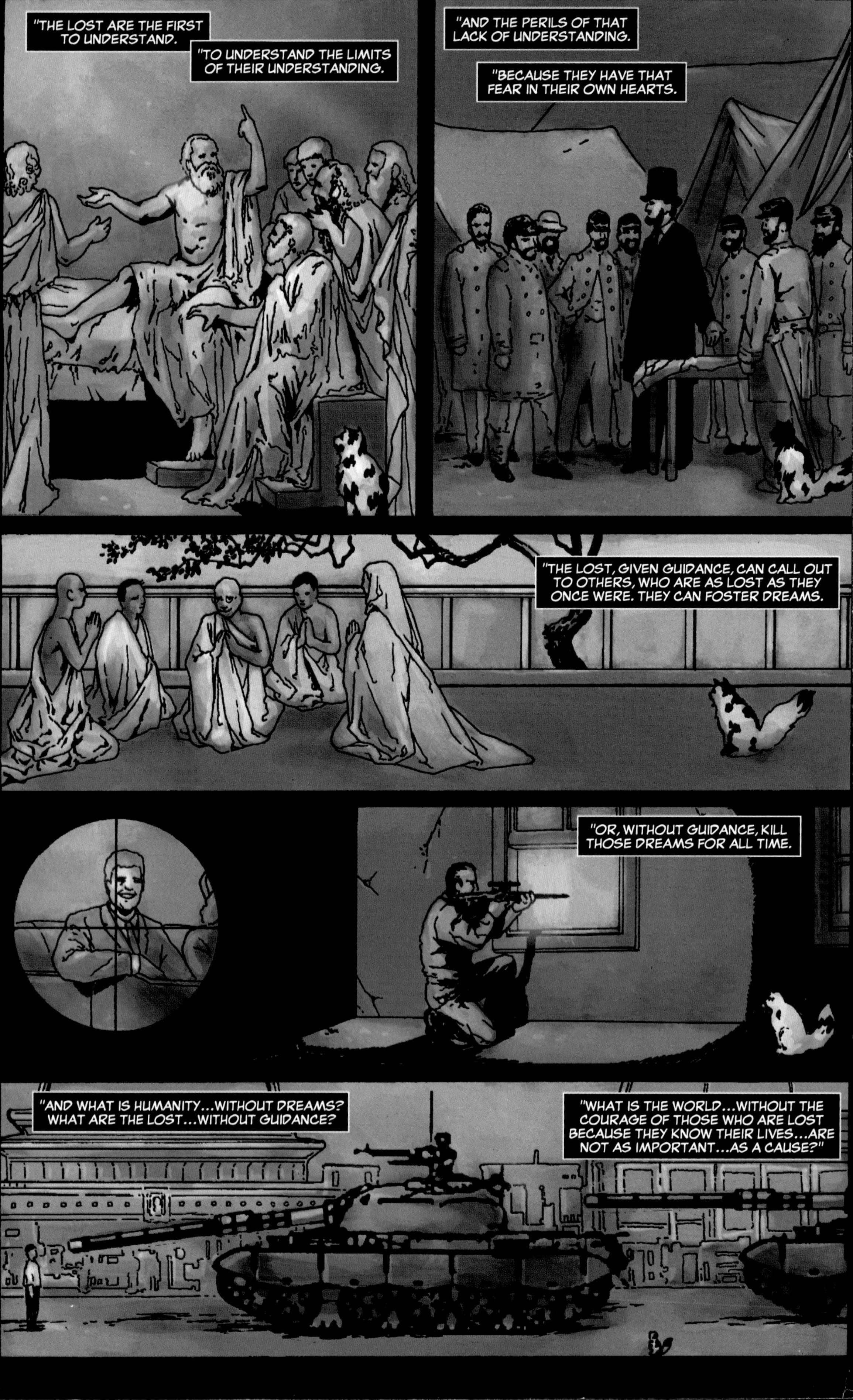
"THE LOST ARE THE FIRST TO UNDERSTAND.
"TO UNDERSTAND THE LIMITS OF THEIR UNDERSTANDING.
"AND THE PERILS OF THAT LACK OF UNDERSTANDING.
"BECAUSE THEY HAVE THAT FEAR IN THEIR OWN HEARTS.
"THE LOST, GIVEN GUIDANCE, CAN CALL OUT TO OTHERS, WHO ARE AS LOST AS THEY ONCE WERE. THEY CAN FOSTER DREAMS.
"OR, WITHOUT GUIDANCE, KILL THOSE DREAMS FOR ALL TIME.
"AND WHAT IS HUMANITY...WITHOUT DREAMS? WHAT ARE THE LOST...WITHOUT GUIDANCE?
"WHAT IS THE WORLD...WITHOUT THE COURAGE OF THOSE WHO ARE LOST BECAUSE THEY KNOW THEIR LIVES...ARE NOT AS IMPORTANT...AS A CAUSE?"

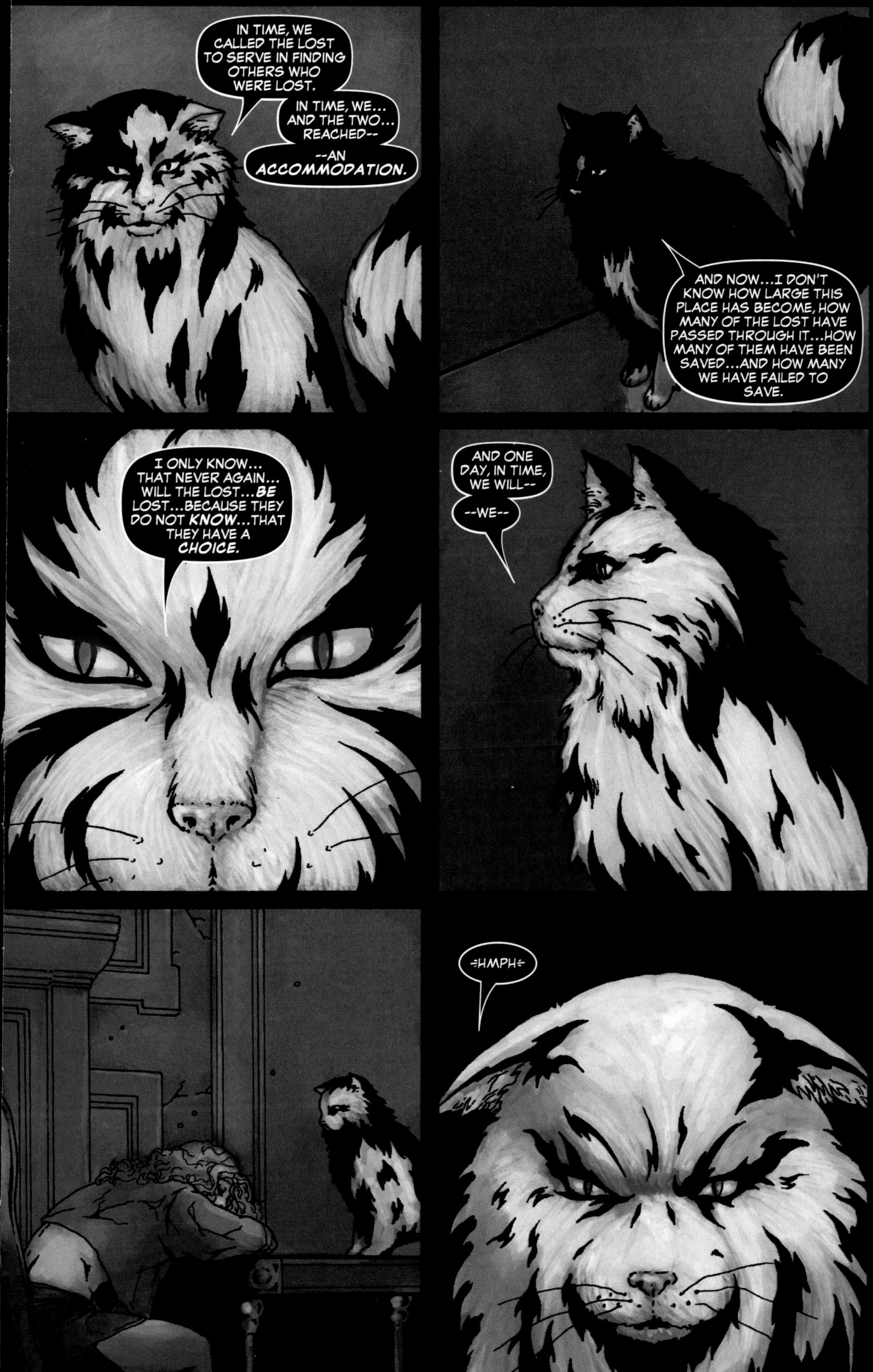
IN TIME, WE CALLED THE LOST TO SERVE IN FINDING OTHERS WHO WERE LOST.
IN TIME, WE... AND THE TWO... REACHED--
--AN ACCOMMODATION.
AND NOW...I DON'T KNOW HOW LARGE THIS PLACE HAS BECOME, HOW MANY OF THE LOST HAVE PASSED THROUGH IT...HOW MANY OF THEM HAVE BEEN SAVED...AND HOW MANY WE HAVE FAILED TO SAVE.
I ONLY KNOW... THAT NEVER AGAIN... WILL THE LOST...BE LOST...BECAUSE THEY DO NOT KNOW...THAT THEY HAVE A CHOICE.
AND ONE DAY, IN TIME, WE WILL--
--WE--
=HMPH=

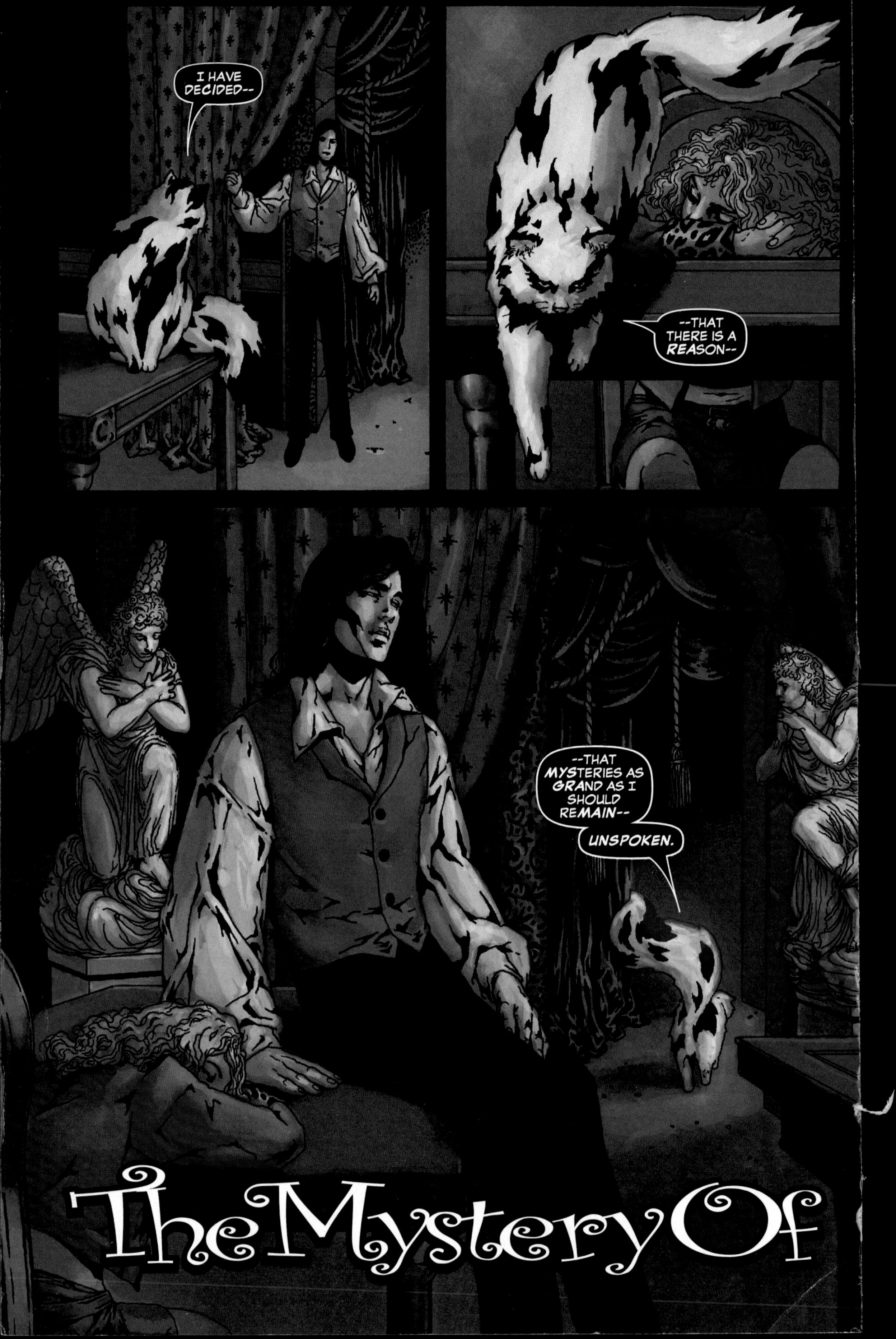
I HAVE DECIDED--
--THAT THERE IS A REASON--
--THAT MYSTERIES AS GRAND AS I SHOULD REMAIN--
UNSPOKEN.
The Mystery Of